Sustainable Customer Experience Design

D1766528

Experiences are an important part of our lives and increasingly represent a crucial topic to address for businesses and professionals. This book focuses on designing, staging and managing experiences within the context of the events, tourism and hospitality industries. It also illustrates current and future developments in these industries and wider society, with an emphasis on sustainable development.

The book offers an innovative approach for successfully creating experiences for (potential) customers that is based on combining insights and methods from the world of design and the social sciences. Moreover, it shows how the experience economy and sustainable development both reinforce one another and create challenges that businesses and professionals can address through this approach.

Critical thinking questions, practical examples and international case studies are integrated throughout the text. Combining a design science and a social sciences perspective in one inclusive hands-on approach to designing, staging and managing experiences, this is essential reading for all students of Events, Tourism and Hospitality Management, but also related fields.

Bert Smit is a Senior Lecturer in Experience Design at the Academy of Hotel and Facility Management, NHTV Breda University of Applied Sciences, the Netherlands.

Frans Melissen is a Professor of Sustainable Business Models at the Academy of Hotel and Facility Management, NHTV Breda University of Applied Sciences, the Netherlands.

ST030023

CORNWALL COLLEGE

Sustainable Customer Experience Design

Co-creating Experiences in Events, Tourism and Hospitality

Bert Smit and Frans Melissen

LONDON AND NEW YORK

First published 2018
by Routledge
2 Park Square, Milton Park, Abingdon, Oxon OX14 4RN

and by Routledge
711 Third Avenue, New York, NY 10017

Routledge is an imprint of the Taylor & Francis Group, an informa business

© 2018 Bert Smit and Frans Melissen

The right of Bert Smit and Frans Melissen to be identified as authors of this work has been asserted by them in accordance with sections 77 and 78 of the Copyright, Designs and Patents Act 1988.

All rights reserved. No part of this book may be reprinted or reproduced or utilised in any form or by any electronic, mechanical, or other means, now known or hereafter invented, including photocopying and recording, or in any information storage or retrieval system, without permission in writing from the publishers.

Trademark notice: Product or corporate names may be trademarks or registered trademarks, and are used only for identification and explanation without intent to infringe.

British Library Cataloguing-in-Publication Data
A catalogue record for this book is available from the British Library

Library of Congress Cataloging-in-Publication Data
A catalog record has been requested for this book

ISBN: 978-1-138-65854-7 (hbk)
ISBN: 978-1-138-65855-4 (pbk)
ISBN: 978-1-315-62074-9 (ebk)

Typeset in Bembo
by Florence Production Ltd, Stoodleigh, Devon

Visit the eResource: www.routledge.com/9781138658554

Cornwall College Learning Centres
Classmark: 790·069 SMI
Barcode: STO30023
Month/Year: MAY 22
Campus: STAC

For Marijntje, Lotte, and our students

Contents

Figures

Case studies

Acknowledgements

First, we would like to express our gratitude to Emma Travis and Carlotta Fanton at Taylor & Francis/Routledge for their support for this book and their guidance during the preparation. We would also like to thank Lars Moratis and Danny Han, for proofreading the manuscript, and Gienke Osinga and Anne van Delft, for giving us the time and freedom to complete this journey. We also thank our colleagues at the NHTV Breda University of Applied Sciences for their understanding and allowing us to (try to) reach a state of flow during the writing process.

We would especially like to thank Joe Pine, Jeroen Nawijn, Ondrej Mitas, Geoff Marée, Ron Swidler, Vincent Neveu, Xander Lub, Moniek Hover, Ady Milman, Anita Zehrer, David Strafford, Phil Crowther, Lars Moratis and Xavier Font, who contributed case studies that sustain this book's storyline in an excellent way.

Finally, we would like to thank Roy Wood for encouraging us to embark on this journey. We loved it!

Bert Smit and Frans Melissen
Breda
December 2017

Introduction

This book focuses on designing, staging and managing experiences within the context of the events, tourism and hospitality industries. It presents an approach for successfully creating experiences for (potential) customers that is based on combining insights and methods from the world of design and the social sciences, while taking into account current and future developments in these industries and wider society. With respect to the latter, one of the key issues addressed and incorporated in the presented approach is sustainable development.

Combining a design perspective and a social sciences perspective in one inclusive hands-on approach to designing, staging and managing experiences is both innovative and much needed. This approach can assist in creating the necessary adjustments to current business practices and models within the events, tourism and hospitality industries, other service-oriented industries and beyond. It can assist professionals in successfully tackling two key developments in our society:

1. The needs and wishes of consumers have changed and continue to change over time, with one specific trend – often succinctly referred to as the rise of the experience economy – standing out.
2. Businesses and professionals who try to provide experiences for consumers that meet those needs and wishes need to incorporate sustainable development principles in the way they do, to ensure long-term success and a (sustained) social licence to operate.

These two developments are already prompting new business models within the service industry and other industries, which increasingly make use of business logic and tools originating from the service industry. Both developments are introduced in short in the remainder of this introduction and together they form the thread that links all chapters that follow.

THE RISE OF THE EXPERIENCE ECONOMY

The basic premise of the so-called experience economy is that experiences can be sold and that, more and more, consumers are looking for experiences instead of individual/separate products or services. Sometimes these experiences include specific products and services but, ultimately, what you as a consumer pay for is the entire experience and not just those products and services. Some very clear examples of such experiences are going to see a musical, visiting a theme park or attending a music festival. If you visit a theme park, you pay a fee to be allowed to spend time in that theme park with your friends or family. You do not pay for the individual attractions and rides but rather for the whole experience of enjoying a day out with your loved ones, to have fun together, to forget about your everyday worries and to create new memories.

At Xavier Artisan, it is not just the ice cream, sandwiches and coffee that you pay for but also the fact that they are home made, on the spot, and that you can enjoy them in a special atmosphere with a view of Montreal's Notre-Dame Basilica. However, the events, tourism and hospitality industries are not the only ones offering experiences to their customers. Companies like SuitSupply – a men's fashion brand – aim to make buying a suit feel like visiting your personal tailor. Experiences are also widely offered online in web shops and provided through games and apps. If you think about it, you can probably come up with numerous examples from your own day-to-day life. What all these examples have in common is that you, as a customer, are not just paying for a specific product or service but also for a specific location, the ambience, the ease of use, the interaction with friends and staff that come with it. In other words, the way it makes you feel: the experience.

Academic interest in the experience economy gained momentum around the turn of the century. Many refer to Hirschman and Holbrook's (1982) paper on the rise of hedonic consumption as the starting point or catalyst for this wave. The work of Giddens (1991) and others on postmodernism, identity formation and aesthetics also plays a crucial role in the way we interpret and explain changes in consumers' needs and wishes. Finally, books such as *The Experience Economy* by Pine and Gilmore (1999) and *The Dream Society* by Jensen (1998) have further increased attention for a so-called shift in the way people consume and thus the way in which businesses and professionals can and must create competitive advantage. Price and quality of products and services are still important but usually not enough to differentiate your company from the competition. Nowadays, almost any company needs to pay attention to the way it delivers its products and services to its customers. Creating a brand experience, also through additional products and services and specific distribution choices, is now part of the game.

In itself, offering and selling experiences is nothing new. The Romans staged gladiator fights and chariot races in the Colosseum, where thousands cheered their heroes. In medieval times, circuses and fairs travelled from city to city to provide entertainment for those who could afford it. In other words, selling experiences has been around for centuries. However, new technologies, education and economic development have made them available to and demanded by an ever-increasing portion of the world's population. In fact, one could argue that people who have more time and money available than required for satisfying their basic needs such as food, housing and clothing almost always and automatically start craving experiences that move beyond simply meeting those basic needs.

New technologies have always played a crucial role in designing, staging and managing (new) experiences and making them available to more and more people in society. The invention of the printing press created the first types of mass media in the shape of books and pamphlets. A printed book was a lot cheaper and faster to produce than a handwritten or stamped book. As a result, the content of those books became accessible to more people, and literature, music, poetry and knowledge became something that the middle class could afford and wanted more of. In the same way, the steam and combustion engine created new ways of transportation and thus new experiences such as day trips and short vacations. Consequently, experiencing new cultures and surroundings was no longer something only available to those with a lot of time and money.

More recent technologies such as photography, radio, film, television, computers and the Internet have had similar effects and have further increased the significance of experiences in the daily lives of most people, especially if you combine them with the effect of social developments such as increased wages and the introduction of labour agreements. Most people now have something called leisure time because working is something you do for a limited number of hours a day and a limited number of days a week. Higher salaries and leisure time make it possible to spend money and time on other things than housing, food and clothing. For quite some time now, many people go to restaurants and theatres. People of all ages enjoy sports, either actively or passively. Owning a television has been commonplace for decades. New industries, such as the tourism and events industries, have emerged and grown considerably over the years.

In other words, experiences have been around for a long time. Simultaneously, a concept such as the experience economy is still a relatively new concept. The fact that price and quality are no longer the only and oftentimes not even the most important influencers in consumer decision-making is something that still needs to fully sink in for some companies. Those that have fully grasped the consequences of technological developments, increased prosperity and various other societal developments and trends have sometimes found it difficult to find new and successful ways to differentiate themselves from the competition. Those that have managed to do so have gained a considerable competitive advantage but retaining that advantage is proving difficult for many of them.

21ST-CENTURY EXPERIENCES AND CONSUMERS

The question that follows from all this is: why is it so difficult (for businesses and professionals) to create successful experiences and to sustain that success?

Part of the answer is certainly technology and, more specifically, how technological developments have truly transformed the way in which experience providers and experience consumers (can) interact. Virtual reality, 4G mobile Internet (probably 5G or 6G by the time you read this), social media and so on are changing the way we work, the way we organise our lives and the way we connect with not only friends and family but also companies. The same technologies are also changing many of the experiences that those companies offer. Virtual reality makes it possible for us to see the world through the eyes of Van Gogh and visit the places he painted and lived in. Shooter games have been incorporated in roller coasters to create so-called 4D-rides. We, the viewers, decide on the ending of a movie through apps that we use while watching the latest 3D adventure movie in our own homes on our own television, computer or in our own home theatre including full surround real-time responsive sound and light system. Michelin star restaurants add smells, sights and sounds of the ocean to the oysters they serve. Added stimuli and interactive elements are becoming integral elements of experiences. This is not every company's cup of tea (yet) but most consumers will not wait until it is.

What is more, living up to consumers' expectations is also not just a matter of adding stimuli and interactive elements to existing products and services. For some companies, becoming successful in the experience economy might require them to drastically adjust or redesign their core products and services and/or the way they distribute them to their customers. In their efforts to bring customers back to their bookstores and to secure a solid market share in a market more and more dominated by online bookstores, Barnes and Noble transformed many of their stores to cafés where you read your book while having coffee or tea – even if you decide not to buy the book. Some of their stores include mini science centres to inspire kids with knowledge from the fields of biology and physics.

The experience economy also leads to completely new business models based on old(-fashioned) products. At Build-a-Bear workshops, kids can create their own teddy bear by choosing the fabric, stuffing, body, head, arms, legs and clothing and then embroidering a name of their own choice on it. These kids create their own unique teddy bear in five or six stages while enjoying their time in the store. Even though these teddy bears are more expensive than their off-the-rack siblings, many parents seem more than happy to spend the extra money in return for the experience offered to their children.

In fact, as argued by Pine and Gilmore (1999), uniqueness is more and more becoming the norm. They described this as a shift from mass production of standardised goods and services to mass customisation and stated that this is what is required to satisfy the needs and meet the wishes of today's consumer. Vargo and

Lusch (2004) refer to a similar shift from creating products and services to creating customer experiences through applying so-called Service Dominant Logic. Businesses and professionals need to realise that the way they create value for their customers needs to be based on looking at products and services through the eyes of the customer and constantly re-addressing and re-answering the question: What do our customers actually want (from us)? Does someone crave a high quality cup of coffee or a moment to relax on the terrace in the sunshine? Does that customer want a flashy bike or simply a means to get from A to B?

The answer to those questions is not the same for all consumers – not even remotely. In fact, to highlight the changes to the circumstances in which today's businesses and professionals operate, Prahalad and Krishnan (2008) formulated two new 'laws' for doing business: N=1 and R=G. N=1 means that businesses need to be able to customise their products and services to the needs of each individual customer, thereby creating a unique experience. R=G means that as a result of N=1, businesses and professionals should not focus on ownership of resources to create and customise those products and services but rather on access to global resources. Only through this access can they create, offer and customise their products anywhere, anytime. This might sound rather abstract but this is exactly what AirBnB, Uber and Netflix are trying to do; not focusing on owning property, machinery and content but on providing access to them through online platforms.

The above portrays just a few issues and challenges involved in the overall shift from products to services and from services to experiences. Successful business models need to accommodate for addressing these issues and tackling these challenges. A smart approach to designing, staging and managing experiences based on truly understanding today's and tomorrow's consumer is a key ingredient of these business models. The rationale for such an approach and the steps it contains are discussed in Part I of this book. However, changing needs and wishes of consumers is not the only challenge businesses and professionals in the events, tourism and hospitality industries, and beyond, are faced with.

THE WIDER CHALLENGE OF SUSTAINABLE DEVELOPMENT

Switching attention from exciting, customised, sometimes virtual experiences to discussing momentous, omnipresent, real-life problems in relation to sustainable development of our society might be rather poignant. Simultaneously, these problems are linked to the second key challenge businesses and professionals are faced with. They will need to address both challenges, in an integrated way, if they want to be and remain successful.

One of the biggest and scariest problems that we, as society, are faced with is global warming. In some parts of our world, we can already see the consequences quite clearly. Extreme weather conditions leading to flooding, droughts, wild fires and changing landscapes are threatening animals, plants and people across our globe.

Yet, climate change is just one of a range of interconnected threats. On-going acidification of our oceans, pollution and deforestation aggravate the problem and combined with climate change they undermine the long-term functioning of our planet's ecosystems. This not only leads to biodiversity loss and direct health problems for people, such as the spread of diseases, but also damages the functioning and capacity of our planet as our food production system. In turn, these developments can cause and can be argued to already have caused armed conflicts, terrorism and migratory flows.

These are just a few examples of the many complicated and interrelated environmental, socio-cultural and economic problems we are faced with. Resolving them or, at least, trying to minimise their impact is probably the biggest challenge we face as society as a whole. Postponing or shying away from dealing with this challenge will threaten the future of our planet and the quality of our lives and the lives of our children. Tackling this challenge is referred to as striving for sustainable development, which is defined by the United Nations as 'development that meets the needs of the present without compromising the ability of future generations to meet their own needs' (United Nations' World Commission on Environment and Development, 1987, Chapter 2, item 1).

This definition incorporates two crucial elements that complicate the challenge we have to overcome. First, it refers to the needs of current and future generations. Second, it refers to the needs of generations, not just those fortunate enough to have a job, enjoy freedom and live in wealthy parts of our world. Together, these two elements highlight the systemic and ethical dimensions of striving for sustainable development. Somehow, we will have to ensure that the way in which we meet the needs of people living today does not make it impossible for our children and grandchildren to meet their needs. If you realise that we already use more resources per year than the Earth can provide in the long term and that, based on predicted growth of the Earth's population, we would need two Earths by 2030 to accommodate our current consumption patterns, the gravity of the situation becomes clear. Especially if you realise that these predictions do not take into account the detrimental effects of global warming and the additional resources that are needed to meet the needs of the less privileged, such as people currently living in poverty.

Businesses and professionals have a crucial role to play in mitigating these problems and realising true sustainable development of our society. Fulfilling this role and sustaining a social licence to operate within a society that will (increasingly) struggle to deal with some of the consequences of decisions made in the past, also and maybe even especially by the business world, requires them to adjust their business models and develop new business logic. Part II of this book discusses the challenge of sustainable development and the role of businesses and professionals in more detail, explains the implications for the business models they (need to) apply, and highlights that the rise of the experience economy and the need to pursue sustainable development represent two developments that not only fit in with each other but also strengthen and reinforce each other.

EXPLORING THE FUTURE OF CUSTOMER EXPERIENCES

The third and final part of this book is devoted to exploring how the comprehensive approach to designing, staging and managing successful experiences presented in Part I can be combined with the reference points for sustainable business models established in Part II. These final chapters synthesise the insights developed in the first two parts in discussing how businesses and professionals – especially those in events, tourism and hospitality – could concurrently address the requirements linked to the rise of the experience economy and the need to realise sustainable development. They explore the experiences they will (need to) create, how to do that successfully, and the business models and technologies they will (need to) apply in doing so. Finally, this part of the book discusses what all this means for (future) professionals working in these and other industries, the competencies they need to master and the way they can benefit from applying the insights and tools presented in previous chapters.

AN OVERVIEW OF THE REMAINDER OF THIS BOOK

As indicated earlier, this book consists three main parts.

Part I: Designing, staging and managing experiences

Chapter 1 illustrates the relevance of designing, staging and managing experiences to (business) success based on theoretical insights and through discussing (international) examples and case studies. It also provides theoretical insights and examples/case studies to explain and illustrate the rise of the experience economy. It concludes by highlighting the need for a comprehensive yet hands–on approach to designing, staging and managing customer experiences.

Chapter 2 focuses on developing a better understanding of customer experiences and covers relevant theoretical insights from psychology, social psychology and sociology – the social sciences perspective. It answers questions such as: Why do consumers want (or need) experiences? Why are they willing to spend (scarce) resources on them? How do consumers perceive experiences? How do combinations of stimuli influence our experience of an event or situation?

Chapter 3 explains that any product, service or experience that is offered to consumers, needs to be designed properly to make sure that it responds to the needs and wishes of those consumers. This chapter covers theoretical insights and practical examples from the design world and design science to explain the various approaches to and steps of a design process.

It also explains how design methods, tools and techniques that are usually focused on designing tangible products could also be applied to designing intangible products, such as services and experiences, and highlights the advantages of using a structured approach to doing so.

Based on the reference points established in the previous chapters, Chapter 4 presents a comprehensive hands-on approach to designing experiences that merges the social and design sciences perspectives. This step-by-step approach is illustrated with (international) examples and case studies. It also presents specific tools and formats that can be used within the various steps of the design process.

The final chapter of Part I, Chapter 5, explains how experiences that have been designed using the approach presented in the previous chapter can be staged and managed in 'real life'. It illustrates the relevance of Human Resources Management, Quality Management and Leadership through discussing (international) examples and case studies and presenting additional tools and formats for staging and managing experiences.

Part II: Sustainable development and the role of businesses and professionals

Chapter 6 introduces theoretical insights and provides examples related to the concept of sustainable development. It explains why this concept is much more than greening and why it is so important for any business or professional aiming at long-term success. It also addresses how combining the rise of the experience economy with the challenges linked to sustainable development explains why boundaries between systems and industries are shifting and sometimes even disappearing, especially if you relate those developments to technological progress. Examples and case studies are used to illustrate this blurring of industries: retail is mixing with hospitality; products, services and experiences are no longer separate entities; and web-based services are influencing the way offline services are/need to be offered.

The need for sustainable development of our societies implies that businesses and professionals need to rethink the business models and technologies they apply; this is the topic addressed in Chapter 7. Theoretical insights, examples and case studies are used to explore how businesses and professionals could incorporate sustainability principles in the way they operate, as well as the complications linked to specific self-reinforcing mechanisms ingrained in our current socio-economic system. Finally, this chapter explains the basics of sustainable business models, establishes some key reference points for businesses and professionals who want to make a significant contribution to realising sustainable development, and describes the apparent match between staging experiences and pursuing sustainable development.

Part III: Co-creating sustainable experiences

Chapter 8 builds on the insights developed in the first two parts of this book by describing how the apparent link between sustainability and experiences can be turned into a healthy, blossoming relationship. It establishes four levels of ambition for businesses and professionals who stage experiences with respect to incorporating sustainability principles in the way they operate. It also explores ways to convince consumers to (buy and) consume these (more) sustainable experiences. Finally, it establishes that successfully staging sustainable experiences requires addressing all reference points and complications involved with doing so in their design.

Consequently, Chapter 9 merges the comprehensive approach to experience design, as presented in Part I, with the insights developed with respect to incorporating sustainability principles in the experiences staged by businesses and professionals. Through examples and case studies, it illustrates how this design approach could assist in incorporating sustainability principles in the design of experiences for all four ambition levels described in Chapter 8. Finally, it explains how all the reference points, theories, models, tools and techniques this book presents could prove helpful for businesses and professionals in concurrently addressing the challenges posed by the rise of the experience economy and the need to realise sustainable development of our societies, as well as developing the business models and technologies to do so successfully.

Finally, Chapter 10 describes and illustrates what competencies – defined as a combination of specific knowledge, skills and attitudes or behaviours – (future) professionals need to master to successfully design, stage and manage experiences in today's and tomorrow's market place and society. It relates each of these competencies to what is discussed in the first nine chapters.

REFERENCES

Giddens, A. (1991). *Modernity and self-identity: Self and society in the late modern age.* Stanford, CA: Stanford University Press.

Hirschman, E.C. & Holbrook, M.B. (1982). Hedonic consumption: Emerging concepts, methods and propositions. *The Journal of Marketing*, 92–101.

Jensen, R. (1998). *The dream society: How the coming shift from information to imagination will transform your business.* New York: McGraw-Hill.

Pine, B.J. & Gilmore, J.H. (1999). *The experience economy: Work is theatre & every business a stage.* Boston, MA: Harvard Business Press.

Prahalad, C.K. & Krishnan, M.S. (2008). *The new age of innovation: Driving co-created value through global networks* (Vol. 1). New York: McGraw-Hill.

United Nations' World Commission on Environment and Development (Brundtland Commission) (1987). *Our common future (The Brundtland report).* Oxford: Oxford University Press.

Vargo, S.L. & Lusch, R.F. (2004). Evolving to a new dominant logic for marketing. *Journal of marketing*, 68(1), 1–17.

PART I

DESIGNING, STAGING AND MANAGING EXPERIENCES

1 The concept of experiences

INTRODUCTION

Experiences are an important part of our lives and increasingly represent a crucial topic to address for businesses and professionals. However, what exactly is an experience? What does the term experience mean? Some would say life itself and everything we do and encounter while living our lives are experiences. There is definitely some truth in this statement because through our senses – seeing, hearing, tasting, smelling and touching – we continuously experience the world around us. Moreover, we constantly compare this sensory input with what we know and expect of specific events, situations and encounters, even though doing so might not always be something that we are (fully) aware of. Most of these comparisons are made unconsciously and only draw our conscious attention if and when a situation is different from what we expected.

This book explores how businesses and professionals can design, stage and manage experiences successfully, with a specific focus on doing so within the context of the events, tourism and hospitality industries. Obviously, these experiences represent a particular subset of the complete range of experiences that shape our lives. In the first instance, the types of experiences addressed in this book are experiences that are purposely designed, staged and managed by businesses and professionals who offer these experiences to consumers in exchange for money. Some of these experiences might very well trigger strong emotions and many of them have been customised to fit the social norms and rules of a specific consumer or consumer group. Ultimately, however, the experiences addressed here represent a specific product or service offered by a specific company to specific consumers as part of the economic transaction that these two parties have agreed on. These experiences have been designed, and are staged and managed, with an explicit objective in mind: to satisfy the needs of both the consumer and the company involved. Reaching this objective requires a full understanding of all features of these experiences and how they relate to satisfying those needs. Therefore, the remainder of this chapter focuses on those features and the various types of experiences they can create, as well as the resulting challenges for businesses and professionals who offer them.

EXPERIENCES

Research specifically dedicated to experiences first emerged in the 1960s, with Thorne (1963) and Maslow (1964) publishing their studies on so-called peak experiences. Thorne refers to a peak experience as one of the most exciting, rich and fulfilling experiences a person has ever had, which is often described as the highlight of one's life. The opposite of a peak experience would be a nadir experience: an experience that was extremely unpleasant and that represents one of the low points in one's life. Maslow describes a peak experience as an experience leading to a person transcending ordinary reality and truly perceiving 'being' or ultimate reality. He explains that peak experiences are short in duration and accompanied by intense positive emotions and feelings of affection. Contrary to some of his contemporary colleagues, Maslow claims that any person can have a peak experience, whether that person is religious or not. By virtue of this statement, he contributed to peak experiences no longer being the exclusive territory of theology and becoming a topic studied by psychologists and others.

An optimal experience or flow (Csikszentmihalyi, 1990) relates to a different type of experience. Flow represents a mental state in which a person is fully focused on a self-rewarding activity. Flow generally occurs if and when a person is challenged by engaging in an activity to a level that is only just within the reach of that person. If the challenge posed by a specific activity is not in balance with the skill level of the person undertaking it, engaging in that activity will lead to a different experience. If the perceived challenge is higher than their skill level, people will report feelings of arousal, worry or anxiety, whereas a challenge perceived lower than their skill level will lead to people reporting feelings of control, relaxation or boredom. Given that an activity at just the right level requires full attention, people engaged with this type of activity generally lose track of time and place but are also less likely to pay attention to feeling hungry, thirsty or sleepy. Reaching this state is called reaching a state of flow. A state of flow is more likely to occur in work situations than during leisure time. However, artists, such as painters and musicians, and gamers can also experience periods of flow. In one of his follow-up publications, Csikszentmihalyi (2000) describes flow as a state of peak enjoyment, energetic focus and creative concentration experienced by people engaged in adult play but even children can reach that same state while playing.

The flow concept as described by Csikszentmihalyi is similar to how several other authors have described or defined experiences. For instance, O'Sullivan and Spangler (1998) indicate that experiences require involvement and participation of individuals in the consumption stage and those individuals reaching a state of being physically, mentally, emotionally, socially or spiritually engaged. Mossberg (2007) describes experiences as many elements coming together and involving a consumer emotionally, physically, intellectually and spiritually. What all of these descriptions have in common is that they refer to a situation, activity or event requiring involvement and full attention of the consumer. In some way or another, they also all point out that, as a result, the consumer will temporarily forget about his or her environment, worries, everyday routines and so on.

However, there are also differences in these descriptions. The skill level of a person in a state of flow could very well increase as a result of engaging in that activity and thus the challenge involved with that activity will need to increase as well for that state of flow to be maintained. In other words, flow often incorporates an element of learning, which is not necessarily the case for other types of experiences. This is the reason why some authors make a distinction between an experience, representing a one-off event, and gaining experience or knowledge acquisition. Pine and Gilmore (1999), for instance, refer to staging experiences versus guiding transformations – often also referred to as transformative experiences. Whereas the outcome of staging an experience is a (positive) memory of that particular moment or period, the outcome of guiding transformations is a sustained change in a person with the term guiding referring to both a steering element and the, generally, longer duration of such experiences.

Some researchers have observed similar changes in people as the result of short events, specific situations and encounters that would not necessarily be classified as guiding transformations. Denzin (1992) calls them turning point experiences or epiphanies that 'rupture routines and lives, and provoke radical redefinitions of the self' (p. 26). Carù and Cova (2003) observe similar phenomena and call them philosophical experiences. They also make a clear distinction between consumption experiences and consumer experiences. The first relate to staged experiences and the latter to experiences that are facilitated by third parties. A consumption experience would then be a restaurant staging the experience of enjoying a great dinner with high quality food and beverages. A consumer experience could take place in that same restaurant but the actual experience revolves around catching up with an old friend, which you do while enjoying that dinner and which is thereby facilitated by the restaurant.

A final type of experience that deserves mentioning here is the so-called extra-ordinary experience (Abrahams, 1986) or extended experience (Arnould & Price, 1993). Both refer to experiences that are not based on a single event, situation or encounter but on a temporary extended series of events that include elements of novelty and discovery, but not necessarily learning. People that have had such an experience would usually refer to it as a single entity because they were immersed in that specific environment for a longer period of time. This type of experience is different from flow and guiding transformations because it does not necessarily lead to a sustained change in a person. A multi-day river rafting trip, a visit to Disney World or backpacking in the Himalayas represent examples of experiences that could qualify as an extraordinary or extended experience. They would almost certainly create strong memories and involve new discoveries but do not have to lead to changes in people and their behaviour, or increase their skill levels. If they do, you would refer to (specific events, situations or encounters during) these experiences as turning points, guiding transformations or a state of flow.

By now, it is clear that the word 'experience' can refer to many different things and is interpreted differently by different people. However, it is also clear that all of these different types of experiences have some elements in common: they all relate to events, situations or encounters that demand attention and involvement of people experiencing them and they all lead to some form of memories or learning in combination with specific emotions. In fact, we could categorise (see Figure 1.1) almost all of the different types of experiences mentioned earlier based on their position on two axes or dimensions. The first dimension relates to the duration of the experience, ranging from short, one-off events or encounters that could literally only last a few seconds or minutes to series of events and encounters or specific situations that could last days or even weeks. The second dimension relates to the outcome of the experience and ranges from a (positive or negative) memory to a (radical) sustained change in the person(s) involved.

Truly understanding and distinguishing between all the various types of experiences and their features can be quite a challenge – let alone purposely designing, staging and managing the particular experience that a particular consumer craves at a particular moment in time in a way that also benefits the company offering that experience. The purpose of this book is to assist businesses and (future) professionals in doing so. However, it focuses on only three out of the four categories of experiences displayed in Figure 1.1. So-called epiphanies or philosophical experiences are not explicitly addressed because they represent a category of experiences that would normally be beyond the scope of experience providers in the domain of events, tourism and hospitality. In fact, this applies to businesses and professionals in most other domains as well. Epiphanies and philosophical experiences are psychologically complex and their occurrence is highly dependent on the situation, history and mental state of the person(s) involved. As such, these experiences are almost never purposely designed, staged and managed within the context of an

FIGURE 1.1 Typology of experiences

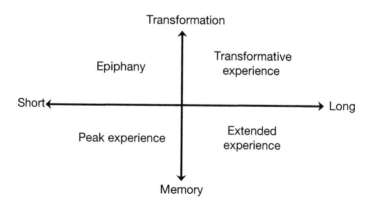

economic transaction between a company and a consumer. In contrast, experiences that fall into one of the other three categories displayed in Figure 1.1 could all very well be at the centre of such transactions.

A peak experience or memorable encounter

Peak experiences or memorable encounters constitute the first category of experiences that could purposely be designed, staged and managed by businesses and professionals. They usually relate to one-off events or encounters, or situations that do not last for a long time, and their outcome is a (lasting) memory of that event, situation or encounter. Obviously, this memory could be linked to positive emotions but also to negative ones. These emotions have usually been triggered by an element of the event, situation or encounter that was out of the ordinary or different than expected. A typical example of an encounter that could trigger positive emotions would be a waiter in a restaurant responding to customers in a way that makes them feel special, whereas a typical example linked to negative emotions would be that same waiter being rude. A specific dish tasting like something you have never experienced before could have the same effect, both in a positive and negative way – serving raw chicken will do the trick when it comes to the latter. Obviously, this type of experiences is key to being successful in the events, tourism and hospitality industries and many other domains.

An extended experience or extraordinary experience

Extended and extraordinary experiences differ from peak experiences and memorable encounters with respect to their duration. This type of experiences usually lasts for several days or even weeks. However, they are not aimed at changing people or learning. Extended and extraordinary experiences are also mostly self-steered rather than guided. Based on these characteristics they also differ from transformative experiences. Similar to peak experiences and memorable encounters, their ultimate effect is a (lasting) memory linked to specific emotions. Even though these experiences consist of several events or encounters that take place over a longer period of time, the whole period is remembered as one entity or story. They are also immersive by nature because these events and encounters take place within the same physical context, such as a city, a region, a country, a national park, or a walking or biking trail. Backpacking in Australia represents a typical example of an extended or extraordinary experience. The actual trip could cover weeks or even months and consists of numerous events, situations and encounters but the backpacker will probably remember them as being part of one overall experience. Once again, it is obvious that this category is highly relevant to businesses and professionals in various domains, especially those operating in the events, tourism and hospitality industries. Typical examples of experiences offered by businesses and professionals in these industries are multi-day music festivals, fly-drive holidays, and all-inclusive resorts.

A transformative experience or flow

Transformative experiences and flow cannot be distinguished from extended and extraordinary experiences based on their duration. However, what makes them different is that they are absorbing by nature rather than immersive and, as a result, usually provoke learning or, at least, sustained changes in the person(s). These changes can relate to an increased skill level – getting better at playing the violin, performing heart surgery or rock-climbing – or an increased knowledge level – knowing and/or understanding more of architecture, haute cuisine or history. As discussed earlier, experiences that are labelled flow usually occur in work situations. Flow refers to situations that require such intense concentration on a particular (set of) task(s) that one loses track of time and place. Obviously, you would not automatically associate this type of experience with the events, tourism and hospitality industries. However, similar experiences, then usually referred to as transformative experiences, most certainly do occur within this context. These experiences are often directly linked to people's hobbies, such as sports, gaming, arts, and even studying – not because you need a diploma to get a job but simply because a specific topic interests you and you would like to know more about it. Many of these experiences can be purposely designed, staged and managed by others, such as businesses and professionals. Typical examples would be guided tours in museums, visiting historical sites as part of a fully organised holiday, rock-climbing expeditions to the Alps, and a weeklong LAN party. Transformative experiences often require facilitation, for instance by a guide, coach or expert, but can also be the outcome of a co-creation process that involves other players, students and guests as well as officials, instructors and hosts.

ECONOMIC TRANSACTIONS BASED ON EXPERIENCES

As indicated in the previous section, specific types of experiences can play a crucial role in the economic transactions between companies and consumers in the events, tourism and hospitality industries, and many other industries for that matter. In fact, it seems that experiences have gradually replaced (tangible) products and services as the ultimate promise made by those companies to their (potential) customers. Within the context of an economic transaction this promise is usually referred to as the value proposition and it represents what businesses or professionals promise to deliver to their customers in exchange for their money.

The experience economy

To highlight this increased importance of experiences in economic transactions between companies and consumers, the work of Pine and Gilmore is often used as a key reference point. In their influential book *The Experience Economy: Work is Theatre & Every Business a Stage* (1999) they describe and elaborate on this transition of our economy. The basic premise of this book is that customising products and services to the needs of customers and differentiating them from those offered by competitors can increase the economic value of those products and services. In fact, the more products and services are customised to the needs and wishes of individual customers and the more the way this is done is unique, the more they will be worth within the context of economic transactions. Customisation and uniqueness of the way companies deliver their products and services to their customers – together shaping the ultimate experience offered to those customers – create the value propositions of those companies. The actual product or service is just one element of that value proposition. Obviously, some competitors will probably try to copy or imitate value propositions that prove successful. If they manage to do so, the value proposition will lose its uniqueness and its economic value will decrease accordingly. Pine and Gilmore refer to this risk as the commoditisation trap, with commoditisation representing the counterpart or opposite of customisation. In other words, a higher degree of customisation leads to increased economic value, whereas a higher degree of commoditisation leads to decreased economic value.

CASE STUDY 1.1   FUTURE BUSINESS MODELS FOR THE EXPERIENCE ECONOMY

Joe Pine

It has been more than 20 years now since we first wrote about the Experience Economy in 'How to profit from experiences' in *The Wall Street Journal* (Pine and Gilmore, 1997). And it has even been 25 years since Harvard Business School Press published my first book, *Mass Customization: The New Frontier in Business Competition* (Pine, 1993). Both of these publications highlighted critical changes in the way companies were thinking about value creation, providing frameworks that would help other companies learn how they, too, could create greater economic value for their customers. Today, we see a very different business world as a result because of the ways companies have embraced these ideas.

Companies have adopted the principles of the Experience Economy in a wide range of industries, not just in the 'usual suspects' of experience staging in tourism, events, and hospitality. No, the Experience Economy has also gone mainstream in manufacturing, business-to-business services, healthcare, and numerous other arenas. In many of those same industries (and more) customer centricity and Mass Customisation are now the standard rather than the exception.

Does this mean the Experience Economy has reached its full potential? Far from it. I still get puzzled looks when I am on a stage stating my case that companies should actually charge for the time customers spend with them (via an admission, membership, or other time-based fee) rather than just charging a premium for their goods and services. I still see question marks in the eyes of some CEOs and even CXOs (Chief Xperience Officers) when I challenge them to go beyond experiences and start guiding transformations as an economic offering (and then charging for the outcomes customers achieve!). For in so many industries the big incumbents are getting disrupted by new players that apply these Experience Economy principles.

Any company that understands that the value it creates can be visualised along a journey through time should understand that it can in fact charge for the time it designs. If you mass customise this journey – smartly weaving together elements of space, time, and matter with digital technology in a dance of personal value – then you can minimise customer sacrifice while maximising engagement. If, throughout the journey, you employ smartly designed theming and engaging dramatic structure, then you can stage a very distinctive experience that attracts customers and furnishes competitive advantage. We see this for instance at Carnival Corp. Its Ocean Medallion programme enables them to recognise and mass customise to every individual guest along the journey of their cruise experience – before, during, and after they are on-board. It smartly blends the physical and the virtual worlds to co-create individual experiences, elevating every guest's experience in ways they could not imagine.

And do recognise that experiences are not the end all be all. Understand that experiences are merely the memorable events for the transformations they guide. And there is no greater economic value you can create than in helping someone achieve his aspirations – become who he wants to become. Chances are that if you are reading this book, you are in the middle yourself of the transformational experience of education, for we are all the product of our experiences.

So shouldn't more businesses start to think about charging for impact – for the demonstrated outcomes their customers achieve – rather than for stuff (commodities), things (goods), activities (services), or even time (experiences)? Shouldn't your university charge you for the impact it has on you both now and in the future? Think of what it would do differently if the university's income were dependent not on its inputs (classes, readings, assignments, etc.) but on *your* outcomes (lessons learned, skills attained, earnings obtained, etc.)!

The business models of the future will be exactly about that impact. Impact on the customer, impact on the community, impact on employees, impact on partners across the business model, even impact on the planet.

Sources

Pine, B.J. & Gilmore, J.H. (2013). The experience economy: Past, present and future. In J. Sundbo & F. Sørensen. (Eds.), *Handbook on the experience economy* (pp. 21–44). Cheltenham: Edward Elgar Publishing.

Norton, D.W. & Pine, B.J. (2013). Using the customer journey to road test and refine the business model. *Strategy & Leadership*, 41(2), 12–17.

Pine, B.J. (1993). *Mass customization: The new frontier in business competition*. Boston. MA: Harvard Business School Press.

Pine, B.J. and Gilmore J.H. (1997, August 4). How to profit from experience. *The Wall Street Journal*.

Read more about Carnival Corp.'s Ocean Medallion: https://strategichorizons.com/joe-pine/mass-customizing-guest-experiences-at-carnival-corp/

The effect of these principles on the price customers are willing to pay for a specific product, service or experience can best be illustrated through some practical examples. If you consider cocoa beans, it is clear that demand and supply on the world market determine the price traders will have to pay. However, the price you, as an individual customer, will have to pay for those same cocoa beans when you buy them in a gift-wrapped box at Harrods in London will be considerably higher. Part of this difference can be explained by the actual costs involved with transporting those cocoa beans from Ivory Coast to London. Another part can be explained by the fact that Harrods needs to pay for the gift-wrapping and the box, as well as the salary of their employee who puts the cocoa beans in the box, gift-wraps it and then hands it to you. However, the price you will (be willing to) pay for this gift-wrapped box of cocoa beans is probably higher than the price for the same cocoa beans from Ivory Coast in a similar box and gift-wrapped with the same type of paper printed with the same ink sold in another department store. The same applies to chocolate bars made out of those cocoa beans sold at a supermarket or a Sacher Torte made out of the same cocoa beans that you buy in Hotel Sacher in Vienna. Somehow, the way the ultimate product is delivered to us, and the environment in which this takes place, influences the price we are willing to pay for it.

Similarly, some of us are perfectly happy buying a standard pair of sneakers, whereas others want to have a say in every little detail because sneakers represent so much more than just shoes: sneakers reflect your identity! This explains why people are willing to spend extra money and use the online NIKE ID store to create their own personalised sneakers. Various hotel chains are currently experimenting with similar concepts, letting guests pick the specific room they want to stay in, the stuffing of the pillow on a bed covered with sheets in almost any colour imaginable and, if required, what the room will smell like.

However, the ultimate experience that you (are willing to) pay for, as a customer, is not just based on a customised product or the combination of specific products and services. It is also the way this combination of products and services is tailored to your needs, exceeds your expectations and makes you feel. Petrol station staff members who not only fill up your tank but also clean your window and stop traffic for you so that you can safely continue your journey add something to the rather commoditised product at the core of the experience you are paying for – petrol. Waiters in a restaurant who know not to ask you what you would like to drink in the middle of you proposing to your girlfriend will increase chances of you and your wife returning to that same restaurant to celebrate your wedding anniversary. Ultimately, it is the specific combination of the menu, the quality of the food, the atmosphere created by the music and lighting, the behaviour of the waiters and many more elements that shape the experience and determine whether that experience lives up to your expectations or even exceeds them. And, obviously, your girlfriend saying *yes* would certainly help in making it a perfect night.

Branded experiences

The result of the rise of the so-called experience economy is that consumers are willing to spend time and money on experiences. In fact, consumers more and more base their buying decisions on how products and services make them feel. Consequently, many theme parks and zoos nowadays state that they do not sell tickets or merchandise; what they actually sell are fond memories of a day out with family or friends. These companies aim to stage meaningful experiences for their visitors. In fact, these companies invest a lot of money to ensure that these experiences create memories that are linked to their park in an effort to not only create positive word of mouth and mouse but also loyalty. Creating a positive image and a group of loyal customers who repeatedly visit your premises or buy your products and services is key to beating the competition in most domains.

Simultaneously, many companies offering those products, services and experiences are part of or at least linked to a bigger whole. In the hotel sector, hotels are often part of a chain or have a contract with a specific hotel company to use their brand name. The same applies to many restaurants and theme parks. The petrol station referred to in the previous section could be a Shell one but also a BP or Chevron one. The personalised sneakers we discussed are NIKE sneakers, not ADIDAS or Puma. Some of us would never dream of buying a Puma outfit, others would never dream of wearing anything else. How is a Coca-Cola or Heineken experience different from experiences offered and staged by their competitors? What makes a stay in a Hilton hotel feel different from a stay in a Hyatt hotel?

Brands have been around for more than a century. The first brands appeared in sectors such as porcelain, tobacco and clothing, and you could recognise them based on logos and trademarks representing the manufacturer of those products. Over the years, brands have evolved from these manufacturer emblems into marketing tools that try to create a certain image of products or the company offering them. This evolution of the concept of brands can be illustrated through the way various authors have defined brands. In the 1960s, the American Marketing Association (1960) defined a brand as a name, term, sign, symbol or a combination of these that identifies the maker or seller of a product. A few decades later, Aaker (1991) defined a brand as a set of assets (or liabilities) linked to a brand's name and symbol that adds to (or subtracts from) the value provided by a product or service. The difference between these two definitions shows how brands have evolved from simply identifying the maker or seller to a set of attributes that have value through the image or personality of a company, created through marketing messages. Kapferer (1997) further highlights this evolution by stating that a brand does not represent a product but the product's source, its meaning and its direction. He explains that a brand defines the identity of specific products and services in time and space. More and more, brands are almost seen as living organisms that behave in a predictable way and interact with their surroundings. They tell the consumer what to expect from products, services and experiences linked to this brand and even what this brand *feels* is important.

FIGURE 1.2 Kapferer's brand prism

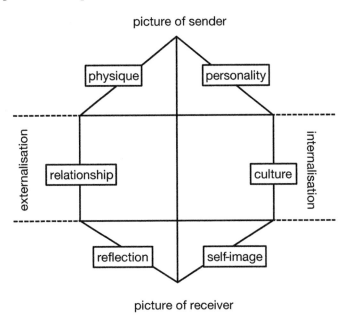

Adapted from: Kapferer, J-N. (1997). *Strategic brand management: Creating and sustaining brand equity long term.* London: Kogan Page.

Figure 1.2 shows the so-called brand prism that can be used to review the various elements that together shape a brand. The brand prism uses the analogy of a lens to zoom in on these elements. Brand lenses can be used to see and analyse how a brand is internalised and how it is externalised. Internalisation relates to the companies behind specific brands and what they stand for, whereas externalisation relates to how this is expressed and communicated to consumers.

The internalisation lens is used to review how the brand relates to the personality and culture of the company or organisation behind the brand but also to what the brand intends or aims to do for customers' self-image. Brand personality refers to the identity of the brand – it is the set of (human) characteristics that can be associated with the brand because of the way it communicates about itself and its products. Language and symbols are often key ingredients of this communication and these reflect a character and attitude that represent the brand's identity. The brand culture comprises specific values that reflect what the brand stands for and what it will and will not do – how the brand looks at and interprets the world. If we consider NIKE and its marketing messages over the years as an example, it is clear that this brand promises to help individuals to reach their potential. They refer to (potential) customers as athletes and repeatedly use words as inspiration and innovation to further strengthen this message. Adverts by this company are known for portraying *normal* people engaging in sports and interacting with famous top athletes. A brand uses a coherent set of words and symbols to communicate its personality and culture and what those can bring to its customers and their self-image. Consumers that favour a specific brand often use these brands to highlight certain aspects and characteristics of themselves or who they would like to be. This means that these consumers internalise certain characteristics of the brand. For instance, going to Starbucks for a cup of coffee might make you feel young and hip – or at least it used to, whereas having a cup of coffee at the Ritz Carlton might make you feel respected and successful – or, at least, it might assist you in sending that message to others, especially if you back that up with wearing Lacoste and driving a Porsche.

Similarly, the externalisation lens can be used to review the way this personality, culture and self-image are expressed and come to life. The three elements crucial to this externalisation are physical facets, relationships and the reflected consumer. Physical facets of a brand are the tangible elements that make the brand visible and recognisable. A physical facet could relate to furniture – which will be very different at Starbucks from the Ritz Carlton; a person – think of Elon Musk for Tesla or the late Steve Jobs for Apple; a logo – almost everybody in the world will recognise the golden arches of McDonalds; a flagship product – No. 5 immediately comes to mind when thinking of Chanel; and so on. The relationship element refers to the typical mode of conduct associated with a brand and the way it interacts with its customers, including the language used to do so. Apple focuses on user-friendliness and connection – in every sense of the word, whereas Ritz Carlton will treat you with respect and Starbucks tries to be informal and personal. Finally, the reflected consumer is the prototypical customer of the brand or, more precisely, the type of customer that the brand would like you, as a potential customer, to see as typical consumer of that product or service. This is why Coca-Cola creates commercials with young, happy people and CitizenM likes to emphasise that their hotels are meant for a new breed of travellers: the mobile citizen of the world. Obviously, Coca-Cola is quite willing to sell beverages to older, possibly not so happy people and CitizenM welcomes all kinds of travellers. However, by portraying the typical consumer of their products and services in a specific way, brands hope to attract consumers from various target groups who feel attracted to that image.

If constructed and applied correctly, the six elements of the brand prism create a coherent brand. Coherent implies that the way the brand portrays itself through physical facets and communicating about its personality – the constructed source – matches the way it portrays its customers and the way actual customers view themselves or who they would like to be – the constructed receiver. The way the source and the receiver interact is determined by the culture and relationship elements of the brand prism.

EXISTING THEORIES, METHODS AND TOOLS

Staging successful experiences depends on communicating a value proposition that appeals to consumers – for instance through physical assets, behaviour, words and

THE CONCEPT OF EXPERIENCES 25

images – but also what role these businesses and professionals would like consumers to play if and when they interact. It is crucial that not only tangible products and services but also this interaction matches the needs and wishes of customers to ensure that the ultimate experience lives up to or even exceeds their expectations. It is also clear that these needs and wishes can differ significantly between different (groups or segments of) consumers, as do the types of experiences they are looking for. All of these reference points apply to branded experiences but also to experiences offered by independent businesses and professionals, such as so-called bed and breakfasts, independent hotels, restaurants, theme parks, museums and other types of tourist attractions, music and other types of festivals, and an ever increasing range of other types of experiences offered both within and beyond the events, tourism and hospitality industries.

Numerous theories, methods, tools and techniques have been developed to assist these businesses and (future) professionals in better understanding and tackling these challenges. The remainder of this section provides an overview of some of the best-known and widely applied theories, methods, tools and techniques relevant to designing, staging and managing experiences.

Pattern of affective dynamics

Solomon and Corbit (1974) looked into patterns of single moment experiences, such as peak experiences and memorable encounters. Their research shows that a relatively standard pattern of so-called affective dynamics manifests itself in most of these experiences:

1. the introduction of a stimulus;
2. a sudden affective or hedonic reaction to the stimulus, which quickly reaches a peak and then slowly declines;
3. a steady level of affective reaction as long as the stimulus is maintained;
4. a peak of affective after-reaction following termination of the stimulus, different from the original reaction;
5. an after stage in which this second reaction slowly decreases.

This sequence might seem rather abstract. However, if you think about the last time you had an exceptionally good dish in a restaurant, it is actually quite easy to recognise these five stages. The first stage is what happens when you have your first bite of the dish. The second stage relates to the moment the combination of flavours and texture of the dish makes you realise this is not an ordinary dish but a really good, especially tasty dish that you really like. In the third stage you continue enjoying the dish while finishing your plate. The fourth stage relates to the moment you finish and you realise that this was the type of dish you simply have to tell your friends about. Finally, in the fifth stage life slowly goes back to normal but probably only after complimenting the staff and a final peek at the menu to make sure you remember the name of the dish. Such an experience is a typical example of a peak experience – a sudden and unexpected peak of enjoyment that ensures you will remember this dinner and this restaurant for quite some time. It goes without saying that most businesses and professionals would love to be able to stage such experiences because they are likely to result in return visits of customers, as well as positive word of mouth and mouse.

Touch points and customer journeys

Simultaneously, a peak experience like the one linked to eating an exceptional dish is not the only event or encounter that will occur during your visit to a restaurant. You will probably also interact with restaurant staff, get an impression of the interior of the restaurant, check out or interact with other guests, and enjoy or dislike other dishes and beverages. Like many experiences in events, tourism and hospitality, the overall experience consists of a series of events, situations and encounters. Together, such a series of events, situations and encounters can also create an extended or extraordinary experience, or even a transformative experience or a state of flow. In any case, together they make up your so-called customer journey (Tseng et al., 1999). A customer journey incorporates all relevant events, situations and encounters a customer experiences prior, during and after consuming a specific product or service. Whether this customer journey includes specific peak experiences and memorable encounters or turns into an extended, extraordinary or transformative experience, depends on the characteristics of those events, situations and encounters. Within the context of customer journeys, these would normally be referred to as touch points.

In other words, the characteristics of specific touch points within a customer journey determine what types of experiences, if any, will be linked to consuming a specific product or service, or a combination of specific products and/or services. To understand the mechanisms involved, Falk and Dierking (1992) developed the so-called interactive experience model (see Figure 1.3). They studied people in museums and established that the way a person participates in and assesses experiences offered and staged by the museum depends on the combination of three specific contexts. The first context relates to the personal context of a visitor: his purpose or motivation to visit the museum, his personality, his expectations of the museum and the experiences it offers, and his skills, knowledge and previous experiences. The second context relates to the social context in which that visitor finds himself during the visit. This social context consists of the people accompanying him – most people behave and experience things differently when visiting a museum with family compared to visiting the same museum with colleagues – but also other visitors and staff, and the way these people behave. Obviously, a museum visit will be experienced differently when it is extremely crowded compared to when it is relatively quiet and you have a curator all to yourself to explain details of and backgrounds to specific objects and artefacts displayed in the museum. This social context also, to some extent, dictates the type of behaviour expected from a visitor. For instance, the fact that most people are very quiet in a library is likely to

FIGURE 1.3 Falk and Dierking's interactive experience model

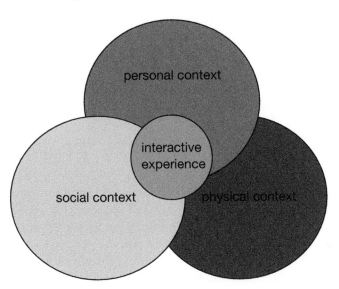

Adapted from: Falk, J. H. & Dierking, L. (1992). *The Museum Experience*. Ann Arbor: Whalesback Books.

influence the volume at which you will talk to your friend sitting next to you in that same library. The third and final context relates to the physical context: the layout of the museum, signage, ambient conditions such as air quality, temperature, smell and lighting, and the interior design of the museum. Ultimately, these three contexts together shape the so-called interactive experience.

Within the context of a customer journey, each touch point can be interpreted as an interactive experience. At different stages of the customer journey linked to consuming a specific product, service or combination of products and services, the contexts shaping the customer's overall experience might be different. For instance, booking your tickets for a theatre show on your laptop at home is done within a very different physical and social context than enjoying the actual show in the theatre itself. The website you visited to book those tickets might have influenced your expectations of the show and the same applies to a conversation you had with other visitors while leaving your coat in the cloakroom of the theatre. Whether the overall customer journey linked to visiting a theatre show contains memorable encounters or even turns into an extraordinary experience depends on the characteristics of all of these touch points, and the impact of each individual touch point depends on the combination of the personal, social and physical contexts linked to it. Some of these touch points might create peak experiences for you as a customer, whereas others might be rather uneventful or even prove to be an unexpected low point in your overall customer journey.

Dramatic structure

Together, these peaks and lows create a so-called storyline or dramatic structure linked to the customer journey. In fact, dramaturgy and literature (studies) provide valuable insights for those responsible for designing and staging the optimal combination and sequence of peaks and lows in the experiences offered to customers. Lawrence and Hormass (2012) refer to the overall outline of peaks and lows as the dramatic structure and use the term dramatic arc to point to the build up to individual peaks within that structure. Analogous to plays and movies, each dramatic arc represents a scene, whereas the combination of dramatic arcs together creates the dramatic structure.

Businesses and professionals, especially in the events, tourism and hospitality industries, often purposely try to design and stage the experiences they offer to customers in such a way that they are based on a specific storyline or dramatic structure. Music festivals usually intend to create a peak at the beginning but also try to build up to the biggest peak near the end of the festival. By scheduling an interesting artist in the first few hours of the festival, organisers try to ensure that visitors arrive early and thus consume more food and drinks. However, the most popular artist usually performs near the end of the festival, so that visitors stay till the end, leave the festival on a high and already look forward to next year's festival. This final high is usually also the first thing that comes to mind when visitors are asked about their memory of the festival – a typical peak experience. Similarly, James Bond movies always start with an action scene but actually catching the bad guy and rescuing the beautiful girl is postponed until a few minutes before the titles

FIGURE 1.4 Dramatic structure 1: build-up to a peak experience

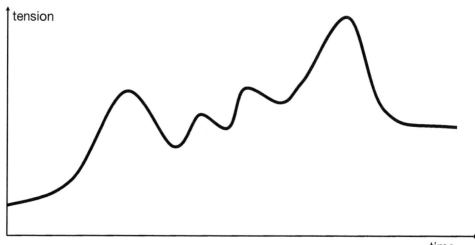

appear. This dramatic structure is similar to the structure of many myths and is generally referred to as the hero's journey. It is applied frequently in (designing new) tourism and gaming experiences (see for instance Calvi et al., 2015 on the 'hero's journey' of Vincent van Gogh).

Hotels and restaurants tend to aim for a different dramatic structure. If the strategy of a hotel is to focus on encouraging return visits, the storyline they try to apply for regular guests is often similar to soap operas. Every visit to the hotel should have its own (predictable) little peak(s) – a reasonably memorable encounter or a little bit more than just a pleasant experience, with a season finale every now and then – a true peak experience or memorable encounter – to keep those guests curious about their next visit. Such a season finale can for instance come in the form of a free upgrade to a more luxurious room or a complimentary dinner. The balancing act that these types of companies have to engage in is to make every visit a little bit special without continuously raising the bar for the next return visit. Otherwise, exceeding or even meeting the expectations of guests will become a mission impossible in the long run.

Even though theme parks usually do not have (full) control over the order in which their guests will experience the various rides and attractions in the park, guests' affective reactions are still predictable to some degree. Generally, theme park guests will have their first peak early during their visit because they arrive full of anticipation. A first ride will create a first peak, which is followed by several more peaks linked to subsequent rides and attractions. However, as time passes, guests will get used to the effect of these thrills and their affective reaction will decrease

FIGURE 1.5 Dramatic structure 2: the soap-opera approach

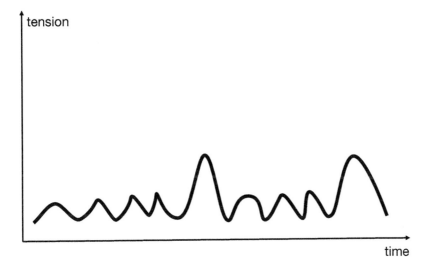

FIGURE 1.6 Dramatic structure 3: the theme-park experience

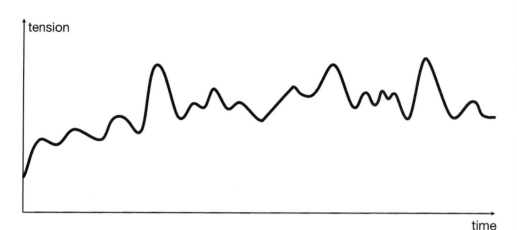

accordingly, with the possible exception of an especially extraordinary ride or attraction. Therefore, theme parks purposely try to create a high end-peak by organising shows, fireworks and parades just before the park closes. The downside of this dramatic structure is that guests who leave early will not experience this final peak. However, a well-designed theme park will offer enough peaks and thematic consistency to its guests to create an extended experience, meaning the memory of the day out will be related to the overall experience and not so much to a particular attraction.

Satisfiers, dissatisfiers and exciters

Most businesses and professionals offering experiences aim to stage experiences that result in happy, excited and satisfied guests. Their objective is to create a customer journey that will be remembered for the right reasons, and that will lead to repeat purchases, return visits and positive word of mouth and mouse. Therefore, peak experiences during that customer journey should not be offset by negative experiences and disappointing touch points.

In designing, staging and managing experiences it is important to realise that different touch points will have different impacts on different (types of) customers. Depending on people's personal context, some touch points will be more important to them than others. Some visitors to music festivals are quite happy as long as they can see and hear the performance of a specific artist, whereas satisfaction of other visitors might depend on them being able to dance without being knocked over. The elements that determine whether a customer is satisfied with the ultimate experience are called satisfiers.

Simultaneously, a customer journey can also contain potential dissatisfiers. Dissatisfiers are those elements that will result in customers not being satisfied with the ultimate experience if they fall below a certain minimum level. During a music festival, typical dissatisfiers would be quality of the food and restroom hygiene. For most visitors good quality food and clean restrooms would not compensate for not being able to see and hear their favourite artist but poor quality food and filthy restrooms could lead to them being dissatisfied despite witnessing a top performance. As such, dissatisfiers relate to specific minimum requirements that need to be met to prevent dissatisfaction.

A third and final type of element that deserves attention is a so-called exciter. An exciter relates to an unexpected event, situation or encounter with a positive influence on the overall satisfaction of customers. An unannounced guest performance by a famous artist, mind-blowing special effects or an invitation to come on stage and hug your favourite artist could certainly do the trick.

Designing, staging and managing successful experiences needs to account for these different types of touch points – satisfiers, dissatisfiers and exciters (Kano et al., 1984). Not only overall satisfaction but also whether the customer journey can be turned into an extraordinary or even transformative experience depends on including the right satisfiers and exciters, timed and executed to perfection within the context of the right dramatic structure, but also on avoiding potential dissatisfiers.

Layers in experiences

Roscam Abbing (2010) distinguishes five possible layers that together shape experiences and individual touch points within a customer journey: aesthetics, interaction, performance, construction and meaning. Each of these layers and their combination can be the source for satisfaction or excitement of consumers. In fact, consumers *peel off* the layers from a well-designed touch point one by one, like an onion. The aesthetics layer relates to what a touch point looks, feels, smells, tastes and sounds like, in other words, the sensory input linked to a specific touch point. The interaction layer relates to the behaviour the touch point elicits and what type of interaction with consumers it creates. This interaction could involve staff but also software or tangible products. The performance (or functional) layer relates to what the touch point does, the problem it solves, the service it provides: its functionality. The main question linked to this layer is: does the touch point do or deliver what it is supposed to do or deliver? The fourth layer, construction, relates to the physical attributes of the touch point: the technology and materials used. The final, inner layer of the touch point is the meaning layer. This layer relates to communication of the vision and values of the brand(s), business(es) or professional(s) offering the experience. As established in discussing the brand prism, the affective reaction the touch point elicits should match these values. If the value proposition stresses hospitality, touch points should make you feel welcome. A value proposition highlighting user-friendliness should be backed up with touch points that are indeed user-friendly.

Even though consumers experience a touch point outside-in, starting with the aesthetics layer, Roscam Abbing states that experience designers should start with the inner layer of meaning in designing touch points. In fact, throughout the customer journey, this inner layer should be present in a consistent way in every touch point and linked to the other layers of that touch point in a logical and coherent manner.

Two schools of thought in service marketing and management

Given that experiences are often linked to providing a specific (combination of) service(s) to consumers, especially in the events, tourism and hospitality industries, insights from the fields of service marketing and service management offer potentially useful assistance to experience providers. Consumer perception of services – a concept closely linked to experiences – has been a much-debated topic in this field. This debate revolves around the question how people choose and distinguish between services offered to them. Two main schools of thought have emerged from this debate. The first school of thought focuses on how consumers buy and perceive services, whereas the second focuses on how companies can best manage service performance from a quality and efficiency point of view. Regardless of favouring a perception or actual performance perspective, representatives from both schools agree that it is important to continuously improve service quality because competition will do the same.

The best-known theory linked to the first school of thought is the ServQual model and the related standardised test published by Parasuraman, Zeithaml and Berry (1988). The ServQual model addresses how to provide the best possible service to consumers based on their expectations. The reference point for this model is the disconfirmation paradigm (Grönroos, 1984), which states consumer satisfaction depends on comparing expected and perceived service quality. ServQual identifies five gaps that can influence the difference between a consumer's expectations of a service and his perception of the service actually provided to him. Identification of these potential gaps is, in turn, based on the reference point that providing a service to a consumer involves interaction between service provider and consumer. A consumer will evaluate the service provided to him based on his expectations and these expectations are influenced by personal needs, word of mouth and mouse, and past experiences but also by the service provider communicating with their (potential) customers.

In order to meet expectations, service providers must translate those expectations into a service strategy. This translation is the source of the first (possible) gap: a misinterpretation or mistranslation of consumer expectations into a service strategy. The second (possible) gap relates to not properly applying this strategy in designing actual services and establishing service specifications. The third (possible) gap occurs when the service is not provided according to this design and those specifications. Given that most services, especially in today's experience economy, rely on staff interacting with consumers and thus on people instead of machines, it is not at all uncommon for this gap to occur. Even if expectations are properly translated into a service strategy, which has been accurately used to design services, which have then been provided according to specifications, a fourth gap can occur when different promises have been made to consumers. Given that both service delivery and communication with consumers are interpretations of the service strategy, any difference between these interpretations, for instance by separate departments, would create such a gap. A fifth and final gap then relates to ultimate possible differences between what a consumer expects and how he perceives the ultimate service provided to him. This final gap can be analysed using a standardised test that accompanies the ServQual model. This test addresses five dimensions relevant to this gap:

1. tangibles, which relates to the physical characteristics of the service provider, such as the building, equipment, furnishings, staff and visual communication;
2. reliability, which relates to the trustworthiness of the service provider, usually based on timeliness, punctuality, problem-solving ability and error-free execution of the service;
3. responsiveness, which relates to the behaviour of staff involved in terms of communication, pro-activeness and eagerness to help;
4. assurance, which relates to how confident consumers are that staff involved are able to provide the service in terms of knowledge level, skill level and courteousness, but also how safe consumers feel in terms of personal safety and safety of data and money involved in the economic transaction taking place;
5. empathy, which relates to the ability of the service provider to adapt to the needs and wishes of consumers in terms of opening hours, personal attention and flexibility.

The main criticism of the second school of thought on approaches such as the ServQual model is that too much emphasis is placed on perceptions and expectations. Perceptions and expectations differ between individual consumers and are difficult to predict, let alone control. This makes it extremely difficult, maybe even impossible, to use these concepts as guiding principles for providing services to those consumers. Professionals and academics representing this second school therefore claim that the best way to ensure customers will be satisfied is to focus on actual service performance.

Service performance researchers have developed a number of techniques and frameworks to better understand how interaction between customers and company (staff) can be analysed and improved. A typical example of such a technique is service blueprinting (Shostack, 1987; Bitner et al., 2008), also known as service experience blueprinting (Patricio et al., 2011). Over the years, many businesses and professionals have used this technique and its popularity is still increasing as a result of the rise of e-services and e-retailing. A service blueprint represents the process that creates a service and resembles what would be called a technical drawing for tangible products. It shows when and where customers and the company offering the service interact, the communication channels used, how providing the service is organised, and – if applicable – physical evidence provided to indicate that the service has been provided. A typical example of the latter would be a chocolate on your pillow to highlight that housekeeping has cleaned your hotel room. Service blueprinting can be used to analyse service performance in terms of sources of mistakes, efficiency and effectiveness, but also to redesign the service delivery process.

The starting point displayed in a service blueprint is a (potential) customer action that requires a reaction from an employee or system of the service provider. The blueprint then shows how this employee or system needs to react and what this reaction entails. By applying principles similar to those used in process charts and flow charts, a service blueprint shows the sequence of customer actions and organisational reactions involved in providing a specific service. It also shows how staff involved need to interact with systems and how individual systems need to interact with each other. In other words, it displays not only the interaction between customer and company, but also internal interactions within the company. A simple example would be the blueprint linked to buying a book on Amazon, as shown in Figure 1.7. The process starts with a customer searching and finding a book she is looking for on the Amazon website. After deciding that she wants to buy this book, the customer will add the book to her shopping cart and click the order button. This will result in a new page appearing where the customer will need to log in to her account, choose the delivery address and payment method, and then pay for the book. The system then needs to process this payment and a storehouse system subsequently checks availability of the book in Amazon warehouses. Once the appropriate warehouse is selected, this system sets a robot in motion that grabs the book and transports it to the packaging line, where it gets packed and appropriate labels are attached to the package. The package is then transported to the location in the warehouse where a third-party mail delivery company picks up the package and then transports it to the address displayed on the label. The customer can track progress of this process by logging in to a dedicated system and the customer is alerted to this through an email message sent to her by this system a few hours after she ordered the book.

A very different example would be the blueprint representing dinner at a fancy restaurant – shown in Figure 1.8. The starting point for the service delivery process displayed is a reservation made by guests via a telephone call or through the restaurant website. The blueprint shows the next steps: the guests entering the restaurant, the host checking the reservation, taking guests' coats and then escorting them to their table. At the table, the guests order some wine, which is served together with an appetiser. Subsequently, a waiter brings the menu and explains the specials. The guests are then given some time to make up their minds. The waiter comes over to take their orders which are communicated to the kitchen,

FIGURE 1.7 The buying a book on Amazon service blueprint

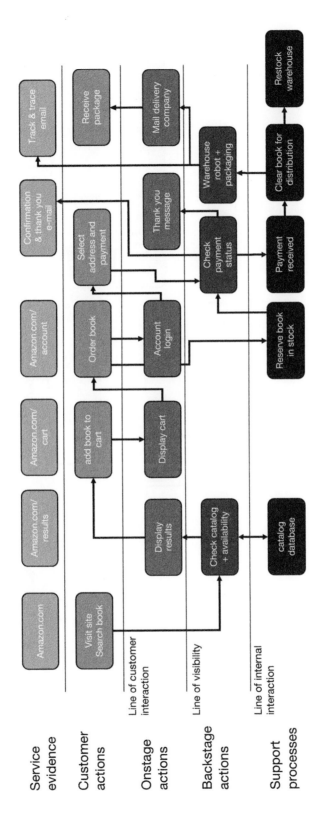

FIGURE 1.8 The dinner at a fancy restaurant service blueprint

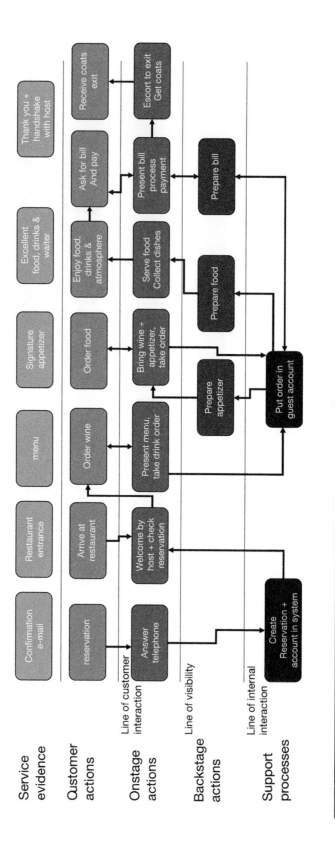

and staff in the kitchen start preparing the food. The various courses ordered by the guests are served at just the right time – not too fast but also not making them feel like they have to wait too long – and empty plates are collected at just the right time as well – not too soon, because guests might feel rushed, but also not too late, because guests do not want to be staring at an empty plate. The final few steps in the process relate to presenting the bill, the payment, and handing the guests their coats and seeing them out.

These two service blueprints are obviously very different, given that they represent two very different services, but they are also similar in some respects. Both blueprints show that customer actions lead to one or more organisational reactions and connected internal interactions. They also show that the specific reactions and interactions required depend on the characteristics of the service request by the customer and the communication channels used for making this request.

Service blueprints combine well with so-called service scripts – another tool widely used by service providers in various sectors. Whereas a service blueprint focuses on the sequence of steps in the service process, including choices available for completing those steps, scripts focus on what staff should say and do within each step of the process, especially those steps that involve direct interaction with customers. Scripts used in practice range from being very generic to being extremely detailed. For instance, the staff manual for junior staff at a five-star Hilton lobby contains more than 400 pages of Standard Operating Procedures (SOPs). These SOPs instruct the staff members to make sure that guests have a glass of water within 28 seconds of them sitting down in the hotel lobby. This particular SOP includes instructions on the type of glass and napkin to use and the exact words and phrases to use in conversations with guests in order to promote Hilton products and services and meet brand standards. Other SOPs relate to grooming standards, how to register guest information, how to approach and interact with VIP guests, and so on. Equally detailed scripts can also be found in customer service departments of insurance companies. Some of these scripts are actually embedded in software that assists staff members in handling telephone calls. Ultimately, these scripts and SOPs can be useful tools in standardising services across staff members, departments and locations, and can prove helpful in ensuring effectiveness, efficiency and reliability of services provided.

Combining these two schools of thought

Over the years, various researchers have tried to combine the insights from both schools of thought discussed in the previous subsection. In fact, Berry, one of the authors of the initial paper on the ServQual model, published a second influential paper together with Wall and Carbone (2006). It aims to bridge the gap between the service perception and service performance perspectives by focusing on service performance clues that influence customers' assessment of service experiences. This is done by stressing that most services involve more than (tangible) objects and also involve (staged) performances by people who interact with customers. This paper highlights that customers evaluate their service experience during and after the delivery of the service by filtering clues and organising them into sets of impressions. In fact, three types of clues can be distinguished: functional, mechanic and humanic. Functional clues are linked to the technical quality of the service. Based on his service experience, a customer answers specific questions. Was the service delivered on time? Did I get exactly what I ordered? Functional clues are thus concerned with the reliability of the service, a key element also present in the ServQual model and service blueprinting. Mechanic clues relate to sensory input and the environment in which the service is provided. These clues include elements such as interior design, packaging design, materials, textures, smells, sounds and taste. Restaurants, hotels, event venues, supermarkets and websites all have mechanic clues that influence how customers evaluate services provided by them. Think of the smell of freshly baked apple pie in a coffee shop, the interior design of a McDonalds restaurant, and the photographs displayed in H&M stores. Obviously, mechanic clues are closely related to the tangibles dimension of the ServQual model and the concept of service evidence used in service blueprinting. Humanic clues are linked to the behaviour and appearance of staff involved in the provision of services. These clues include elements such as words, body language and clothing, but also the effort, enthusiasm and passion of staff involved. Humanic clues are closely related to the empathy, assurance and responsiveness dimensions of the ServQual model, and to scripting and SOPs. These clues have the highest potential to create peak experiences and memorable encounters within the context of labour–intensive, highly interactive services. Together with mechanic clues, humanic clues elicit emotional reactions, whereas functional clues usually elicit more rational, calculative reactions. By acknowledging the relevance of both types of reactions, service clues can be helpful in uniting the service perception and service performance perspectives on providing successful services.

Another way to do so is to translate perception dimensions into performance variables – an approach proposed by Brady and Cronin (2001). They compared and combined various service perception quality models, including ServQual, to come up with their hierarchical approach to service quality. This approach assists service managers in better understanding customer satisfaction and ways to improve satisfaction. Based on their comparison of a number of existing theories, models and tools, Brady and Cronin conclude that most researchers and professionals actually seem to agree on which variables determine service quality. They also distinguish three types of quality and link each variable to one of these three types: interaction quality, physical environment quality and outcome quality. The interaction quality is determined by the following variables: attitude, behaviour and expertise of staff involved in providing the service. The physical environment quality is determined by the design – e.g. spatial layout and furniture, ambient conditions – acoustics, temperature, smell, and so on, and social factors – other people visible and/or audible to customers – of the environment in which the service is provided. Waiting times, tangibles – such as the assortment of products available, and valence determine the outcome quality. Valence refers to personal characteristics and circumstances of customers and how these influence their perception of service quality. Together these nine variables determine overall service quality and each of them can be described in terms of reliability, responsiveness and empathy. Reliability then relates to consistency and trustworthiness, responsiveness to adaptability and flexibility, and empathy to the level of understanding of the customer's needs shown by the service provider.

Both of these approaches stress the importance of the environment – both the physical environment and (characteristics of) people present in it – in which a service is provided for customers' perception of service quality. Bitner (1992) has created a framework to explain environment-user relationships and refers to this environment as the servicescape. She defines a servicescape as the artificial and designed landscape in which a service takes place. Her framework explains which physical elements influence both customers and staff of the service provider who are present in the servicescape. Their responses to these elements can be cognitive, emotional and physiological. In turn, these responses lead to one of two basic types of behaviour: approach or avoidance. Finally, these behaviours and (resulting) interactions between and among customers and service staff create new responses, new behaviours, and so on. Bitners' framework confirms that careful design of the physical environment is required, given its significant impact on customer satisfaction, loyalty, word of mouth and mouse, and so on.

THE RESULTING BUSINESS CHALLENGE

The previous sections have shown that experiences are an increasingly important element of economic transactions between businesses and professionals on the one hand, and their (potential) customers on the other. This is especially true for businesses and professionals operating in events, tourism and hospitality. However, purposely designing, staging and managing these experiences is anything but a sinecure.

One of the reasons why doing so is complicated is that the term experiences can actually refer to very different types of experiences. In some circumstances, businesses and professionals would need to aim for staging one-off events or encounters that lead to peak experiences or memorable encounters. In other circumstances, it might be more appropriate to try and create series of events and encounters that lead to extended experiences or extraordinary experiences, or even transformative experiences and a state of flow for customers involved. The subsection on service marketing and management has shown that doing so requires purposely creating and controlling the environment in which these experiences are staged. Within this environment, a customer journey needs to be created with the right storyline and dramatic structure. This customer journey consists of a number of touch points, some of them designed to satisfy or even excite customers, others simply to not dissatisfy them. Shaping these touch points needs to account for aspects such as aesthetics, interaction, performance and meaning, and how each of these aspects influences both customers and staff involved. You need to ensure that staff members involved engage in the right type of behaviour at the right time, without always being able to predict beforehand what the *right* type of behaviour would be and at what exact point in time this behaviour would need to be displayed. The reason for that is that experiences involve various types of interactions between the environment and people, and between the various people involved. All kinds of stimuli, clues, responses and behaviours will lead to new stimuli, clues, responses and behaviours. Together, all of these elements will determine how a customer will evaluate the experience you are offering. What's more, not all customers will react in the same way to the same stimuli, clues, responses and behaviours. Customers bring their own individual expectations, preferences, personal circumstances and contexts to the table. Regardless of your efforts to design, stage and manage a flawless experience, fully accounting for seemingly objective measures such as waiting times, cleanliness and expertise of your staff, different customers are still very likely to perceive the quality of what you are offering differently.

In other words, the previous sections have provided a lot of useful insights for businesses and professionals aiming to design, stage and manage successful experiences. Simultaneously, they have also highlighted that doing so requires answering a lot of interrelated questions. As a business or professional who aims to stage successful experiences, you really need to understand the people to whom you will be offering these experiences. You need to understand their backgrounds, their needs, their wishes and even the way they will react to specific stimuli, clues, responses and behaviours. This is the topic of the next chapter.

Once you understand your (potential) customers, you also need to be able to translate this understanding into a value proposition that fits your identity and competencies as a business or professional. And, obviously, you then also need to ensure that you live up to the promise you made. Designing, staging and managing the experiences that do so cannot be based on trial and error. Failing to deliver on your promises will seriously damage your reputation and your ability – as an individual business/professional or as a brand – to persuade existing customers to stay loyal to you and to attract new customers. In other words, you need to be able to get it right straight away and for as long as you offer those experiences. Accounting for all relevant aspects discussed in the previous sections requires an inclusive approach to designing them. This is why Chapter 3 elaborates on existing methods for designing products, services and experiences, and then describes the contours and steps of a design approach that would allow for incorporating all of these aspects.

Both elements – i.e. understanding your (potential) customers and understanding the process of designing experiences that account for (potential) customers' characteristics and how these characteristics relate to all relevant stimuli, clues, responses and behaviours – then need to feed into the actual design process applied by businesses and professionals aiming to stage successful experiences. This is the topic of Chapter 4, where a comprehensive hands-on approach to designing experiences is presented, explained and illustrated by means of practical examples.

The final chapter of Part I of this book then elaborates on how this approach can form the basis for actually staging and managing those experiences within the context of real-life economic transactions. It will also return to some of the tools and techniques discussed in this chapter that could assist in doing so.

SUMMARY

Based on reading this chapter, we hope you will understand and remember the following:

- Experiences come in many different forms.
- Different people could interpret the same experiences differently.
- Three specific types of experiences could be staged by businesses and professionals within the context of an economic transaction with their customers:
  - o   peak experiences or memorable encounters;
  - o   extended or extraordinary experiences;
  - o   transformative experiences or flow.
- Customising products and services to the needs and wishes of customers can increase the economic value of those products and services.
- Branding can be a crucial element of customising those products and services.
- Most single-moment experiences can be linked to a so-called pattern of affective dynamics.
- The characteristics of touch points within customers' journeys determine what type of experience, if any, these customers will experience through consuming a specific product or service.
- Each touch point in itself could be interpreted as an interactive experience.
- The way a person will participate in or assess a specific experience depends on:
  - o   his or her personal context;
  - o   the physical context;
  - o   the social context.
- The storyline or dramatic structure of an (overall) experience influences how customers will participate in and assess an (overall) experience.
- It is important to distinguish between satisfiers, dissatisfiers and exciters.
- Five possible layers together shape experiences.
- The ServQual model.
- Service blueprints and scripts.
- The Brady and Cronin model (2001).
- All topics discussed in this chapter together shape a crucial challenge for businesses and professionals (in events, tourism and hospitality, and in other industries): how to successfully design, stage and manage experiences.

FOOD FOR THOUGHT

Based on the content of this chapter, the following questions, challenges and topics could serve as interesting starting points for further discussion:

- Could you distinguish specific experiences that you evaluate differently from your friends or colleagues?

- Could you name a few products or services – that you have bought or used – that could clearly benefit from turning them into experiences?

- Apply the ServQual model to explain why a particular product or service that you bought or used recently did not meet your expectations.

- Think of a particular extended or extraordinary experience you have 'consumed'. Try to describe the storyline or dramatic structure of this experience and how this was linked to the various touch points in your customer journey.

REFERENCES

Aaker, D. (1991). *Managing brand equity: Capitalizing on the value of a brand name*. New York: The Free Press.

Abrahams, R.D. (1986). Ordinary and extraordinary experience. In W.E.V. Turner & M. Bruner (Eds.), *The anthropology of experience* (pp. 45–72). Urbana: University of Illinois Press.

American Marketing Association (1960). *Marketing definitions: A glossary of marketing terms*. Chicago, IL: American Marketing Association.

Arnould, E.J. & Price, L.L. (1993). River magic: Extraordinary experience and the extended service encounter. *Journal of Consumer Research*, 20(1), 24–45.

Berry, L.L., Wall, E.A. & Carbone, L.P. (2006). Service clues and customer assessment of the service experience: Lessons from marketing. *The Academy of Management Perspectives*, 20(2), 43–57.

Bitner, M.J. (1992). Servicescapes: The impact of physical surroundings on customers and employees. *Journal of Marketing*, 56(2), 57–71.

Bitner, M.J., Ostrom, A.L. & Morgan, F.N. (2008). Service blueprinting: A practical technique for service innovation. *California Management Review*, 50(3), 66–94.

Brady, M.K. & Cronin Jr, J.J. (2001). Some new thoughts on conceptualizing perceived service quality: A hierarchical approach. *Journal of Marketing*, 65(3), 34–49.

Calvi, L., Hover, M., Ouwens, F. & van Waalwijk, J. (2015). Visualising Vincent's life: An engaging experience into van Gogh's heritage. In L.-L. Chen, T. Djajadiningrat, L. Feijs, S. Kyffin, L. Rampino, E. Rodriguez, & D. Steffen, (Eds.), *Design and semantics of form and movement*, pp. 312–315.

Carù, A. & Cova, B. (2003). Revisiting consumption experience a more humble but complete view of the concept. *Marketing Theory*, 3(2), 267–286.

Csikszentmihalyi, M. (1990). *Flow: The psychology of optimal performance*. New York: Cambridge University Press.

Csikszentmihalyi, M. (2000). *Beyond boredom and anxiety*. San Francisco, CA: Jossey-Bass.

Denzin, N.K. (1992). *Symbolic interactionism and cultural studies: The politics of interpretation.* Oxford: Blackwell.

Falk, J. H. & Dierking, L. (1992). *The museum experience.* Ann Arbor, MI: Whalesback Books.

Grönroos, C. (1984). A service quality model and its marketing implications. *European Journal of Marketing,* 18(4), 36–44.

Lawrence, A. & Hormass, M. (2012). Boom! Wow. Wow! WOW! BOOOOM!!! *Touchpoint – Journal of Service Design,* 4(2), 24–27.

Kano, N., Seraku, N., Takahashi, F. & Tsuji, S. (1984). Attractive quality and must-be quality. *Journal of the Japanese Society for Quality Control,* 14, 39–48.

Kapferer, J-N. (1997). *Strategic brand management: Creating and sustaining brand equity long term.* London: Kogan Page.

Maslow, A. H. (1964). *Religions, values, and peak-experiences.* Columbus: Ohio State University Press.

Mossberg, L. (2007). A marketing approach to the tourist experience. *Scandinavian Journal of Hospitality and Tourism,* 7(1), 59–74.

O'Sullivan, E.L. & Spangler, K.J. (1998). *Experience marketing: Strategies for the new Millennium.* Edmonton: Venture Publishing Inc.

Parasuraman, A., Zeithaml, V.A. & Berry, L.L. (1988). Servqual: A multiple-item scale for measuring consumer perception. *Journal of Retailing,* 64(1), 12.

Patrício, L., Fisk, R.P., Falcão e Cunha, J. & Constantine, L. (2011). Multilevel service design: From customer value constellation to service experience blueprinting. *Journal of Service Research,* 14(2), 180–200.

Pine, B.J. & Gilmore, J.H. (1999). *The experience economy: Work is theatre & every business a stage.* Boston, MA: Harvard Business Press.

Roscam Abbing, E. (2010). *Brand driven innovation: Strategies for development and design.* Amsterdam: Ava Publishing.

Shostack, G.L. (1987). Service positioning through structural change. *Journal of Marketing,* 51, 34–43.

Solomon, R.L. & Corbit, J.D. (1974). An opponent-process theory of motivation: I. Temporal dynamics of affect. *Psychological Review,* 81(2), 119.

Thorne, F.C. (1963). The clinical use of peak and nadir experience reports. *Journal of Clinical Psychology,* 19(2), 248–250.

Tseng, M.M., Qinhai, M., & Su, C.J. (1999). Mapping customers' service experience for operations improvement. *Business Process Management Journal,* 5(1), 50–64.

2 Understanding your (potential) customers

INTRODUCTION

As discussed in detail in the previous chapter, it seems that experiences are more and more replacing (tangible) products and services as the promise made by businesses and professionals, especially in events, tourism and hospitality, to their (potential) customers. Businesses increasingly try to differentiate themselves from their competitors based on customising their products and services and delivering them to customers in a unique way. The reason is that these businesses and professionals have found that customers are actually willing to pay (more) for products and services that are tailored to their specific needs. Businesses and professionals who manage to exceed customers' expectations, and stage the peak experiences, memorable encounters, extended or extraordinary experiences, or even transformative experiences they crave, are the ones who create a loyal customer base and positive word of mouth and mouse.

However, not every customer wants the same type of experience. In order to be able to design, stage and manage successful experiences, you need to know and understand the people to whom you will be offering those experiences. How will they respond to specific stimuli? What are their expectations, preferences, personal circumstances and contexts? How will these characteristics influence their reaction to your value proposition and – if you manage to persuade them to choose your proposition over those of your competitors – how will they react during and after the actual experience you stage for them? In other words, you need to understand why (potential) customers crave specific experiences, why they are willing to spend time and money on those experiences, and how they will perceive the experiences you offer to them and stage for them.

This chapter reviews perspectives and theories from the social sciences, such as psychology and sociology, which could assist in answering these questions. It discusses relevant concepts, such as personality, values, happiness, learning and schemata, as well as interesting methods, tools and techniques linked to these concepts, such as the Kelly Repertory Grid and the Zaltman Metaphor Elicitation

Technique. Finally, it explains how *personas* could be used to translate the outcomes of applying these concepts, methods, tools and techniques into a logical starting point for designing experiences.

WHY DO WE WANT EXPERIENCES?

Sociologists have tried to explain the rise of the experience economy by referring to the consumption of experiences as a way for people to position themselves in the world. By consuming experiences together with specific (groups of) people and by telling other people about it, you actually make a claim about who you are, what is important to you and to what group(s) in society you (want to) belong. This need to create a specific identity and position oneself can be explained by an on-going process of individualisation in Western society.

As a result of technological progress, barriers such as time and space have almost disappeared from our daily lives. Somebody who lives in London can go shopping in New York over the weekend and go online – while travelling – to catch up with friends in Singapore, and complete and hand in an assignment that is part of her economics study at the Kahn Academy. The globalisation process that has made this possible has changed our world rapidly and significantly. Just a century ago, being able to talk to people who live in a town only 50 kilometres away would have probably required a two-day trip. Studying economics would require you to move and live in the city in which the university is located – if you could afford to, that is, and if you were lucky enough to belong to the right social class. In fact, in those days, your parents' religion, social class and place of birth would have largely determined your future in many ways. If your father were a farmer, and you were a boy, you would become a farmer too. If you were a girl, you would become a farmer's wife. If your parents were Catholics, you would be Catholic. Similarly, if your father were a mayor, your chances of becoming a mayor someday would be good, even if you would not be especially talented as a politician. Chances of a farmer's son becoming a mayor would be slim to none. Chances of a farmer's daughter becoming a mayor: zero.

Over the years, though, society has changed and, as a result, many of these predetermined aspects of life have become choices. As a result of technological developments, together with associated economic and democratic developments, education, religion, occupation, beliefs and political views have more and more become a personal choice for most people in developed countries. Our preferences and cultural habits used to be the product of our upbringing, family views and local community characteristics, but these days they are (also) influenced by (social) media, (international) friends, and so on. Consequently, who we are and what we do is increasingly a matter of choice and not predetermined. This process of individualisation means that in postmodern society someone's identity is no longer fixed but has become a task of each individual (Beck, 1992). We, people living today, build and communicate our identity through consumption and membership of social groups. We create our identity through our job, our clothing, our religion, our hobbies, the food we eat, the car we drive and … the experiences we consume! Driving a Tesla instead of an Audi says something about who you are or want to be. People who book an all-inclusive holiday in a beach resort are different from people who go backpacking in another continent. Somebody who makes a point of wearing the latest fashion is communicating something different from somebody who wears second-hand clothes and accessories bought at Oxfam's Online Shop.

Interestingly, Beck (1992) not only states that identity has become the task of individuals but also that this constitutes a problem. Together with influential sociologists like Giddens and Bauman, he considers the on-going process of individualisation a problem because the effect of this process is that people feel less and less bound to their (local) community. As a result, people are more inclined to choose things that are good for them instead of things that support the common good. In other words, individualisation can lead to situations in which individuals will go for a socially defecting choice instead of a socially cooperative choice, even though all individuals would be better off if they all make the socially cooperative choice. Such a situation is called a social dilemma (Dawes, 1980). These dilemmas play a crucial role in some of the challenges our society is faced with, such as an unequal distribution of wealth across our globe and climate change. Many of us are inclined to choose short-term personal pay-offs, such as a holiday on a tropical island that we travel to by plane, over long-term collective pay-offs, such as a liveable planet for current *and* future generations. If enough people would choose not to fly, that would reduce CO_2 emissions, which would significantly contribute to making that liveable planet a realistic scenario. Somehow though, today's society seems to stimulate us to make different decisions. We will return to this issue in more detail from Chapter 6 onwards, where the need to incorporate sustainable development principles in the way businesses and professionals design, stage and manage experiences is explored.

Bauman (2000) warns that individualisation also leads to the collapse of various social institutes that are time and place based. For instance, sports clubs, work and families have become a lot less influential in binding people. A few decades ago, it was common for families to get together in the living room to watch a television programme. Today, each family member can watch his or her favourite programme on demand wherever and whenever they feel like it. A typical scene from a week night in a family home is mother checking her work email on an iPad, while father is watching a football match on TV, their daughter is chatting with a friend through WhatsApp, their son is gaming on his PlayStation, and the family dog is desperately trying to get the attention of one of them because it needs to go out. Individual sports, such as fitness, running and cycling, have never been more popular. More and more people work from home or otherwise apply flexible work places and hours instead of spending eight hours a day in the same office together with the same colleagues.

Simultaneously, people still feel the need to be connected to others, to belong to specific groups. Consumption, also consumption of experiences, is slowly but surely becoming a crucial way for many people to fulfil this need. Within this context, people engage in so-called symbolic consumption (Denzin, 1992; Giddens, 1999). Buying particular brands, visiting specific pubs, admiring certain artists, visiting festivals, playing online games and more help them understand who they are – or prove who they are, which groups they belong to, and which groups they do not belong to. However, this is not the only reason why consumption and, especially, consumption of experiences have gained importance. Consider the following statement by Le Breton (2002, p. 130): 'the risk-free long-term projection, with the assurance that nothing will ever change and that all surprises are excluded, generates boredom and indifference, in the absence of hurdles which give individuals the chance to measure themselves against their existence.' In other words, Le Breton suggests that modern (Western) society is too safe and does not challenge and test us enough. In the old days, when we roamed the plains of Africa, we needed problem-solving qualities and creativity to survive. Our lives were filled with memorable encounters – imagine running into a huge hungry carnivore while looking for food, transformative experiences – learning was not a privilege but a requirement to survive, and a number of other pleasurable and not so pleasurable but definitely intense experiences. Today, these challenges are missing for most of us and, consequently, one could argue that many of us are simply bored. This might explain our innate obsession with novelty, personal development and an almost compulsive need to *move on* (Abrahams, 1986). Arnould and Price (1993) suggest this might explain the explosive growth in popularity of extreme sports, such as downhill racing and skydiving, adventure holidays, and various other dangerous pastimes. Many of us seem to fear boredom and feel the urge to experience strong emotions. Given that our daily lives, both private and professional, have become peaceful and risk-free, it seems we are more and more inclined to look for intense experiences (Le Breton, 2002). Whether consciously or unconsciously, more and more people manoeuvre themselves into risky situations and engage in extreme, and sometimes unethical, behaviours, such as those that could be argued to eventually have caused the financial crisis in 2008. As indicated earlier, this link to ethics – and a so-called social licence to operate – as a key component of incorporating sustainable development principles in designing, staging and managing experiences will be discussed in more detail from Chapter 6 onwards.

Happiness

As logical as this urge to consume extreme experiences may be, one could question whether we, modern-day people, are really equipped to undergo:

> 'intense, personality-shaking experiences all the time. Religious, spiritual, and existential experiences often result in dogmatism, obsession, and serious delusions of reality. Somewhat mundane experiences of medium intensity – and even

fake experiences – may in fact be the precondition for happiness. As such, they [also] have an important role to play in enriching our ordinary, daily lives.

(Schmitt, 1999, pp. 251–252).

In other words, we cannot all be bungee jumping, gambling and rally-racing all the time. You could seriously question whether that would make us happy. Sometimes a friendly game with friends at your local Glow-in-the-Dark miniature golf course is more than enough to feel alive again and to make you happy.

This highlights a crucial aspect of why consumers want experiences and why they want different experiences at different times and in different circumstances. One of the main reasons for people to consume experiences is that they hope and expect that these experiences will contribute to their quality of life, their overall happiness. Happiness could be defined as one's overall appreciation of life as a whole (Veenhoven, 1984). People base this appreciation on two sources of information: (1) a cognitive component, and (2) an affective component (Diener et al., 1985; Veenhoven, 2009). The cognitive component consists of an assessment of how well your life meets your needs. To assess this, you compile a list of things you have, you have done and achieved, such as your possessions, experiences and relationships. You then weigh this list against things that you would like to have, have done or have achieved. This second list is very much influenced by what relevant others have, have done or have achieved. The affective component consists of an assessment of how well you feel most of the time. To come to this verdict, you essentially compare your moods and emotions over a longer period of time with what you consider to be normal. For instance, if you are sad more often than you consider normal, this will negatively influence how happy you feel. And, obviously, if you are cheerful almost all the time, you will probably consider yourself happy. Experiences can contribute to both the cognitive and affective component of happiness. Going on a skiing trip with a group of friends could for instance feed into the cognitive component through creating strengthened relationships with those friends or through conquering that black slope you always wanted to conquer. The same trip could also contribute to the affective component through the positive effect of sunshine, pleasant company, having fun and the adrenaline kick. In fact, your mood will probably not only be influenced positively during that trip, but also before – anticipation makes you smile about what is yet to come – and after – just thinking of all the fun you had immediately brings back the positive emotions you experienced during the trip.

However, experiences not only contribute directly to happiness through, for instance, peak experiences and the associated adrenaline kick; there is also an indirect effect. We also consume experiences to fulfil our social needs. These social needs relate to the fact that we are social creatures and curious and eager to develop ourselves. This is why authors discussing the experience economy, like Jensen (1999), often refer to Maslow's hierarchy of needs (Maslow, 1943) as a further explanation for our desire to consume experiences. This hierarchy of needs is based on the premise that people have a certain order or ranking with respect to (fulfilling) their (personal) needs. For instance, oxygen takes precedence over food and food comes before shelter. The explanation for this order is obvious: you cannot survive for more than a few minutes without oxygen while you could do without food for a few hours or even a few days. Similarly, in order to survive you simply need food, while you could survive for quite some time without shelter if the circumstances are not too unfavourable. Ultimately, Maslow distinguishes five different levels of needs. The first two levels represent our most basic needs, such as oxygen, food, shelter, clothing and so on. The third, fourth and fifth levels focus on social and developmental needs. Together, this creates the following ranking of human needs:

1. Physiological needs: fulfilling these needs enables your body to function properly and they include oxygen, food, drink, sleep, sex, and so on.
2. Safety needs: fulfilling these needs ensures our physical and psychological safety and they include a house, warmth, clothing, freedom from fear, and so on.
3. Psychological and social needs: these include the need to love and be loved, to feel you belong somewhere, but also the need for friendship, family, intimacy and feeling part of a group.
4. Esteem needs: these higher-order psychological needs include the need for self-esteem as well as respect from others in relation to who you are and what you do; you not only want to be part of a group but you also want that group to appreciate and respect you.
5. Self-actualisation needs: these highest-level needs include the need for self-development, learning and reaching your potential.

Jensen (1999) argues, given the economic situation, that for most people in Western society the first two levels of needs are fulfilled to a satisfactory level. The logic of Maslow's hierarchy of needs then suggests that people automatically shift their attention to the higher-level needs. Obviously, the experiences that businesses and professionals could stage for their customers could play an important role in fulfilling them. Memorable encounters and extended experiences could help to fulfil social needs – including opportunities to engage in activities that are appreciated or even admired by your peers, whereas transformational experiences could assist in self-development, learning and reaching your potential.

It is also clear that higher-order needs are closely related to Beck's statement with respect to the possible negative effects of individualisation in modern society. Fulfilling the third- and fourth-level needs within Maslow's hierarchy could assist in feeling bound to your community or group and shaping your identity. By consuming experiences linked to these needs we can indicate who we are and to which social groups we belong. Given that these aspects are no longer predetermined, we actually tend to spend a lot of time, energy and money to establish ourselves as a member of various (offline and online) social groups. Similarly, we consume experiences to build our reputation and self-esteem, as well as to challenge and develop ourselves. Most of us have the resources to invest in education, travel, events, hobbies, and so on, to assist us in shaping our identity. Through (social) media it is easy to compare ourselves to others and to share our accomplishments and views with friends, family and fellow professionals.

Values

A relevant concept in relation to the above is the concept of values. Within this context, the words 'values' or 'value systems' are not linked to economic principles but rather to our personal and cultural beliefs and ethics. Rokeach (1973, p. 5) defines a value as 'an enduring belief that a specific mode of conduct or end-state of existence is personally or socially preferable to an opposite or converse mode of conduct or end-state of existence'. In other words, values are the generalised ideas of what we find important, such as freedom or true friendship, and how we wish to behave in relation to them. Values can play a role in consumption decisions, for instance with respect to (symbolic) consumption of experiences, services and goods. Buying fair trade coffee can symbolise the value of respect for others and equality, whereas skydiving might symbolise the value of excitement in life. Rokeach (1973), one of the first to look into values and value systems as a relevant concept for predicting and explaining (differences in) people's behaviour, identified some of the generic values most people have. He also looked into how values relate to each other and how people organise values hierarchically in a value system. These hierarchies tie in with attitudes and beliefs, two other crucial aspects that are often used in the social sciences to explain behaviour. Rokeach developed a standardised survey that tests how important certain values are to an individual. This test addresses 36 values that can be grouped into terminal values and instrumental values. Terminal values relate to the end-state a person hopes to achieve in life, whereas instrumental values refer to the way people would like to behave to reach that end-state. Typical examples of terminal values are freedom, true friendship, equality, sense of accomplishment, and family safety. Instrumental values include values such as cheerfulness, ambition, honesty, and intelligence. Even though all people will have specific beliefs regarding all generic values, some people might find freedom more important than equality, whereas for others this might be the opposite. Obviously, these personal rankings or preferences impact the behaviour of individual people. Somebody who feels true friendship is extremely important might very well be inclined to try and create shared memories and a strong bond through experiencing extreme circumstances and challenges together. Such a person might, for instance, like to go hiking or mountain climbing together with friends, especially, if this person also scores high for values such as ambition and a sense of accomplishment. An all-inclusive holiday resort would probably not satisfy this person to the same extent. However, this is probably very different for somebody who scores high for values such as family safety.

The Rokeach Values Survey (RVS) is rather extensive and, therefore, not easy to incorporate in market research. Some of its critics have also pointed out that the direct link to consumer behaviour is not always evident and have proposed alternative surveys that could assist businesses and professionals aiming to stage experiences for or sell goods and services to consumers to better understand their target audience(s). One of these alternatives is the List of Values (LOV) (Kahle et al., 1986). This list is based on Rokeach's values, Maslow's hierarchy of needs and various other studies on values and needs. The original LOV consisted of nine values: self-respect, sense of accomplishment, being well-respected, security, warm relationships with others, sense of belonging, fun and enjoyment in life, self-fulfilment, and excitement. At a later stage, the excitement value was merged with fun and enjoyment, resulting in a final list of eight values that consumers are asked to rank. The outcome of this short survey can provide businesses and professionals with input to cluster (potential) consumers into groups and then target these groups with specific, customised offers. It can also assist in setting up more effective and efficient marketing campaigns because this survey helps to understand how people will react to specific types of messages and reveals what types of consumers live where. Finally, understanding the value systems of (potential) customers can also prove essential input for designing and staging appropriate experiences for specific (groups of) consumers. Obviously, there is really no point in trying to design and stage the ultimate bungee jump experience for people with high scores for security and low scores for excitement.

HOW DO WE PERCEIVE EXPERIENCES?

People process sensory information all the time. We see, listen, feel, taste and hear everything that happens in the world around us. However, in a lot of situations we are actually not aware of what our senses detect. Most of the time this information is processed unconsciously. Our brain is trained to organise this information in such a way that situations are interpreted as normal or abnormal. In normal situations, we are usually not aware of the fact that our brain has reached that conclusion; there is simply no reason for us to pay attention to the various sensory inputs that have been processed. In this way, we are protected from having to be fully aware of our senses all the time. The word protection is definitely the right choice of word here because constantly having to process sensory information would place too big a burden on us and would distract us from other activities. Without this protection, we would be unable to concentrate on our work, have a conversation, work out, read a book, and so on. When our senses and our brain tell us a situation is abnormal, the situation is different. When we smell smoke or gas, we stop what we were doing and, if possible and needed, take action. When a sandwich just does not smell or taste right, we will check the expiry date – and probably think: why didn't I do that before I took a bite? In other words, normal situations allow us to focus on activities or tasks that require our full attention, whereas a signal based on sensory input processed by our brain that tells us a situation is abnormal will ensure we switch our attention to that signal and input.

Schemata and learning

To organise information such as sensory input, our brain applies specific organising systems: schemata. We all use schemata; processing information in a normal or standard situation is done through using schemata to generate the appropriate standard reaction to that situation. Schemata assist us in *knowing* how to react or behave in specific circumstances. Some of these schemata have been *given* to us at birth but we also continuously create and adapt schemata through learning. Piaget (1929) first introduced the term schemata to indicate the way young children develop their understanding of the world and the increasingly complex situations they encounter as they get older. The type of situations for which children have or develop schemata ranges from being hungry as a baby – you feel your tummy, you cry, and then someone will pick you up and feed you – to knowing how to safely cross a busy street. Bartlett (1932) and, quite some years later, Anderson, Kline and Beasley (1979) further developed schemata (or schema) theory and highlighted the crucial role of schemata in how people learn – all people, not just children. Throughout our lives, we create and adapt schemata to assist us in knowing how to behave in different situations.

However, learning can be the result of very different stimuli. Psychologists usually distinguish three main ways of learning: (1) classical conditioning, (2) operant conditioning and (3) observational learning. Classical conditioning implies that new behaviour is linked to a new (neutral) stimulus (Pavlov, 1927). Pavlov first recognised this principle when he saw his dog salivating when it saw the lab assistant who normally fed it. This inspired him to test whether the same reaction by the dog could be solicited by linking a different stimulus to food. By sounding a bell every time the dog was fed, it started to associate the sound of a bell with food. After a while, every time someone rang the bell, the dog would start to salivate. Obviously, just in case, Pavlov also checked whether he could create the same type of learning with other dogs – and no, Pavlov's dog was not the exception to the rule.

Operant conditioning (Skinner, 1938) is pretty similar but in this case unsolicited behaviour is rewarded immediately after it is engaged in. If you praise a two-year old every time he tries to put on his jacket, the little one will most likely keep trying. Bizarrely, Skinner actually proved his theory by applying the principle to teach pigeons (!) to play ping-pong and jump through hoops. By now, we know that the effects of operant conditioning are not necessarily limited to two-year olds and pigeons, and that various types of *teachers* apply this type of learning for various kinds of *learners* in various kinds of circumstances.

The third way of learning is through observation. Bandura (1977) was one of the first to prove this. The basic premise of observational learning is that people – and animals, for that matter – tend to copy behaviour of others to see how that works out for them. Children – and many grown-ups – have all kinds of role models, both positive and negative. Copying their behaviour allows them to test whether this behaviour would also work for them. You can find out whether you (intrinsically) like it and whether it results in positive or negative consequences. The latter is often referred to as positive or negative reinforcement. Usually, you would be more likely to copy behaviour from people who you feel are similar to you or who you would like to be similar to, such as an elder sister/brother or senior colleague. Obviously, you are also much more likely to copy behaviour if you have observed that the role model gets rewarded for that behaviour. If you then find out that you receive similar rewards if you display the same behaviour, this behaviour is reinforced and has now become part of your repertoire of behaviours through observational learning.

It is important to realise that schemata play an important role in each of these ways of learning, both for all kinds of simple daily situations but also for more complex situations that involve specific social rules and norms. These schemata explain why most of us behave differently among friends from when we visit our grandparents or the in-laws. Schemata dictate what we consider *normal* behaviour in specific contexts, such as social contexts. The term social context relates to the (socio-cultural) rules and norms that dictate (appropriate) interaction within a specific group or situation – in other words, what *relevant* others or the *average* person would consider *normal* and appropriate behaviour. However, schemata can also assist us in ensuring that we display appropriate behaviour for specific physical contexts – the physical surroundings in which we are immersed. These schemata tell us what type of behaviour would be acceptable in an upscale hotel or in a youth hostel. Most 40-year old people staying in a Ritz Carlton hotel would not dream of displaying the same behaviour that they vaguely remember engaging in during their stay at that shabby hostel when they were 18. Similarly, the social context of the Ritz Carlton hotel will probably also make them interact differently with staff than they did with hostel staff all those years ago.

All of us have a collection of schemata for almost all possible types of situations. The specific schemata, or scheme, that we apply in a specific situation depends on our personal context, our mental state, our values and norms, and the purpose or goal relevant to the situation at hand. In other words, to once again use the example of a hotel, the scheme you will apply depends on whether you are there as a leisure guest or for business, whether you are in a hurry or not, and so on. Two people on their honeymoon will apply very different schemata than two colleagues that stay over to prepare for a crucial business meeting in town.

The above is obviously closely linked to the interactive experience model (Falk & Dierking, 1992) discussed in Chapter 1. Not only which schemata we will apply but also how we experience an experience staged for us depends on our personal context, the social context and the physical context. We evaluate that experience based on what we expected and what actually happened, and schemata will play a crucial role in how we will react to specific (sensory) stimuli. Therefore, ideally, businesses and professionals who design, stage and manage those experiences will not only try to understand your expectations but also how you will process stimuli they create for you.

Memory

Schemata are 'stored' in our memory, which – physically – consists of neurons in our brain and the links or paths between them. Some of these neurons process the sensory stimuli in our direct surroundings to allow us to determine whether immediate action is required. These neurons together form our short-term memory. Information gets stored in these neurons through electrochemical edging but most of the information we process in our short-term memory is deleted quite quickly. Some information, however, is passed on to a different type of neurons – neurons that are used for long-term storage. These networks of neurons, called engrams, constitute our memory. Memories that are stored basically consist of short narratives of our emotional, cognitive and behavioural reactions to certain situations. Our brain stores these memories to allow for retrieval at a later stage by linking them to other, related, narratives and reactions. For example, you might have fond memories of going for ice cream with your parents on carefree, light-hearted childhood afternoons. In your brain, this memory might be linked to times you went for ice cream because you felt bad and needed to cheer yourself up or even console yourself. Going for ice cream on those days made you remember your happy childhood and definitely made you feel better. Somehow, the next time you feel down or worried, it is not at all unlikely that these networks of neurons will make you enter that Italian ice cream shop around the corner before you well and truly realise why you ended up there.

CASE STUDY 2.1 PEAKS AND LOWS DURING OUR VACATION

Jeroen Nawijn and Ondrej Mitas

We studied the emotions of 39 American and Dutch vacationers. Emotions were tracked daily during their vacation through a diary, using the peak-and-end rule, meaning we asked people to rate their strongest experience of each emotion on each day. Findings indicated that fluctuations in emotions are related to length of vacation. Vacationers on an 8- to 13-day trip experienced significant changes in the balance of their emotions over the course of their trip. In general, they felt good, but this feeling began to decline at the end of the vacation. When the vacation was viewed in segments (i.e. first 20%, second 20%, etc.), vacationers felt best during the second, third, and fourth segments of their trip, leaving room for improvement. The absence of a peak emotional segment suggests tourists are likely to remember the end of the holiday instead, which is when they feel the worst. Possibly, tourists' positive feelings are distracted by hassles of packing and making arrangements for the journey back home. As vacation memories are an important predictor of future purchase behaviour, the tourism industry should try to create peaks in positive emotions. These moments could be potentially more memorable than the end of the holiday.

The industry should build off the results of our study by explicitly designing experiences to elicit positive emotions, such as awe and joy, and reduce negative emotions such as fear and anger. Thoughtful experience design is sometimes lacking in the industry, especially at 'neglected' customer journey touch points (e.g., airport transfers and check-in), which then devolve into sources of stress and negative emotion for tourists. Experience design is also often ignored by destination marketing organisations (DMOs) who could work with: (a) locals to create pro-poor tourism projects that elicit tourists' involvement, sparking emotions such as interest, hope, and pride; and (b) product developers to design vacation packages that specifically address individuals' hobbies and passions, eliciting emotions such as interest, amusement and inspiration.

Our study results support compounding evidence that tourists do experience a higher intensity of positive emotions compared to negative emotions on vacation. This finding validates the industry's use of emotions in travel marketing. However, when tour operators such as Kuoni® or Apple Vacations® promise life transformations and profound personal development – in other words, flourishing – from vacations, there may be cause for concern, as our participants did not reach a flourishing level of emotion balance. To ensure truth in advertising and the vacation experience, we recommend that all tourism businesses measure these effects in their own customer research. Measuring emotions also enables more effective management of positive word-of-mouth and loyalty, as emotions are mechanisms of these processes. Measuring emotions is not common practice for tourism and leisure businesses, although new technology is facilitating the process, including mobile surveys, smart service measurement kiosks, and facial expression recognition. Hence, the opportunities for improving tourists' satisfaction with the overall product are substantial.

Based on: Nawijn, J., Mitas, O., Lin, Y. & Kerstetter, D. (2013). How do we feel on vacation? A closer look at how emotions change over the course of a trip. *Journal of Travel Research*, 52(2), 265–274.

However, the memory of enjoying ice cream is just one type of memory. In fact, Zaltman (2003) distinguishes three types of memories: (1) procedural, (2) semantic and (3) episodic. Our procedural memory helps us remember how to do certain things, step by step, and is mostly related to skills. This type of memory provides us with scripts and rules for a wide range of activities with a repetitive nature, from tying the laces of our shoes to completing our tax forms, and from crossing the road to making coffee.

Our semantic memory helps us recall the meaning of words and symbols. We need our semantic memory to engage in conversations and to understand what other people are saying. Obviously, the words stored in this memory can range from simple concepts like pizza and bicycle to more abstract and complex concepts such as democracy and the big bang. This semantic memory not only helps us to decipher the word-based messages from other people and to create our own messages, but it also helps us to interpret symbols. Within this context, the word 'symbols' can relate to a logo representing a brand, such as the Apple logo, but also to very different types of symbols, such as Ennio Morricone's music representing the atmosphere of cowboys and westerns. Our semantic memory enables us to make the connection between a picture and a brand, and between sounds and a specific atmosphere and type of movie. In other words, this memory helps us to make the connection between symbols and meaning.

In contrast, episodic memories are very much linked to a particular place, time and situation worth remembering. For instance, a first date, a trip to Paris, or the birth of a child. However, episodic memories do not only have to be linked to life (changing) events; they can, for instance, also relate to remembering what was said by whom during a specific meeting. Episodic memories also connect the when, where and with whom of a particular situation to other memories related to that point in time or life stage, those people and that location. Another key characteristic of episodic memories is that they have a clear beginning and an end. Obviously, this type of memory is closely related to the memories created by memorable encounters, peak experiences, extended experiences and extraordinary experiences, as discussed in Chapter 1. Understanding how to create positive episodic memories for your customers – or at the very least, ensuring that no negative episodic memories are created – is therefore crucial to businesses and professionals aiming to design, stage and manage experiences. However, procedural and semantic memories can be just as relevant, for instance for designing appropriate scripts for your employees or when you aim to offer transformative experiences.

METHODS, TOOLS AND TECHNIQUES TO PUT THE PUZZLE TOGETHER

Over the years, a number of methods, tools and techniques have been developed to assist in better understanding schemata and memories. Many of these methods, tools and techniques are aimed at improving product development and marketing of goods, services and experiences.

The Kelly Repertory Grid method can be used to create insight into the way consumers rank products, services – and therefore also experiences of which those products and services are a part – and brands based on so-called critical personal constructs. Kelly (1955) first developed this technique to better understand the meaning people attach to certain concepts. His idea was that patterns in this process of giving meaning could be used as indicators of the personality of respondents. Market researchers nowadays apply this tool to understand how consumers position, compare and choose between products, services and brands based on a number of constructs.

A repertory grid always revolves around a specific type of value proposition, for instance a fast-food restaurant or a music festival. For this specific type of proposition, market researchers will then pick a number of competing offers on the market. For a fast-food restaurant, this list could include restaurants such as McDonalds, Pizza Hut, KFC, Spudulike and Nordsee. Based on qualitative interviews with potential customers, constructs are established that apparently give meaning to this type of offer for consumers. These constructs are always bipolar. For fast-food restaurants,

FIGURE 2.1 An example of a Kelly Repertory Grid

Fast-food restaurants					
5-point scale	McDonalds	Pizza Hut	KFC	SpuduLike	Nordsee
Healthy	3	5	2	1	1
Fun	5	1	1	3	2
Cheap	1	2	1	3	5
Sustainable	1	3	5	1	4

these could include constructs such as healthy versus unhealthy, fun versus dull, cheap versus expensive, and sustainable versus unsustainable. During interviews, respondents are then asked to organise the list of competing offers based on those constructs by contrasting them. The interviewer will ask which two offers are the most healthy and which the most unhealthy. These verdicts are recorded on a five- or seven-point Likert scale and then the remaining offers are also scored using the same scale.

Reynolds and Gutman (1984) recognised the potential of the repertory grid method for marketing purposes and developed a means-end chain analysis to assist in establishing a better link between values and beliefs, as recorded in the grid, and actual product and service attributes. The underlying logic for this means-end chain analysis is to link consumer values to product and service attributes as a reference point for improving branding and product development. The analysis itself is based on so-called laddering interviews that can be used to better understand the mental chain – the steps in the thought process – of consumers when assessing the attractiveness of a specific product or service. Establishing the mental chain ultimately allows for connecting product and service attributes to the personal values of (individual or groups of) consumers. The laddering interview technique can follow two different procedures. If the objective is to better understand the brand values that consumers attribute to a particular product or service, the starting point for the interview are the product and service attributes and functions. If the purpose is to identify product improvement possibilities or innovation opportunities, the starting point can also be consumer values. In the first case, the interviewer invites the respondent to a conversation about the product and service attributes he distinguishes. The interviewer then tries to identify the cognitive and/or affective reactions these attributes elicit. In the next stage of the interview – the consequence level, the respondent is asked to reflect on these reactions. Within this context, the term consequence relates to the effect of specific attributes on the respondent. For example, a respondent may like his NIKE running shoes because they make him look good or offer comfort and stability during his workout. Looking good and comfort/stability are consequences this respondent links to attributes of the NIKE running shoes. Then, in the final stage of the interview, these consequences are linked to the respondent's personal values. By asking why specific consequences are important to the respondent, the interviewer can establish this link. Looking good could very well turn out to be linked to values such as self-respect or being successful, whereas comfort/stability could turn out to be linked to values such as security and fun/enjoyment. Based on the answers and explanations of the respondent, the interviewer tries to create the full chain from tangible product features to abstract consumer values.

Another interesting tool in this field is the patented Zaltman Metaphor Elicitation Technique (ZMET). It can assist researchers in trying to understand the thoughts and feelings people attach to certain concepts by examining meaning through metaphors. This tool was developed by Zaltman (1997) in order to create a deeper understanding of consumer preferences. For a ZMET interview, respondents are asked to collect and bring a number of pictures that represent their thoughts and feelings about the topic at hand (Christensen & Olson, 2002). These pictures are then used as the starting point for a two-hour in-depth conversation about that topic. After the interview, both the pictures and the language – the metaphors – used by the respondents to explain the concept are analysed to get a full understanding of how a consumer, or a group of consumers, feels about the topic. ZMET mostly taps into semantic and episodic memories of respondents and uses these to understand the associations they have with certain topics and concepts.

Businesses and professionals aiming to design, stage and manage experiences could benefit greatly from insights gathered through ZMET. Consider, for example, a ZMET session focused on the concept of sports. If people are asked to bring 10 or 12 pictures that illustrate this concept to them, it is very likely that different (groups of) respondents will bring very different sets of pictures. Whereas one person might associate sports with teamwork, perseverance, a sense of belonging, fun and winning, another person might primarily associate sports with being fit, healthy, stress relief, mental wellbeing and self-confidence. By interviewing these different types of consumers, ZMET can result in valuable insights with respect to personal values underlying these associations and clear differences between different consumer groups. Obviously, this could prove to be crucial information for designing, staging and managing successful experiences for specific types of consumers.

PERSONALITY

Truly understanding why specific people like or dislike specific experiences requires a full understanding of what makes people different. Why does one person love the idea of backpacking through the rainforests in Uganda and why does that sound like the worst possible holiday plan ever to another person? As discussed earlier, our upbringing, other people, our memories, our values and a number of other aspects seem to influence what we like and dislike. However, at least one crucial piece of the puzzle is still missing. That piece is usually referred to as personality and represents a concept that brings together a number of the aspects discussed so far.

Even though the term personality is widely used to explain the differences between people, psychologists have not yet been able to reach consensus on an exact definition. What is clear though, is that the concept of personality relates to a set of personal characteristics that reveal themselves in the behaviour of people in various settings. What most psychologists also agree on is that our personality is not necessarily stable throughout our lives; it develops as a result of different life stages and life events, such as the death of a parent, birth of a child, moving out of your parents' house, and landing your first job. The on-going debate amongst psychologists revolves around clustering these characteristics and how specific patterns in behaviour can be established.

Most personality tests are based on the so-called big five personality traits (Costa & McCrea, 1992). The idea behind this big five is that personality traits can be clustered into five separate dimensions:

1. Openness to experience: people differ from curious and inventive on one side to cautious and consistent on the other. A person, who scores low on openness, can be characterised as pragmatic, persevering and factual, and as someone who prefers structure and routines. A person, who scores high on this dimension, prefers novelty and variety in activities, is curious, and likes to engage in new intense experiences.
2. Conscientiousness: this second dimension addresses the difference between people who prefer to be efficient and organised, and people who are easy-going and careless. A person, who scores high on this dimension, is self-disciplined, plans his activities and is achievement or goal driven, whereas a person, who scores low, is flexible and spontaneous but can also be sloppy and unreliable.
3. Extraversion: people's score on the extraversion dimension differentiates them on their behaviour in relation to the social world. A person, who scores high, likes being in the company of others and has a high need for affiliation and attention. A person, who scores low, is introverted and does not seek attention, and is more reflective and quiet.
4. Agreeableness: this dimension indicates whether a person tends to be compassionate, willing to help others and trusting – a high score, or tends to be suspicious of others and competitive – a low score.
5. Neuroticism: this final dimension relates to a person's emotional stability and impulse control. Someone, who scores high, will be calm and stable but could also come across as uninspiring, whereas someone, who scores low, can be sensitive and anxious, and could be perceived as very dynamic but also insecure.

Obviously, a person's scores on these five dimensions could serve as a valuable predictor of the types of experiences that person would like or dislike. Someone who scores high on openness to experience is clearly more likely to prefer the backpacking trip to Uganda mentioned earlier than someone who scores low on this dimension. Similarly, it is probably not very wise to try and sell a group holiday to someone who scores low on extraversion and agreeableness, nor would you be likely to be successful with staging experiences based on surprises and unexpected twists and turns for people who score high on conscientiousness.

The concept of personality also has a direct link with brands, brand personalities and the (types of) experiences they stand for. As discussed in Chapter 1, businesses need to make sure that customers have positive associations with the experiences they offer and the brand under which this is done in order to create loyalty and positive word of mouth and mouse. Kapferer's brand prism illustrates that what a brand – or independent business or professional – stands for, needs to be represented in language, symbols and the relationships it tries to have with its customers. In other words, these facets represent and communicate the brand's personality. In essence, a brand personality and people's personality are very similar concepts. They both consist of a number of characteristics that become visible and apparent through behaviour and behavioural preferences. This also means that cultivating these characteristics can help consumers decide whether they would like to associate themselves with a particular brand and the other people who like it. Ultimately, persuading (the right) people to consume the experiences you offer needs to account for the right fit or *click* between these customers' personality and your personality as a brand, business or professional.

THE ECONOMIC (IR)RATIONALE OF WHY CONSUMERS BUY EXPERIENCES

The previous sections and the previous chapter have provided a number of explanations for the rise of the experience economy. Interestingly enough though, economists especially have struggled to understand – or maybe *accept* – why consumers are willing to spend money on experiences. In many economic models, consumers are treated – or modelled – as fully rational beings that are supposed to look for products of a certain quality level at the lowest possible price. In other words, many economists assume consumers always use maximum utility as the one and only criterion for their buying decisions. However, a rational trade-off consisting of a straightforward exchange of money for goods cannot always explain actual buying behaviour of consumers. Even if one accounts for additional aspects such as time and access, some consumer decision-making seems irrational from a purely economic perspective. Why do consumers, with time and access being equal, sometimes simply refuse to go for the cheapest option?

Valence, expectancy and instrumentality: motivation

To answer this question, economists like Vroom (1964) developed alternatives to the maximum utility concept as the reference point for economic transactions between companies and consumers. Vroom pointed out that some consumer buying behaviour could only be explained if you accept that, rather than maximum utility, maximum pleasure is what consumers are looking for when choosing specific (combinations of) products and services. This pleasure is derived from the product(s) or service(s) a person buys, but can also be created by the transaction itself – the experience. Similar to the happiness concept discussed earlier, this pleasure concept includes a rational and an emotional component. It takes both quantitative and qualitative elements into consideration, such as time and money on the one hand and aspects such as friendship, enjoyment and personal growth on the other.

Vroom further operationalized his perspective on consumer behaviour by establishing that motivation for certain behaviour is the result of a comparison of different behavioural alternatives based on multiplying valence, expectancy and instrumentality for each of the alternatives. The alternative with the highest motivation is the one for which the highest pleasure and the lowest pain are anticipated. In Vroom's formula, valence represents the desirability of the outcome – the value created by specific behaviour, expectancy relates to the belief that more effort – investing more time and money – will lead to a better performance, and instrumentality is the extent to which a person believes that a better performance leads to a better outcome. If you would apply this formula to Europeans who choose to spend a beach holiday in a remote area of Thailand, it would work as follows: Important outcomes for these people, or valence, could be to get away from everyday Western life, being immersed in tropical nature, relaxing and going to a place where friends have not been – the brag factor! Obviously, travelling to this destination is more expensive than a destination nearby, more time consuming, and could very well require some research and planning. Together with the prospect that all these efforts will lead to a *better* holiday, these elements create the value for expectancy. Finally, instrumentality for these people relates to the feeling that such an exotic holiday will actually make them happy – more happy than a beach holiday on the Spanish coast ever could. This example clearly illustrates how Vroom's theory encompasses much more than just quantifiable measurements of tangible items, money and time. This makes it an interesting perspective within the context of the experience economy and for businesses and professionals trying to be successful in an era in which consumer needs and wishes seem to be shifting more and more in a direction that cannot be explained purely based on maximising utility.

Although motivation based on expected gain and pain, as formulated by Vroom, can be considered a good starting point for understanding consumer choices and preferences, it cannot always explain actual behaviour. Over the years, researchers from different fields have tried to create a deeper understanding of how behaviour can be explained and predicted. However, it would be fair to say that no definitive model or algorithm has been established yet. As it turns out, we, people, are rather complicated and sometimes even a bit weird. What we do know, so far, is that real-life decision-making and the desire to do or buy something are not always in line with each other. To illustrate this, consider people with an unhealthy life style. Most of them are fully aware of the fact that in order to stay fit and healthy, they should quit smoking, eat and/or drink less and exercise more. Many of them would actually also like to be more fit and healthy. At some point in time, many of them have also decided to start a diet, quit smoking, or start going to the gym. However, some of these people find it extremely difficult to really change their behaviour, especially over a long period of time, and relapses are no exception. There is no doubt that motivation was high for a number of these people and that motivation is at least one of the predictors of actual behaviour. However, people's behaviour is also influenced by other factors, such as the world around them. If we return to the example, it is not difficult to see how trying to quit smoking is quite a challenge if friends or family members are also smokers. The same applies to trying to drink less alcohol, if people around you consider having a few glasses of wine every night a normal thing. Going to the gym definitely helps in the long run, but it can be disheartening to be confronted with the differences in body size and fitness level between you and other people in the gym. To top it off, regaining your health and fitness is hard work – there is no way of getting around that. Putting in the effort could very well take a lot out of you and have an effect on your mood and temper. In that case, it really does not help to hear other people, in 'real' life and on television, claiming that 'chubby' people are often the most cheerful and friendly.

Motivation, opportunity and capacity

In other words, there is more to explaining and predicting behaviour than just motivation. At least two other types of factors seem to play a role, and these can be referred to as opportunity and capacity. As indicated by Morel, Poiesz and Wilke (1997, p. 467), 'people will engage in [. . .] specific behaviour when their motivation, perceived capacity, and perceived opportunity to execute this behaviour are sufficiently high, that is, above some critical subjective minimum level'. They define motivation as the need, interest or desire to engage in particular behaviour. Capacity refers to a person's perceived and objective capability, instrumentality and skill to engage in that behaviour and to achieve a stated goal. Opportunity covers all the external circumstances that might influence the behaviour – both positively and negatively. This Triad of (types of) factors (Poiesz, 1999) seems to cover all relevant determinants of behaviour. If and when a person engages in particular behaviour, the three Triad factors have all reached a particular minimum level and the overall score resulting from multiplying the scores for the individual factors is higher than for alternative behaviours.

To illustrate the logic of this Triad approach to predicting and explaining behaviour, consider the following practical example: A UK-based man, let us call him Jim, has

FIGURE 2.2 The Triad approach to explaining and predicting behaviour

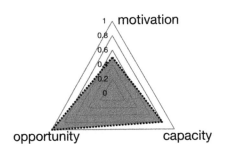

dreamt for years of going on a long road trip with his wife and two kids. He has saved some money to make his dream come true. Now the time has come to make a choice. Jim is considering three alternatives. The first one is the Great Ocean Road along the south coast of Australia. The second option is the Garden Route along the coast of South Africa and the third is Route 66 across the USA. All three alternatives should be wonderful and adventurous, and they share the immersive character Jim and his family are looking for. If Jim would be forced to pick one purely based on what he expects to be the most beautiful road trip – especially because of the chance of seeing African wildlife, he would probably pick South Africa. It is a tight call though because all three alternatives are promising in that respect. In other words, all three clearly score above the threshold when it comes to motivation. However, there are other factors to consider, such as those linked to the capacity category. First of all, money plays a role because there is a price difference between the three options. Australia is the most expensive alternative and South Africa is by far the cheapest, with the USA somewhere in between. Jim is a little worried about South Africa though, because he is not too sure about the infrastructure over there and has some doubts about his capabilities as a driver when it comes to handling different surfaces and potentially unsafe situations. In fact, safety issues also reduce his motivation for South Africa a bit. Australia and the USA definitely score higher in this department, but Australia is a really long flight and Jim and his wife are not too sure their children will be able to cope with that. And then, in the same week that Jim feels he should really make up his mind and book one of the options, his wife watches a travel special on ITV covering a road trip on Route 66. What is more, the programme not only contains a number of interesting tips on how to make the most of your trip across the USA, but is followed by a commercial with a special offer. That offer would allow Jim and his family to extend their trip by another week without going over his original budget. What an opportunity! That settles it: within budget, safe, beautiful – especially if Jim makes sure to follow up on some of those tips, not too long a flight; Route 66 it is! Or in Triad terms, motivation for the USA is now at least as high as for the other two alternatives; opportunity is the highest, and capacity is also at least

FIGURE 2.3 Jim's options assessed based on the Triad factors

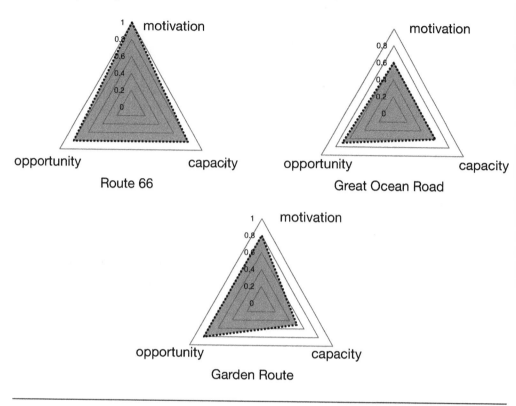

as high, if not higher, than for the other trips. All this means that the overall score for this trip is now clearly the highest.

High-involvement and low-involvement decisions

Obviously, Jim did not actually take out his calculator to do the maths involved with this Triad logic. Estimating the Triad scores for specific (types of) people with respect to specific decisions and behaviour can definitely be a useful tool – also for businesses and professionals offering experiences – to predict and explain ultimate behaviour of those people. However, the people involved are not very likely to consciously make these calculations. They might take some time though, and even draw up a pros and cons list, to make up their mind, especially for decisions that involve a lot of time, money and effort, and that are new to them. Jim's road trip is one of those decisions, as is buying a house or car (for most people). Houses and cars are typical examples of so-called high-involvement goods: purchasing those goods requires significant (investments of) resources from the people buying them. In contrast, margarine, milk, toothpaste and shampoo represent typical examples of low-involvement goods. These are products that you buy regularly and doing so does not involve a lot of time, money and effort. Not too many people would go through the trouble of compiling a pro and con list for seven different brands of margarine.

Over the years, several researchers have tried to translate this high/low-involvement factor to buying services and experiences but have found these types of offers less binary than goods. This is especially true for experiences offered in the events, tourism and hospitality industries. Almost all of these experiences require or provoke a relatively high involvement of the consumer, even if the actual amount of money involved is relatively low compared to a house or a car. One of the reasons for that is that, whereas margarine or toothpaste is something we buy without really thinking about it, these experiences are often directly related to what we like, what gives us pleasure – our so-called hedonic values. Further, for many of these experiences, as discussed before, consuming them also encompasses a certain symbolic value to us – consuming experiences is linked to who we are or want to be and the (type of) people we want to be associated with. This means that for most experiences, involvement is higher than you would expect purely based on the money involved. Going to a rock concert and buying a month's supply of laundry detergent could very well cost about the same – moneywise, but they are very different when it comes to our level of involvement. Another reason for that is that buying the wrong laundry detergent is something that is annoying but the mistake is easily repaired and you would forget about it within minutes. That is not the case if the concert you visit turns out to be a horrible experience because the band clearly forgot to do a sound check and most of the other visitors only had two things on their minds: getting drunk and trying to pick a fight. That is not something you will forget about in a few minutes and also not something you can simply replace or repair. Consequently, the level of involvement for buying experiences is a more complicated issue than it is for goods. The ultimate level of involvement depends on factors such as the personal meaning of the purchase, the risk associated with the purchase, the importance of the negative consequences of a wrong or bad choice, the perceived probability of making a bad choice, and the hedonic and affective value linked to the purchase (Laurent & Kapferer, 1985). Based on the previous sections, it is obvious that different (types of) consumers will score differently on these factors. This means that you could create specific consumer profiles based on these different scores and these profiles could provide valuable information for businesses and professionals trying to sell experiences to these consumers.

STEREOTYPES, ARCHETYPES AND PERSONAS

The previous sections have reviewed a number of concepts, methods, tools and techniques that can assist in predicting and explaining the behaviour of consumers. We pursue happiness based on our (different types of) needs, values and expectations. Within this context, consuming experiences has become increasingly important to many of us. They help us express who we are or want to be. They reinforce our personality, give us pleasure and excitement, or they help us learn and develop ourselves. We are motivated to consume experiences for a number of reasons but so much is clear: we want them; we need them!

However, it is also clear that different people want and need different things and thus also different experiences. Interestingly, most of us would probably feel we could pretty accurately predict the type of experiences that other people would like or dislike. We all tend to distinguish specific groups of people based on specific characteristics – even though we do not know those people personally – and we also tend to ascribe certain preferences and behaviours to those groups in our minds. The elderly cannot work with modern electronic devices and parents do not understand (the value and importance of) social media. Golfers are rich people and Spanish people are laid back. Even though you might not agree with these statements, they probably sound familiar. Statements like these are typical examples of so-called stereotypes and the fact is that almost all of us are inclined to create and/or remember them. Stereotypes are a common way of creating groups of people in our minds. We all, to some extent, use stereotypes to assess people. Typically, people who belong to your group are the cool ones, the nice ones, whereas people outside that group are simply not that cool, not your kind of people. Luckily, the divide is not always so black and white because we actually belong to a number of different (types of) groups simultaneously: a family, a group of friends, a sports club or team, students studying at the same university, colleagues, fans of the same boy band, art lovers, and so on.

Stereotypes generally have the same function as schemata; they help us categorise and structure our surroundings, which frees up brain capacity to focus on other things. Categorisation of groups is based on similarities between people who belong to a particular group and differences between groups. We all know that cars are different from motorbikes but also that Italian cars are different from German cars. With people, we apply the same logic. Unfortunately, this can have severe negative effects, as human history has shown us repeatedly, especially if the logic applied is rather binary by basing stereotypes on just one attribute, such as religion or skin colour. However, if we allow for categorisation based on a range of traits and apply appropriate nuances, stereotypes can actually prove very helpful in understanding various types of consumers for which we design, stage and manage experiences. To avoid confusion with the negative effects of inappropriate stereotyping it might be better to refer to these nuanced stereotypes as archetypes. Archetypes are often used in literature and movies and these nuanced stereotypes reflect a specific fictional character or a role, such as the hero, the innocent child or the jester, that combines a number of typical traits. Ultimately, most of these archetypes are based on the work of early-20th century psychologist Carl Gustav Jung. Jung was one of the first to try and create an overview of personality traits and his archetypes are based on two dimensions: ego versus social, and freedom versus order.

In stories described in books and movies, these archetypes are often used and expanded upon by adding elements such as a personal history, so that the audience

FIGURE 2.4 Jung's dimensions and archetypes

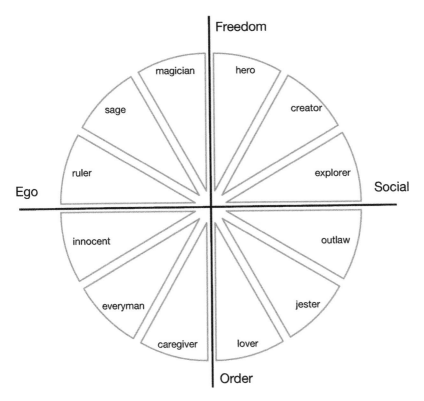

Source: Jung, C.G. (1969). *Archetypes and the Collective Unconscious* [sic], Collected Works of C.G. Jung, Volume 9 (Part 1). Princeton: Princeton University Press.

can understand and appreciate specific traits. Usually, the main characters in a story also develop themselves and, as the story progresses, show new or different traits. Think of the friend who turns out to be the bad guy or the outlaw who ultimately turns out to be the good guy and – obviously – gets to marry the princess. Although research has since shown that Jung's two dimensions do not tell the full story, the archetypes based on them have proven quite appealing and useful for various kinds of businesses and professionals. Marketing and branding specialists have picked up on them and often try to link them to specific brands or try to have the brand behave like one of these archetypes. They emphasise this identity in commercials, events and new products and services. Brands such as LEGO and Apple purposely position themselves as creators, Mercedes as ruler, NIKE as hero, Harvard as sage, and The Body Shop as innocent.

Service and experience designers have also picked up on the ideas behind stereotypes and archetypes, especially ever since they started focusing on customer-centric services and experiences. With the emergence of concepts such as service dominant logic, value co-creation and the experience economy, further strengthened by developments in (information and communication) technology, experience designers now tend to put their customers central in the experiences they want to stage for them. And, given what has been discussed in this chapter and the previous one, they had better! As a business or professional who stages experiences, you simply have to understand the (differences between the) people to whom you will be offering them. You need to understand their personalities, their needs, their values and expectations, as well as the way in which they and their peers are likely to react to specific stimuli, clues, responses and behaviours.

For that reason, the backgrounds and traits of the consumers for whom you will be staging experiences represent the logical starting point for designing those experiences. A logical way of doing so, analogous to books and movies, is to construct so-called personas – the main characters – that represent specific (groups of) consumers with their specific backgrounds and traits. By designing the experience for these personas, you are forced or at least triggered to focus on what they like or dislike – for instance based on their schemata, on what represent the crucial elements in their customer journey – for instance based on their specific needs, wishes and values, and on why and how they expect this experience to contribute to their pleasure and wellbeing or reinforce their identity. Obviously, ideally, you would like 'real' people to provide feedback on your design but this can prove rather complicated for (extensive) experiences made up of combinations of various tangible products, services, behaviours of staff, and servicescapes that specifically have to be created and constructed for staging these experiences. It would be quite tricky to have potential customers provide you with feedback on your theme park before actually building and operating it. For many experiences, reflecting on them basically requires actually experiencing the 'finished product'. That is why designing experiences usually needs to rely on basing them on personas instead. Possible ways to also involve direct feedback from current and potential customers are discussed in more detail in Chapters 3 and 4.

The technique of creating personas in service/experience design was first developed and applied by Microsoft (Pruitt & Grudin, 2003). Microsoft applied personas as part of their efforts to create user-centric interfaces for their software. These personas focused on the type of document that person wanted to create, such as a Word or Powerpoint document, and on the function of the software for the user. This allowed Microsoft to put the purpose of the user central in the development of their software. These days, personas are used by a number of different businesses and professionals, from product engineers to call-centre operators, and from theatres to online insurance agencies and airports. A well-developed persona assists designers and service/experience providers in truly understanding the world through the eyes of their (potential) customers.

Personas are similar to (nuanced) stereotypes and archetypes, and they usually have a specific name, age, marital status, education level but also contain information on the purpose and frequency of consuming a specific product, service or experience and the symbolic meaning attached to that for that persona. Personas can also include statements on values and personality, as well as their preferences with respect to other products, services, experiences and brands. Most businesses and professionals develop between three to five personas as the starting point for their design process. However, such a design process can take on many different forms and include many different steps, stages, methods, tools and techniques. Consequently, deciding on the appropriate process for designing successful experiences is no sinecure. Therefore, understanding the appropriateness of specific types of processes for designing specific types of products, services and experiences is the main topic of the next chapter. Subsequently, Chapter 4 will combine the lessons learnt from Chapter 2 – the so-called social sciences perspective – with lessons learnt from Chapter 3 – the so-called design perspective – and present a comprehensive hands-on approach to designing experiences, including how to incorporate personas as the logical starting point for this process.

SUMMARY

Based on reading this chapter, we hope you will understand and remember the following:

- The reasons why we, customers, increasingly favour experiences over products and services.
- The concept of happiness.
- Different types and levels of needs, such as those identified by Maslow (1943).
- The crucial role of values in explaining and predicting how different people will react differently to the same experience (offered to them).
- The roles of schemata and different types of learning in how we perceive experiences.
- Different types of memory and the link of these types of memories to experiences.
- The Kelly Repertory Grid method.
- The Zaltman Metaphor Elicitation Technique.
- The relevance of these types of methods and techniques for designing, staging and managing experiences.
- The crucial role of the concept of personality in explaining and predicting how different people will react differently to the same experience (offered to them).
- The way the Triad factors approach could assist in explaining and predicting behaviour.
- The difference between high-involvement and low-involvement decisions.
- Stereotypes, archetypes and personas.
- The reason why personas could offer an interesting starting point for designing experiences.

FOOD FOR THOUGHT

Based on the content of this chapter, the following questions, challenges and topics could serve as interesting starting points for further discussion:

- How do you pursue happiness? Is this any different for you from your friends or colleagues? How can these differences be explained?

- How would you score yourself on the so-called big five personality traits and what does that tell you about the types of experiences you prefer?

- If you were to be assigned the task of designing a theme park, what would be crucial personas to create as the starting point for the design process and what are the key characteristics of these personas?

REFERENCES

Abrahams, R.D. (1986). *Ordinary and extraordinary experience. The anthropology of experience* (pp. 45–72). Urbana: University of Illinois Press.

Anderson, J.R., Kline, P.J. & Beasley, C.M. (1979). A general learning theory and its application to schema abstraction. *Psychology of Learning and Motivation*, 13, 277–318.

Arnould, E.J. & Price, L.L. (1993). River magic: Extraordinary experience and the extended service encounter. *Journal of Consumer Research*, 20(1), 24–45.

Bandura, A. (1977). *Social learning theory*. Englewood Cliffs, NJ: Prentice Hall.

Bartlett, F.C. (1932). *Remembering: A study in experimental and social psychology*. Cambridge: Cambridge University Press

Bauman, Z. (2000). *Liquid modernity*. Cambridge: Polity

Beck, U. (1992). *Risk society: Towards a new modernity* (Vol. 17). London: Sage.

Christensen, G.L. & Olson, J.C. (2002). Mapping consumers' mental models with ZMET. *Psychology & Marketing*, 19(6), 477–501.

Costa, P.T. & McCrea, R.R. (1992). Normal personality assessment in clinical practice: The NEO Personality Inventory. *Psychological Assessment*, 4(1), 5.

Dawes, R.M. (1980). Social dilemmas. *Annual Review of Psychology*, 31(1), 169–193.

Denzin, N. (1992). The many faces of emotionality: Reading persona. In C. Ellis & M. Flaherty (Eds.), *Investigating subjectivity: Research on lived experience* (Vol. 139) (pp. 17–30). London: Sage.

Diener, E.D., Emmons, R.A., Larsen, R.J. & Griffin, S. (1985). The satisfaction with life scale. *Journal of Personality Assessment*, 49(1), 71–75.

Falk, J.H. & Dierking, L. (1992). *The museum experience*. Ann Arbor, MI: Whalesback Books.

Giddens, A. (1999). *Runaway world: How globalization is reshaping our lives*. London: Profile Books.

Jensen, R. (1999). *The dream society: How the coming shift from information to imagination will transform your business*. New York: McGraw Hill Professional.

Kahle, L.R., Beatty, S.E. & Homer, P. (1986). Alternative measurement approaches to consumer values: The list of values (LOV) and values and life style (VALS). *Journal of Consumer Research*, 13(3), 405–409.

Kelly, G.A. (1955). *The psychology of personal constructs*. New York: Norton.

Laurent, G. & Kapferer, J.N. (1985). Measuring consumer involvement profiles. *Journal of Marketing Research*, 22(1), 41–53.

Le Breton, D. (2002). *Conduites à risque: Des jeux de mort aux jeux de vivre*. Paris: Puf.

Maslow, A.H. (1943). A theory of human motivation. *Psychological Review*, 50(4), 370.

Morel, K.P., Poiesz, T.B. & Wilke, H.A. (1997). Motivation, capacity and opportunity to complain: Towards a comprehensive model of consumer complaint behavior. *Advances in Consumer Research Volume*, 24, 464–469.

Pavlov, I.P. (1927). *Conditioned reflexes*. Oxford: Oxford University Press.

Piaget, J. (1929). *The child's conception of the world* (J. & A. Tomlinson, Trans.). New York: Harcourt, Brace & World.

Poiesz, T.B.C. (1999). *Gedragsmanagement: Waarom mensen zich (niet) gedragen*. Wormer: Inmerc bv.

Pruitt, J. & Grudin, J. (2003). Personas: Practice and theory. *Proceedings of the 2003 conference on designing for user experiences* (pp. 1–15). ACM.

Reynolds, T.J. & Gutman, J. (1984). Advertising is image management. *Journal of advertising research*, 24(1), 27–37.

Rokeach, M. (1973). *The nature of human values*. New York: The Free Press.

Schmitt, B.H. (1999). *Experiential marketing: How to get customers to SENSE, FEEL, THINK, ACT and RELATE to your company and brands*. New York: The Free Press.

Skinner, B.F. (1938). *The behavior of organisms: An experimental analysis*. New York: Appleton-Century.

Veenhoven, R. (1984). The concept of happiness. *Data-Book of Happiness* (pp. 7–11). Dordrecht: Springer.

Veenhoven, R. (2009). How do we assess how happy we are? Tenets, implications and tenability of three theories. In A.K. Dutt & B. Radcliff (Eds.), *Happiness, economics and politics* (pp. 45–69). Cheltenham: Edward Elgar Publishing Limited.

Vroom, V.H. (1964). *Work and motivation*. New York: Wiley.

Zaltman, G. (1997). Rethinking market research: Putting people back in. *Journal of Marketing Research*, 34(4), 424–437.

Zaltman, G. (2003). *How customers think: Essential insights into the mind of the market*. Boston, MA: Harvard Business Press.

3 Understanding the design process

INTRODUCTION

Chapter 1 has concluded that businesses and professionals in events, tourism and hospitality – but also those operating in other industries – are faced with the challenge of purposely designing successful experiences that can serve as the promise they make to potential customers and the ultimate product they sell to their actual customers. In other words, as a business or professional offering those experiences you need to carefully design the (proposed) customer journeys of all of your (potential) customers, which means designing every aspect of all touch points included in those journeys. However, for those customers to be willing to engage in those experiences, and also (continue) to pay you for staging them, they need to live up to or even exceed their expectations. This means that designing those experiences not only needs to account for those customers' preferences but also how they will react to and perceive (the various aspects of the various touch points in) their customer journeys. In other words, you need to find a way to translate what you have learned from applying the concepts, methods, tools and techniques discussed in Chapter 2 into appropriate experiences.

The process of translating customers' needs and wishes into a product that can fulfil those needs and wishes is called the design process. This process not only needs to account for what customers want but also what the specific business or professional offering that product wants and is able to offer. As indicated in the final section of the previous chapter, this process can take on many different forms and can include many different steps, stages, tools and methods. To assist in deciding on the appropriate process for designing (specific types of) experiences, the remainder of this chapter reviews some of these approaches, tools and methods from the world of the design sciences and their relevance for designing experiences.

WHAT IS DESIGN?

The word design can mean different things to different people in different circumstances. The noun 'design' can relate to a detailed plan, plot or goal, but also to a pattern or composition of physical elements. The verb 'to design' can relate to preparing, drawing or creating a detailed plan of action or sketch of the various components of a complicated machine on paper or digitally, but it can also relate to drawing or creating the aesthetic layer of clothing or wallpaper. As an adjective, the word 'designer' can be added to all kinds of products: a designer chair, a designer car, and a designer dress. Within this context, design refers to the quality of the materials and construction, to the aesthetics of the product, or to the fact that a well-known designer created it. Most of us could probably mention a few famous designers or at least recognise some of their designs, such as Frank Gehry/Guggenheim Bilbao, Fritz Hansen/Egg Chair and Ian Callum/Aston Martin DB9. Finally, the expression 'by design' is often used to indicate whether something happened intentionally or deliberately, or not. If you meet someone by accident and while talking to that person you really like her or him, you might make sure you run into that person again. That second meeting is no longer a meeting by accident but rather by design. Similarly, an experience could scare or confuse someone by accident but it could also be purposely designed to do so. Some people simply like to be spooked and are even willing to pay for it!

Science and/or art?

Somehow, design seems to relate to carefully planned actions *and* the air of exclusivity linked to a specific brand. Design refers to complicated mechanisms and parts that ensure something works but you cannot see from the outside *and* to aesthetics – the look and feel of something, irrespective of its functionality or objective quality. Design can link to hard-core science and extensive calculations *and* to reputation, craftsmanship and art. Sometimes the design of specific artefacts can relate to both simultaneously: some of the most famous designs in architecture, electronics, cars and fashion combine both aspects. A Ferrari Testarossa and a Porsche 911 are high-performance cars based on the hard work of smart engineers and technological marvels. However, this is not the only reason why they make some – mostly men of a certain age – salivate. They are both also simply a sleek piece of design: they look good! Similarly, the Guggenheim in Bilbao looks amazing but could never have been created without a very detailed and well thought-out plan for constructing it, as well as for the routing and functions of the different layers it consists of.

The importance of combining these two perspectives on design is not only relevant for tangible objects, such as cars and buildings, but also – and maybe even more so – for experiences. Experiences combine tangible and intangible elements. Customers evaluate what you as a business or professional offer to them based on objective performance measures, such as quality and price, and subjective performance measures, such as how the experience makes them feel. As discussed in Chapters 1 and 2, customers can base their perception of the quality of the experience you stage for them on the physical characteristics of the building in which you host them but also on the appearance and behaviour of staff involved, or even on the effect of engaging in that experience on their self-esteem or social status. In their definition of service design, Mager and Gais (2009) combine these various perspectives by stating that service design needs to 'ensure service interfaces are useful, usable and desirable from the client's point of view and effective, efficient and distinctive from the supplier's point of view' (p. 42). Once again, this highlights two perspectives that need to come together through design: (1) the objective or scientific perspective, which is represented by aspects such as useful, usable, effective and efficient, and (2) the subjective or art perspective, which is represented by aspects such as desirable and distinctive. This definition also points to another interesting joining of different perspectives that is extremely relevant to designing experiences; somehow, an experience needs to be designed in such a way that it satisfies both the needs and wishes of the customer and the needs and wishes of the supplier – the business or professional staging the experience.

In other words, designing, especially designing experiences, relates to combining tangible and intangible elements, physical characteristics and behaviours, technical aspects and emotions. This not only applies to the end product of the design process – the ultimate design (of the product, service or experience) – but also to the design process itself. As indicated by Cross (1994), sometimes this process will resemble a straightforward logical process of problem solving, whereas at other times it requires creativity and the sudden illumination of a bright idea. This means that sometimes design equals perspiration and carefully taking all necessary steps, and at other times it equals inspiration and a so-called eureka moment. Usually, though, design requires both. The typical design process involves both rational and creative methods. It involves (re)combining existing elements and coming up with new ones. It involves science *and* art!

Design theories, models and methods

The world of design science is just as diverse as the social sciences. Whereas the social sciences have created a variety of theories, models, tools and techniques to assist in understanding and predicting human behaviour, such as the ones discussed in Chapter 2, the world of design science has created a variety of theories, models and methods to assist in creating new products, services and related technological innovations. These theories, models and methods are linked to various, quite different approaches to design. Some approaches could be described as very precise, quantifiable and calculative, whereas others resemble a more free-flowing process, usually focused on identifying opportunities for New Product Development (NPD) or New Service Development (NSD) and operating at the so-called fuzzy front end of product development.

Despite these very different approaches to design, most professionals and academics in this field agree that successfully creating new or improved products, services and technologies usually requires a step-by-step design process. Together, these steps make up so-called design models. Two main types of design models can be distinguished: descriptive models and prescriptive models.

Descriptive models, such as the one depicted in Figure 3.1, focus on creating a solution concept early in the design process, similar to the fuzzy front end approach to design mentioned earlier. Applying this model can be risky because zooming in on a particular solution concept early in the design process – and then improving it through analysis, evaluation, refinement and development – could result in ending up with a product, service or experience with some fundamental flaws. In other words, applying this model is known for sometimes leading to beautiful solutions for the wrong problem. Just imagine a design team that has been given the assignment to come up with something to sit on. They might come up with a beautiful and extremely comfortable sofa, which is not only pleasant to sit on but also allows you to lie down while you read your book or makes you feel like closing your eyes for a few minutes. Sounds good, doesn't it? Well, not if the ultimate client, an insurance company, actually wanted office chairs for staff at their head office. Checking your email on a desktop computer while trying to sit upright on a saggy sofa is probably not the solution they were looking for. Therefore, a heuristic approach to design through applying a descriptive model for the design process only works in specific circumstances. It requires a very experienced designer or design team that is able to empathise with users while relying on previous experiences, rules of thumb and assumptions. Nevertheless, in some contexts this

FIGURE 3.1 An example of a descriptive model of the design process

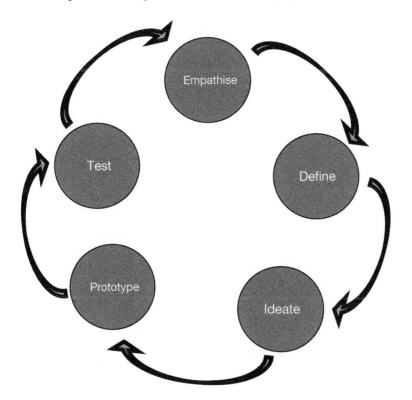

approach is definitely the preferred option. A typical example would be in user-centred companies in the service sector for adding or updating elements of a website or service, if doing so is relatively easy, prototypes can immediately be tested with users and time to market is a crucial competitive advantage. However, for building aeroplanes or skyscrapers this approach clearly is too risky.

If more analytical work is needed before solutions can be generated, it is wise to apply a prescriptive model for the design process. These design models incorporate a more systematic and/or algorithmic approach to design. The first steps in these models focus on identifying and understanding the actual problem, its (sub)components and the requirements possible solutions must satisfy before creating solutions. This is to prevent creating solutions for the wrong problem or solutions that are not feasible. After analysing the problem, prescriptive models then focus on finding possible (sub-)solutions and combining these into complete designs – the synthesis stage. To pick the best design, each (complete design) alternative is then evaluated against the (performance) requirements set in the first stage. A typical example of a prescriptive model is the well-known model for manufacturing design by Pahl and Beitz (2013; see Figure 3.2). However, sometimes a design process needs to be even more detailed than would be the case if you base it on this model. Typical examples would be the design of nano bots or satellites. For these products, it is essential that designers ensure every component is exactly the right size and every moving element moves at exactly the right speed. For such products, designers can go beyond systematic or algorithmic approaches suggested by models such as the Pahl and Beitz one and apply a so-called axiomatic approach. In simple terms, axiomatic design is not based on algorithms – such as pattern recognition or extrapolation – or tools – such as brainstorming or multi-criteria analysis – but on principles and methodologies. Ultimately, you could say that axiomatic design is based on actually calculating the best possible design through applying two axioms or fundamental truths: (1) maintain the independence of the functional requirements, and (2) minimise the information content of the design. It is beyond the scope of the discussion presented in this chapter to elaborate further on this specific approach to design but if you are keen to know more, make sure to have a look at the book *Axiomatic Design; Advances and Applications* by Nam Pyo Suh (2001). Be warned though; you should not try to read this book if formulas scare you!

Obviously, design processes applying a systematic, algorithmic or even axiomatic approach might be more precise but they usually also take longer than design processes applying a heuristic approach. The latter can cause problems if speed is of the essence. In fact, in some situations it might not be necessary to create a perfect design right away, as long as you are the first to come up with an interesting new product or service. In software development, it is not at all uncommon for companies to launch a new software package before all possible bugs and mistakes have been eliminated. New software is simply labelled as a beta version and customers will accept that it might not be perfect yet and will actually often offer assistance in tracing and eliminating possible bugs and mistakes. In other words, the specific context for a design process determines what approach will work best and produce

FIGURE 3.2 Pahl and Beitz's prescriptive model of the design process

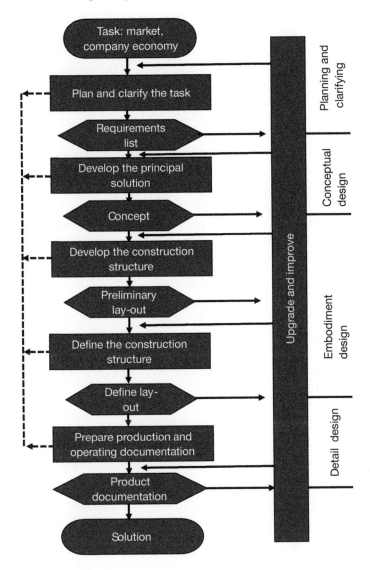

Adapted from: Pahl, G. & Beitz, W., Feldhusen, J., & Grote, K.H.; translated by K. Wallace, L. Blessing, & F. Bauert; edited by K. Wallace (1996). *Engineering Desgn: A Systematic Approach*, 3rd Edition. London: Springer-Verlag.

appropriate products and services. The type of product or service, whether you are designing a combination of products and services such as those that together shape experiences, the type of (potential) customers, the market circumstances, and so on, all of these factors influence what the optimal design process will look like. What is more, some design models combine descriptive and prescriptive elements and are not purely heuristic nor purely systematic and/or algorithmic or axiomatic. In other words, you could pick and mix based on what the specific circumstances require.

THE DESIGN PROCESS

This section describes seven generic design steps that together cover the whole design process. These steps are based on the work of influential design expert Nigel Cross, more specifically on his book *Engineering Design Methods: Strategies for Product Design* (1994). Nigel Cross based his description of the design process on an analysis of a wide range of descriptive and prescriptive models. Consequently, his model should not be interpreted as a one-size-fits-all approach or so-called recipe for design but rather as a generic overview of all relevant stages of a design process, how these stages relate to each other, and what specific methods, tools and techniques could be applied in each of these stages. As indicated above, the choice of applying a heuristic approach to design or a more systematic/algorithmic one and, consequently, the specific design methods, tools and techniques to be applied in each of these stages depend on the specific design task in hand. Therefore, this chapter first presents (the reference points for) the generic stages of a design process and the next chapter then translates these into an approach specifically dedicated to and suited to designing (specific types of) experiences.

Seven generic steps of a design process

As shown in Figure 3.3, the first three steps of a design process focus primarily on analysing the problem or task at hand to ensure that the ultimate solution is made up of sub-solutions that together actually solve that problem or fulfil that task.

FIGURE 3.3 Cross's generic model of the design process

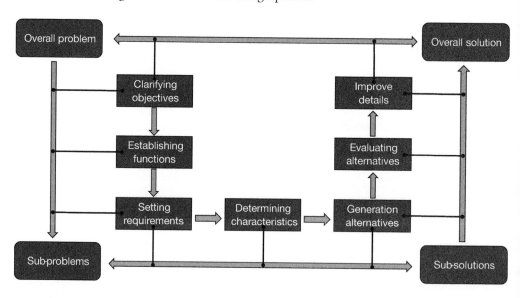

Adapted from: Cross, N. (1994). *Engineering Design Methods*, Second Edition. Chichester: John Wiley & Sons.

The *first step, clarifying objectives*, focuses on answering the question: what is the purpose of what we are going to design? The objectives that the final design must meet may (still) change (a bit) during the design process, for instance as a result of developing a better understanding of the actual problem once you start working on possible solutions. However, to be able to control and manage the design process, it is important to have a clear overview of all relevant objectives – the original ones or, if applicable, updated versions as the design process progresses – at all stages of the design process. This overview of objectives should clearly indicate which specific (overall) problem the ultimate design is going to solve and should be easy to understand for all parties involved, such as all members of the design team and the client or commissioner. For instance, if an investor asks you to design a comfortable, safe and attractive hotel, this step in the design process needs to ensure that you and that investor have a common understanding of the terms 'comfortable', 'safe' and 'attractive', as well as how these objectives relate to each other. Usually, the overview created at this stage of the process comprises one of more overall objectives and various sub-objectives. This means that this overview also needs to incorporate a description of the hierarchical relationships between all of these objectives and sub-objectives.

The *second step, establishing functions*, needs to answer the question: what should the design (be able to) do? This might sound like a straightforward question but answering it unequivocally is crucial to (the success of) the design process. As illustrated by the example of the insurance company wanting to buy office chairs for staff at their head office, it makes a huge difference whether you answer this question with 'offering comfortable support while sitting' or 'offering comfortable support while sitting behind a desk and answering emails or writing reports on a desktop computer'. Similarly, for designing a hotel it is crucial to answer this question with a lot more detail than a simple statement like 'the hotel needs to offer guests a place to sleep, take a bath, relax and eat'. Otherwise, you might end up with a design for a hip hostel while the investor actually wants to invest in a traditional five-star hotel. In other words, this stage of the design process needs to ensure that the design team has a clear understanding of the essential functions that the ultimate design needs to satisfy, regardless of the specific (sub-)solutions they come up with.

The *third step, setting requirements*, answers the question: what are the performance specifications for the ultimate design? These specifications determine the range of acceptable solutions and, as such, they specify the manoeuvring space for the designers. Typical examples of performance specifications are cost, size and production time but also specific legal or safety regulations that need to be satisfied. Performance specifications are different from objectives and functions because they do not specify what the design must do but rather set the limits for possible solutions. For example, if your objective is to design a successful hotel or theme park, the functions relate to the type of experiences the hotel or theme park needs to stage for guests or visitors to be successful, whereas the requirements relate to aspects such as the money and space available to build the hotel or theme park.

However, requirements could link to functions quite closely. For instance, if the investor in our hotel example is quite clear on the type of hotel he wants to invest in: a five-star traditional conference hotel with approximately 100 rooms. In those circumstances, it makes no sense for the design team to explore different types of accommodation that could offer guests similar experiences. For this specific design task, it is a requirement to create solutions of a specific product alternatives category – accommodation that combines facilities for sleeping, bathing, eating and having meetings instead of, for instance, a combination of a separate facility for sleeping and bathing, one for eating, and one for having meetings. In fact, the investor is also already clear on the fact that he wants a specific product type – a hotel – with specific product features – five stars, 100 rooms and conference facilities. In those circumstances, these qualifications by the commissioner limit the range of acceptable solutions and should be regarded as requirements. However, as a designer it might be worthwhile to reflect on and even return to the very first stage of the design process in a situation like this and make absolutely sure that this is what the investor really wants. Maybe, just maybe, you will find out that what the investor really wants is a healthy return on his investment and that his preference for a conference hotel is based on the (possibly incorrect) assumption that this specific product alternative of a specific type with specific features is the only way to do that.

Once these first three steps of the design process are finished, the design team should have a clear view of what it is that needs to be designed. Together, the information gathered in these first three stages is often referred to as the design brief or project scope. The hotel example has shown that ending up with the correct design brief not only requires going through these three steps but might also require some iterations – returning to earlier steps in the process. It is important to realise that doing so is a crucial element of almost any successful design process, even though this might take some extra time and effort. Otherwise, you might end up with the proverbial saggy sofa instead of office chairs!

Then, the *fourth step, determining characteristics*, focuses on linking customers' needs and wishes to so-called (engineering) characteristics of the end product. In essence, this step translates marketing information into designable elements. Marketing information relates to information gathered through applying the concepts, methods, tools and techniques discussed in Chapter 2 and explains what (potential) customers are looking for, their expectations, how they will react to specific stimuli, and so on. This information needs to be linked to actual characteristics of the end product to be designed, so that designers understand what they need to focus on. For the hotel example, this could imply translating specific preferences of potential customers with respect to spending time in their hotel room into designable elements such as the size of the room, the materials and colours to be used in furnishing the room, the type of bed and the type of bathing facility.

The *fifth step, generating alternatives*, focuses on creating design alternatives that fulfil customers' needs and wishes through performing all essential functions established in step 2, while satisfying the requirements set in step 3 and achieving the objectives laid down in step 1. Doing so means creating specific combinations of existing sub-solutions for all relevant characteristics established in step 4 but could also involve creating new sub-solutions for some of those characteristics. This stage of the design process represents what most people think of when hearing the term 'design'; coming up with proposals for something new! Sometimes, this can certainly require creativity, inspiration and possibly even eureka moments. However, in reality, many if not most design processes actually apply a number of existing sub-solutions, and focus more on creating new combinations of these sub-solutions and improving specific details. As indicated by Cross (1994), 'making variations on established themes is therefore an important feature of design' (p. 105). What's more, given the large number of ways in which separate elements can be combined, this process

---

CASE STUDY 3.1 AHA!

Geoff Marée and Ron Swidler

Good design is a result of a good design process. That makes sense. But still. . . Sometimes good design can suddenly happen, as if the idea drops from a clear sky. Most of us have had it – the 'aha' moment, also known as the Eureka moment. Eureka stands for 'I found it!' in ancient Greek. It is well known that the Greek scientist Archimedes discovered a way to measure the gold in a crown by immersing it in a bucket with water to illustrate this effect. The aha was triggered by watching spilled water when he entered a bathtub.

A recent example? The Gettys Group of Chicago are renowned for their hotel design for projects around the world. They design for renovations, but also conceptualise new hotels from the start. They were asked to design a complete makeover for the Park Vue Inn in Anaheim, California, just across the street from Disneyland. On the premises of the current building, a new structure with new looks and services has to come into being. At the beginning of 2017, Principal Ron Swidler and one of his colleagues sat together with the client, flipping through mood pictures to support the inspiration process, when one of them caught his eye. It showed an old automat vending machine in New York, with lined up cubby holes filled with sandwiches and pies. In a flash, he realised that a similar set-up could be a promising answer to a breakfast problem they had been toiling over for some time.

Since the Park Vue Inn is located opposite Disneyland, many of the hotel guests do not want to linger too long at breakfast, as they can't wait to get to their day-destination. That's partly the reason why the room price included breakfast. The Gettys Group studied what happened during high demand periods: how many guests sat down; how many had breakfast on their way out; hot food versus cold, and so on. And that information triggered the aha when Ron looked at the picture. Why not offer a breakfast opportunity to hotel guests via an automat vending machine? And as a result, the plans now show two options: a pick up window and the machine. Guests can order what sort of breakfast they want beforehand. And at their convenience, they can pick it up at their cubby hole with their room number.

might resemble a straightforward problem solving process at first glance but for most design processes it still requires dedication, expertise and also inspiration. This is especially true for designs that need to combine a large number of elements that also represent different types of characteristics, such as for designing experiences. Combining the right physical characteristics of all tangible elements involved – such as the layout of a specific servicescape and the colours and materials used for creating it – with the right non-physical characteristics of all intangible elements involved – such as the behaviour of staff interacting with customers – in an overall experience that will be appreciated by customers is usually anything but a sinecure.

In the *sixth step, evaluating alternatives*, the design alternatives generated in step 5 are evaluated based on specific criteria. Obviously, these criteria are closely linked to the original objectives established in the very first stage of the design process. However, they can also relate to the requirements set in the third stage. In principle, step 5 has ensured that all alternatives meet these requirements but that does not necessarily mean they meet them in the same way or to the same extent. For instance, even though two alternatives might both be within budget, it is quite possible that the actual costs involved with these two designs are significantly different. Similarly, some designs might take longer to realise or implement, or some designs might be more risky than others. Together, all of these criteria need to be incorporated in an evaluation of all alternatives to decide on which design alternative is the best one.

Once the best alternative is known, the final and *seventh step* of the design process, *improving details*, is all about fine-tuning and optimising the design. At this stage of the design process, designers look for ways to further increase the overall added value of the end product, either by increasing the value to customers or decreasing costs for the producer or supplier. For the hotel example, this could, for instance, imply changing the tiles in the bathroom to a different type of the same price because those tiles create a more luxurious atmosphere in the bathroom – something you know potential guests will appreciate. Another option would be to change the tiles in the bathroom to a different type with the same appearance because they are easier to clean and allow for saving housekeeping costs. Obviously, designers will not change essential functions of the design at this stage but rather focus on small changes to optimise the ultimate design.

Different processes for different problems

Sticking to the seven generic stages of a design process described in the previous subsection really is good advice for any designer. These stages are generic enough to allow for applying specific design methods, tools and techniques that fit specific circumstances, while following these steps ensures that you address all relevant aspects of the design process. This reduces the chances of ending up with beautiful solutions for the wrong problems or the wrong solutions for the right problems.

Simultaneously, the specific circumstances for the design process, such as the design task at hand but also the preferences and expertise of the designers involved, could very well imply that some stages deserve or receive special or more attention compared to others. The circumstances also impact not only the time and effort spent on each stage but also the timing and number of iterations required. For example, for specific products and within specific contexts it might very well be possible to gather immediate feedback of actual end-users on your preliminary design. A typical example – working with beta versions for software development – has been discussed earlier in this chapter. In those kinds of circumstances, you might choose to rapidly go through steps 1, 2 and 3 based more on assumptions than on extensive analyses. Subsequently, you would try to come up with a prototype solution (step 4 and 5), which you can then present to the end-users for testing and feedback. The test results and feedback can be used to adjust or refine the assumptions on which the prototype was based, after which a second prototype can be created and tested. If necessary, assumptions can be adjusted and refined even further, and so on, thus creating a number of iterations in the design process. This approach to design is called rapid prototyping. Essentially, it focuses on creating solutions as soon and as quickly as possible and then these solutions are used to define the problem more accurately or in more detail.

Sometimes though, rapid prototyping is not an option. Some problems first require extensive analyses to understand what type of solutions could work. In those circumstances, immediately focusing on solutions would not only be difficult but also extremely time-consuming and inefficient. Typical examples of these kinds of problems are designing (costly) tangible products such as cars and buildings. Creating a prototype of a skyscraper only for you to then find out that nobody would like to work or live in that building clearly is not the way to go. The same very much applies to designing the types of experiences this book focuses on. It would not be realistic to create a prototype of a theme park or hotel and then ask (potential) customers to test it. Imagine the time and money wasted if you got it wrong! Not many companies, if any, could afford to apply this approach to designing experiences. And, even if a company could afford it from a financial perspective, the possible negative consequences from a publicity and marketing point of view could very well prove to be irreversible. How would you prototype a three-day music festival? The answer is clear: you do not.

Simultaneously, experiences are made up of a combination of various tangible and intangible elements. This means that it might very well be possible to apply rapid prototyping for some of those elements. Specific touch points in the overall customer journey could benefit from a more heuristic approach to design rather than a systematic one. However, the way these elements (need to) fit into the overall experience offered to (potential) customers is something that requires a full understanding of how customers will react to specific stimuli within the context of a sequence of stimuli, together creating a specific overall dramatic structure for the customer journey as a whole. Therefore, designing experiences usually requires a combination of heuristic and systematic approaches, applied within a design process that allows for continuously checking the impact of separate elements on the overall customer journey. The ultimate process resembles what is often referred to as concurrent or agile design; designing an overall product by going through a series of smaller design processes or so-called design sprints, in which a number of elements are designed in parallel yet connected processes.

DESIGN METHODS, TOOLS AND TECHNIQUES

Before addressing the details of a design process specifically dedicated to designing experiences in the next chapter, the remainder of this chapter first explores some of the methods, tools and techniques that could be applied in the various steps of a design process. Over the years, a large number of methods, tools and techniques have been developed to assist in executing the various design steps. Some of them are linked to a heuristic approach to design, whereas others are linked to a more systematic or algorithmic approach, or a combination of both. In this section, some specific examples are discussed for each of the seven generic steps of a design process.

Step 1: clarifying objectives

The *objectives tree method* is a tool to categorise objectives and create a full understanding of the underlying (hierarchical) relationships. The crux of this method is to create an overview of all relevant objectives and related sub-objectives for the design in the shape of branches that are directly or indirectly connected to the trunk, which represents the main objective. Quite often, a first briefing or request that forms the starting point for a design process leaves a lot of room for interpretation. The objectives tree method can assist in specifying and qualifying terms used in that briefing or request. This may sound complicated but doing so essentially boils down to asking simple questions that start with 'why', 'how', 'when', 'for whom' or 'what'. The answers will help to get to the problem behind the problem and will highlight how objectives are related to each other – which objectives represent the higher-order ones and which objectives are the lower-order ones. Asking why the commissioner wants this design will usually provide answers linked to higher-order objectives, whereas questions about how to achieve this and how to define success will provide answers linked to lower-order objectives. For instance, if you are asked by a commissioner to design a fun networking event for young artists, you really need to ask why the commissioner wants to organise this event. If the answer is that he wants to give young artists the opportunity to show their work to prospective clients, this suggests that the main objective is actually to organise an event that links artists to clients in a way that increases the artists' chances of selling their work rather than simply having fun. You definitely also want to ask what outcomes of the event would mean the commissioner would consider it a success. Answers could range from 'attracting at least 50 artists and 25 clients' to 'if one of the artists sells his or her work for at least €200,000' or 'if at

FIGURE 3.4 An example of an objectives tree

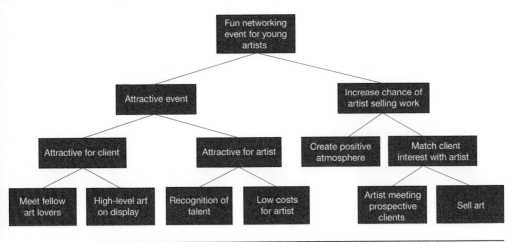

least 75% of the people present indicate they would be interested in a next edition of the event'. Obviously, these answers represent very different types of objectives and could therefore result in very different types of designs for the ultimate event. The first and third answer point to a fun event with quite a few people present, whereas the second answer actually represents an objective that could also be reached by means of a well-prepared serious meeting between one artist and one prospective client. In other words, these answers and the resulting overview of hierarchical relationships between objectives and sub-objectives could prove to be essential in ensuring that you end up with the right solution for the right problem instead of the right solution for the wrong problem.

Another tool to visualise the goals and boundaries of a design process is *design road mapping*. It is a tool that could be especially interesting to apply in circumstances that allow for frequent interaction with and immediate feedback by end-users. This tool is used to illustrate the purpose of the design process as an end goal and all the steps that need to be taken to get there. A design road map typically includes milestones and moments of co-creation with users or commissioners. A design road map can also include moments for rethinking previous steps or moving forward to the next step, for instance after a co-creation or feedback session with users. Basically, design road mapping is a tool that designers can use to consciously think about all the steps in the design process that are required to reach a particular end goal without having to resort to a prescriptive design model for guidance. By reflecting on all necessary steps, designers are stimulated to think about (and if necessary discuss with commissioners) what defines success for each step, who would need to be involved in each step to realise that, the interdependencies between steps, when to iterate or prototype, and so on. In other words, road mapping is a typical example of a tool from the world of descriptive design models and a heuristic approach to design. Interestingly, by applying it at the start of a design process you are actually forced to reflect on aspects such as the objectives you want to reach, the way in which the design needs to contribute to doing so, and the requirements for both the design process and the ultimate design. In other words, maybe without explicitly framing it like that, you are still going through the same steps as the ones described in the previous section – i.e. setting objectives, establishing functions and setting requirements. Thus, design road mapping is a typical example of a non–rigid, non–linear approach to design that still applies the same logic as the seven generic steps of a design process identified by Cross (1994).

Step 2: establishing functions

Previous sections have already highlighted the importance of not thinking in solutions at this stage of the design process but rather in functions: what is it that the ultimate product, service or experience needs to do? Thinking in functions prevents designers from focusing on beautiful solutions for the wrong problem. A method to assist designers in doing so is the so-called *function analysis method*. This method helps to understand the specific functions and sub-functions that the ultimate design needs to incorporate. The crux of this method is to think of the final product, service or experience as a system or a process. This system or process transforms inputs into outputs. This transformation is the overall function of the system or process. A simple example of such a system would be a light bulb, which transforms electricity into light – or lumen to be more precise. Similarly, you could also think about a restaurant as a system or process; a process that transforms hungry people into satisfied guests. In these examples, the system or process itself is still a black box at this stage of the design process because the way inputs are transformed into outputs is still unclear. Function analysis aims at unravelling the black box and specifying what sub-tasks or sub-functions are needed to make this transformation happen. In other words, the first step of the function analysis method is to formulate the overall function: the transformation that needs to take place. Subsequently, you need to break down the overall function – or open the black box – to establish the sub-functions required for that overall function. You then draw a block diagram that shows the interactions between and chronology of these sub-functions, and how outputs of specific sub-functions form the inputs for other sub-functions. Ultimately, your diagram should allow for identifying specific components of the ultimate design for each sub-function. These components could refer to a person performing a specific task but also to a machine, an electronic device, or parts of a machine or a device. For instance, for a restaurant the sub-function taking orders could be executed by a waiter but also by a touch screen or an intercom. At a later stage of the design process, the specific choices made with respect to these components will determine what the ultimate design will look like – a fancy à la carte restaurant, a hip self service restaurant, or a convenient drive-in restaurant.

Quite a different approach to this step in the design process is represented by the *reverse engineering technique*. This technique studies an existing product or service by literally or figuratively taking it apart and studying its components to understand how it works. This technique is used a lot in product engineering to understand and

FIGURE 3.5 An example of a function analysis block diagram

copy products of competitors, for instance with respect to engines in cars. Reverse engineering can be used in combination with the function analysis method, also for services and experiences. It could be very helpful in designing an event such as a multi-day festival to check the way the overall function has been divided into specific sub-functions in successful existing festivals. Why reinvent the wheel if your objective is to design a new bike, especially if the wheel represents bathroom facilities for festival visitors and your objective and passion is to bring together artists and an audience that appreciates soul music?

System mapping is a tool that helps designers to visualise the system that the ultimate product, service or experience they are designing will be part of. Understanding which role or function your design will have in the so-called bigger picture can be crucial to understanding and specifying the functions and sub-functions that will have to be incorporated. For instance, it is quite useful for a designer who is asked to design a playground to know the system that playground will be part of. This system could be a zoo where parents and children come to watch and learn about animals, with the playground located near the restaurant so that parents can have a moment to relax after lunch while their kids can try to climb like a monkey. This system could also be a rough neighbourhood in a big city, where the playground should serve as a safe haven for children and where they can develop their motor skills while learning to cooperate and make friends, while parents can meet their neighbours thus creating more social cohesion. Obviously, these two systems would result in very different functions and sub-functions to be incorporated in the design of the playground. Similarly, it makes a huge difference whether you are designing a restaurant as a stand-alone value proposition or as part of an overall experience provided by a theme park.

Sometimes, it can prove rather difficult to establish functions, for instance because the product, service or experience you are designing actually performs very different functions for different customers. A typical example would be a railway station. Some people are there because they need to catch a train to work, and others might be there to pick up relatives who have come from abroad to visit them, while some

CASE STUDY 3.2 DIFFERENT TYPES OF ZOO VISITORS

Bert Smit

In 2013, visitor experiences of four different zoos in the Netherlands were surveyed. Based on a large number of interviews, visitor types were identified based on personal context and experience needs and wishes. The research showed there are four types of visitors to zoos. The first group visit a zoo as a form of education and entertainment for children; the second group because they love the aesthetics (of animals, plants and nature in general); the third group visit as a form of outdoor recreation, strolling and walking through a natural surrounding; the fourth and final group visit because the zoo is a location for a birthday or family reunion.

The differences between these groups became apparent in two ways. First, for different groups different touch points turned out to be important and unimportant. Second, for different groups, the alternative to a zoo visit was very different.

For the first group, focusing on edutainment for kids, touch points such as animal shows, stroking animals and playgrounds were important, besides being able to do or learn something together. For this group, a visit to a farm, a petting zoo or a theme park is a good alternative.

For the second group, the aesthetics lovers, a zoo needs to have observation platforms – where animal behaviour can be observed and animals can be photographed, together with the landscaping and botanical elements of the zoo. This group wants to get close to rare animals, but not touch or distress them. For this group, the zoo visit can be exchanged with a visit to an art museum. A city centre with famous buildings could also be an alternative.

The third group wants to be immersed in natural surroundings. They want good paths, picnic facilities and quiet areas. Part of the fun for them is in the strolling and enjoying the day outdoors. They are not necessarily keen on seeing a specific animal, but enjoy soaking up the sun on a terrace while being immersed in nature. Their natural alternative is going to a forest or park for hiking or biking.

The fourth group is somewhat odd as the zoo for them is the location of a get-together with friends and family. They want to have a good restaurant or terrace, paths to stroll and chat on, visit a show to create a shared memory and get a group picture taken. For this group, togetherness is more important than the animals and exhibits. The alternative to the zoo for this group would be another accessible and famous location, like a museum or a national park.

Based on: Smit, B. (2015). Customer experience by design. *Proceedings of the Second Global Hospitality and Tourism Conference*, 1, 204–2013.

might be there to get a cup of coffee or have a business meeting in one of the meeting facilities in the same building. All of these people will be part of the same system but for very different reasons. In these situations, it might be useful to apply *ethnographic tools* such as *context mapping* and *walking a mile in your customers' shoes.*

The latter, as the name suggests, involves participatory observation to gather customer insights. Designers that use this technique immerse themselves in the world of the customers by observing them, talking to them and listening to them. The objective is to really understand the purpose or function of specific (parts of) products, services or experiences for these customers. This could assist those designers in establishing a complete list of functions and sub-functions that the ultimate design needs to incorporate.

Context mapping also gathers insights from customers with respect to the context in which a product, service or experience plays a role. It focuses on involving customers in the design process as experts of their own experience and tries to establish goals, needs, emotions and purposes but also social, cultural and physical aspects of the context. Context mapping aims to make tacit knowledge of customer experiences visible by applying a variety of techniques, ranging from asking customers to take pictures during or write postcards about their experiences, to group sessions in which customers are asked to reflect on their experiences and associated emotions, or to create mood boards and engage in role playing. These generative techniques can prove especially helpful for creating a deeper understanding about what customers want and feel in situations in which those feelings are hard to put into words (Stappers et al., 2003) and translating these feelings into functions and sub-functions to be incorporated in the design. Obviously, a number of the methods, tools and techniques discussed in Chapter 2 could also assist in doing so, especially if the design task at hand is to design an experience.

Step 3: setting requirements

The *performance specification method* aims at making an accurate specification of the performance that is required of the ultimate design. It starts with determining what level of generality is required for the solutions created in the design process. Three main levels of generality can be distinguished: product alternatives, product types and product features. If the highest level of generality is allowed – product alternatives, the designer is free to choose the means to achieve the overall objective. For instance, the objective is to design something that makes hotel guests appreciate nature (more). The designer could look at planting trees near the hotel, placing plants in the hotel, creating movie clips about nature that automatically start playing on the television set in your hotel room once you enter, explanations on the restaurant menu about the relationship of menu items with local ecosystems, and so on. At the lowest level of generality – product features, the designer would be assigned the task to come up with a selection of appropriate plants of a certain size to be placed in the hotel lobby at designated spots. From this example, it is clear that deciding on the appropriate level of generality is extremely important because the decision has a huge impact on the range of solutions that will be considered in the design process. The examples of the sofa versus office chairs and the conference hotel discussed earlier in this chapter clearly illustrate the damage that can be done by making the wrong decision. Once the level of generality has been decided, appropriate attributes need to be established. Attributes relate to issues such as the level of comfort that is required but also the cost, size and time that is allowed, as well as relevant safety regulations. The key is to formulate these attributes in a way that is independent of specific solutions or solution types; otherwise you will create the same problem as with specifying the wrong level of generality. For example, regarding the design of the bathrooms in a fitness centre, you should not formulate attributes in terms of the type of tiles that need to be used but rather in terms of being easy to clean and not too slippery. Simultaneously, attributes like easy to clean and not too slippery do need to be specified and, if possible, quantified in ranges between limits. Some of these specifications will be rather technical – not too slippery could be translated into a specific measure for surface roughness – while others will be formulated in terms directly linked to customer needs and wishes – such as visually appealing to specific consumer target groups with specific aesthetic preferences.

With respect to establishing attributes that are directly linked to customer needs and wishes, it could prove helpful to apply the so-called *Kano method*. This method assists in developing a better understanding of the relation between those needs and wishes and attributes to be included in the performance specification. Through assigning attributes to one of five categories, it helps designers to establish the appropriate level of performance required for specific attributes. These five categories are:

1. Required attributes: attributes that cause dissatisfaction if they are not included in the final design but they do not create extra satisfaction if they are included.
2. Desired attributes: attributes that lead to higher satisfaction if the performance level for that attribute is higher and cause dissatisfaction if they are not included in the final design.
3. Exciters or delighters: attributes that do not cause dissatisfaction if not included but if they are included in the final design they can create satisfaction or even a positive surprise because most consumers would not think of including them themselves.
4. Neutral attributes: attributes that do not significantly impact customer satisfaction, regardless of whether they are included in the final design or not.
5. Anti-feature or reverse attributes: attributes that should be left out or avoided because they cause dissatisfaction if included and no dissatisfaction when not included in the final design.

To establish in which category a specific attribute belongs, customers are asked two questions:

1. If product attribute X were present, how would you feel about that? I would like that; I would have expected that; I would be neutral about that; I could live with that; I would dislike that.
2. If product attribute X were not present, how would you feel about that? I would like that; I would have expected that; I would be neutral about that; I could live with that; I would dislike that.

FIGURE 3.6 The Kano evaluation table

Attribute is included \ Attribute is not included	Like	Expect it	Don't care	Live with	Dislike
Like	Q	E	E	E	D
Expect it	A	N	N	N	R
Don't care	A	N	N	N	R
Live with	A	N	N	N	R
Dislike	A	A	A	A	Q

Q = questionable answer   R = required   D = desired   E = exciter   N = neutral   A = anti-feature

Source: Kano, N., Seraku, N., Takahashi, F., & Tsuji, S. (1984). Attractive quality and must-be quality. *Journal of the Japanese Society for Quality Control*, 14, 39–48.

Based on the answers, a table like the one shown in Figure 3.6 can assist in determining the appropriate category.

Obviously, the ultimate design not only needs to please (potential) customers but also the business(es) or professional(s) offering the product, service or experience to those customers. In other words, requirements can relate to customer needs and wishes but also to the provider's needs and wishes, for instance with respect to properly communicating and reinforcing company or brand values. A new product sold at the Body Shop will need to live up to brand values in terms of animal welfare and sustainable production, and communicate this message for instance through smart packaging. A new attraction at Universal Studios will have to use storylines and characters from their movies. Tools and techniques such as *storytelling* and *dramatic structures* are vital in ensuring that appropriate attributes are included at this stage of the design process, especially for designing experiences. Therefore, these specific tools and techniques are addressed in more detail in Chapter 4.

Step 4: determining characteristics

At this stage of the design process you need to translate customer and provider needs and wishes – which have been linked to specific attributes in step 3 – into characteristics included in the final design. *Value analysis* can assist in doing this in a way that ensures that the final product, service or experience would appeal to (potential) customers and be different from competing products, services and experiences. This technique can also help designers to decide on what characteristics of an existing product, service or experience to focus on in creating a redesign. Value analysis involves asking potential customers to rate how important specific attributes are to them. It also involves asking them to rate the performance for those attributes for a range of existing products, services and experiences that represents the competitive set for the design you are creating. By plotting these two sets of ratings, you can create a so-called value-curve for each competitor. These curves highlight the opportunities to differentiate your design from competitors based on customers' preferences and thus what characteristics are most important for a new design or the ones to focus on for a redesign.

A more precise way to determine what characteristics to focus on is to apply *quality function deployment*. Like value analysis, this technique aims to understand the key links between attributes that are important to customers and design characteristics. It thus highlights key characteristics and it can also be used to set specific targets for design characteristics. These targets are based on what customers value and how to differentiate your design from that of competitors. For instance, rollercoaster fans usually prefer rollercoasters that travel at high speed – a product attribute. The speed of a rollercoaster is determined by design characteristics such as the initial drop, the weight of the carts, and so on. By adjusting these characteristics, the speed at which the carts travel can be adjusted and thus the ultimate satisfaction levels of customers can be influenced. However, speed is probably not the only attribute that those customers find important. The number of loopings and visual or audio effects could also influence satisfaction. However, changing or optimising one attribute could impact other attributes. It could very well be that the number of loopings influences the speed at which the carts (can) travel. To create an overview of and be able to analyse the relationships and interdependencies between the various attributes and design characteristics, designers can create a so-called House of Quality. Essentially, a House of Quality is a combination of connected matrices that depict all relevant relationships, interdependencies, current or expected performance of the design and competing designs, and resulting focus points and targets. It is extremely useful in facilitating collaboration between marketing/customer research specialists and designers because it really links customer needs and wishes to actual design decisions. An example of a House of Quality is depicted in Figure 3.7. Creating a set of connected Houses of Quality could be a smart way to appropriately link various touch points to the design of an overall customer journey. Therefore, the specific steps involved in creating one are addressed in more detail in Chapter 4.

Another useful technique to determine design characteristics is to make use of the *fish trap model*. This technique uses three iterative steps to systematically explore alternative solutions on three product levels: topological, typological and morphological. The iterations involve going back and forth between defining the overall problem and related sub-problems (steps 1, 2 and 3 of the design process) and generating sub-solutions and overall solutions (steps 5 and 6 of the design process). The topological product level relates to the overall purpose and function

FIGURE 3.7 An example of a House of Quality

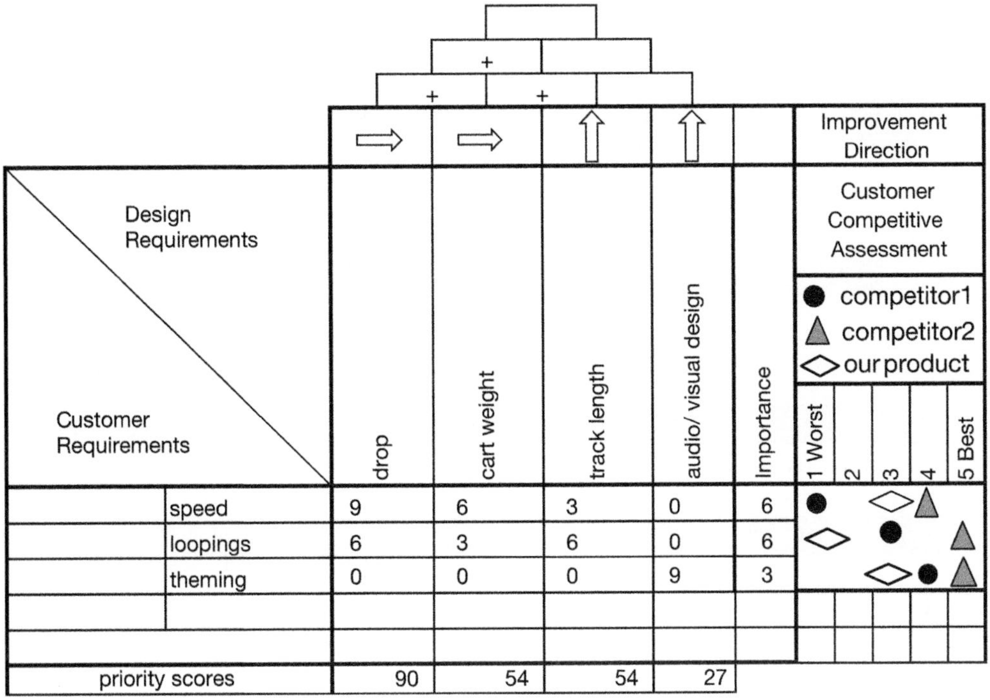

Customer Requirements		drop	cart weight	track length	audio/ visual design	Importance	Customer Competitive Assessment				
							1 Worst	2	3	4	5 Best
	speed	9	6	3	0	6	●		◇	▲	
	loopings	6	3	6	0	6	◇	●			▲
	theming	0	0	0	9	3			◇ ●	▲	
priority scores		90	54	54	27						

Improvement Direction

Design Requirements

competitor1
competitor2
our product

of the new product, service or experience, for instance something to sit on. The fish trap model takes this starting point to get a better understanding of the sub-functions involved to create a structural concept, such as something to sit on comfortably at a table, adjustable to different users, including armrests and headrest. Based on these specifications, designers can start thinking about different types of solutions, for instance a chair, a couch or a bench. Choosing one of these alternatives takes the designer to the next step in the fish trap. By sketching a number of alternative solutions at the typological level, using simple geometrical forms, alternative solutions can be compared and a so-called formal concept is created. For instance, if the outcome of the topological step is to create a bench, rough sketches of what this bench could look like and how users can interact with it can be created, resulting in a new moment of choice. When a specific solution is chosen, we get to the third level – the morphological level – in which the material concept is created and alternatives for manufacturing, assembly and specifications of materials to be used are generated. We are now ready to make a final choice for one of the generated solutions. By going back and forth between these steps, designers need to ensure that the choices made satisfy the criteria set in previous steps. For instance, before choosing a specific type of bench, you need to check whether all alternatives that were generated actually meet the criteria set in the formal concept. As with

FIGURE 3.8 An example of applying the fish trap model

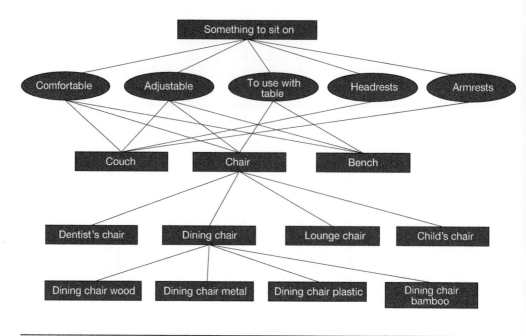

design road mapping, you could argue that this technique is not necessarily linked to one of the seven generic steps of a design process but definitely applies the same logic. The reason for mentioning it here, in discussing tools for step 4 of the design process, is that it connects defining the overall problem and sub-problems to generating sub-solutions and overall solutions – exactly what determining characteristics is supposed to do!

Step 5: generating alternatives

The term morphology stems from biology – morphology studies the physiology of animals in relation to the functions of their body parts. For instance, how do joints and muscles in the legs of frogs enable them to jump so far? In design, the same kind of reasoning can be applied. How can sub-solutions be combined to generate overall solutions for the overall function that the design needs to be able to execute? As discussed in the previous section, most designs – especially designs for experiences – need to combine a large number of elements that also represent different types of characteristics. This means that the number of potential combinations of sub-solutions that together shape the overall solution is huge. A *morphological chart* can assist in systematically generating all possible combinations and checking which combinations are feasible. Essentially, creating a morphological chart starts with listing all sub-functions established in step 2 of the design process. Subsequently, you then create a matrix by filling the row behind each sub-function with all possible (new and existing) sub-solutions that could execute that sub-function. In doing so, the designer needs to make sure to account for the requirements set in step 3, as well as the links between attributes and design characteristics established and analysed in step 4. Once the matrix is complete, generating overall solutions is relatively straightforward by selecting one of the sub-solutions per row. Obviously, in reality, not all sub-solutions can be combined with each other, for instance because together they would result in an overall solution that is too big or too expensive, or because the technologies applied in separate sub-solutions are not compatible. In other words, the trick is to only generate overall solutions that make sense and that are feasible. An example of a morphological chart is shown in Figure 3.9 and how to apply this method to designing experiences is explained in more detail in Chapter 4.

A *touch point matrix* is pretty similar to a morphological chart. However, it is a matrix specifically dedicated to designing service concepts. In a touch point matrix, some sub-solutions link to more than one sub-function. It is also allowed to pick more than one sub-solution per row in generating the overall solution. This way of generating alternatives ensures that the final design incorporates a network of options that is interesting to a diverse group of (potential) customers. In theory, customers can simply pick and mix the elements that they would like to be included in the service provided to them. A typical example would be the design of a cruise ship that incorporates multiple restaurants with live music after dinner, a bowling alley, a casino, two cinemas, three pools, a gym, various room types, and so on. By including multiple sub-solutions for the same sub-problem – for instance, live music, a bowling alley, a casino and cinemas as ways to entertain guests after

FIGURE 3.9 An example of a morphological chart

Sub-solutions / Sub-functions	Alternative 1	Alternative 2	Alternative 3	Alternative 4
Present food options	Paper menu ◆	Signs ●	iPad	Explained by waiter
Take order	iPad	Waiter ◆	Web application	Counter ●
Provide food	Served at a table ◆	Pick up at counter ●	Self-service buffet	
Thank guests	Thank you message on receipt ●	Formal handshake ◆	Staff saying good-bye	

● Design alternative 1   ◆ Design alternative 1

dinner – the cruise ship becomes an attractive holiday destination not only for different types of customers but also for longer holidays. Obviously, the same principle applies to a number of experiences offered in events, tourism and hospitality but also in other industries. In essence, a touch point matrix is the same as a morphological chart but adjusted to allow for concurrently designing multiple – different – customer journeys offered by the same (group of) provider(s), as is shown by the way morphological charting is applied in the next chapter.

A radically different way of approaching this stage of the design process is to apply *rapid prototyping*. As discussed earlier, this heuristic approach to design could be very useful in circumstances that allow for co-creation with and immediate feedback by end-users. However, one of the downsides is that it can prove impractical, time-consuming or expensive to involve a lot of different (types of) users. This could lead to a final design that is only appreciated by the end-users actually involved in creating it and not by all customer segments that are targeted by the final product, service or experience.

Step 6: evaluating alternatives

A *Harris profile* is a graphic representation of the strengths and weaknesses of a design alternative with respect to the requirements established earlier in the design process. A matrix is created in which the requirements are listed on the left side in order of importance. Each row behind a requirement is filled with evaluation options representing a four-point scale from -2 to +2, excluding 0. Each design alternative is then evaluated by checking or filling the appropriate box for each requirement, thus creating a specific profile for that alternative. By comparing these profiles, the differences between alternatives can be highlighted and discussed. Obviously, the better alternatives will have more checks or filled boxes in the top right of the matrix than the others. Even though the Harris profile is not a very exact or precise way of evaluating alternatives, it can be very useful in deciding on which design alternatives to discard and which ones to take into account in a more detailed and elaborate evaluation.

A *multi-criteria analysis* is similar to a Harris profile but more precise and detailed. A list of criteria is generated based on the objectives and requirements created earlier in the design process. Subsequently, each criterion is assigned with an importance score ranging from 1 – not important – to 10 – extremely important. Then, each alternative is assigned a score for its performance with respect to each of the criteria. Finally, multiplying each alternative's score per criterion with the importance score for that criterion, and then adding the resulting scores, generates the final score per design alternative. The design alternative with the highest overall score is deemed the best alternative based on the criteria.

The *stated preference method* is another simple, yet effective method to evaluate alternatives and is especially useful for directly linking consumer preferences to the ultimate choice for a design alternative. This method involves asking (potential) customers to choose between two (or sometimes more) alternatives based on an elaborate series of questions linked to the attributes of those design alternatives. For instance, a London based travel agent could apply the stated preference method to check whether customers interested in fly-drive holidays to South Africa prefer day-time or night-time flights. If most customers prefer day-time flights, she might want to include a lowered price for the trips with night-time flights to see whether that changes customers' preferences. Similarly, the stated preference method could be applied to check for self-driving versus car with driver, different types of hotels, various options for excursions, and so on. By involving a large number of (potential) customers in a stated preference study, the travel agent might even be able to distinguish specific groups of customers with similar preferences and decide to offer more than one travel package alternative or make it adjustable. The latter implies including iteration in the design process by returning to the generating alternatives step and possibly applying a touch point matrix instead of a morphological chart to allow for generating alternatives that include more than one sub-solution – such as multiple excursions to pick from – per sub-function/touch point and alternatives that allow for switching the order of sub-functions/touch points. Obviously, in turn, the latter might require the travel agent to revisit the third stage of the design process and check for consequences with respect to storytelling and dramatic structure.

Step 7: improving details

In the final stage of the design process, the designer focuses on trying to decrease costs and/or negative environmental/social impact of the ultimate design without decreasing value for customers, or on increasing value for customers without increasing costs and/or negative environmental/social impact. *Value engineering* represents a method that can be used for this. It is closely related to reverse engineering and value analysis because it requires the designer to list all components of the final design and then critically assess the (sub-)function(s) this component executes and the value it adds to the overall product, service or experience. Therefore, one could argue that this stage really represents a reminder to revisit some of the earlier stages of the design process to check whether specific changes to details of the design alternative that was chosen in stage 6 could make it even better.

Within the context of designing experiences, it might also be useful to apply *blueprinting* and *spaghetti diagrams* at this stage of the design process. As discussed in Chapter 1, blueprinting can be applied to analyse the expected performance of the design in terms of potential sources of mistakes, efficiency and effectiveness. Carefully reviewing this map of all customer and employee actions and reactions that are designed to take place, including backstage processes, could very well highlight that it might be wise to revisit one of the earlier stages of the design process. For instance, it might highlight that from the perspective of trying to minimise mistakes it would be better to decrease the amount of verbal communication that is required to assess a specific customer's wishes and preferences. A spaghetti diagram could assist in improving efficiency of the final design by visualising employee actions on a floor plan of the servicescape. For designing a restaurant this diagram might, for instance, highlight that it would be wise to place a workstation at a different spot in the restaurant to reduce the overall distance that waiters need to walk to serve guests. Once again, though, you could argue that this type of analysis actually represents a cue for iteration.

In fact, many of the methods, tools and techniques discussed in this section are not necessarily exclusively linked to one particular stage of the design process. This is especially true for design processes aimed at designing experiences. This particular type of design task requires designers to continuously focus on customers' wishes, needs, preferences, expected reactions to stimuli, and so on. For some touch points in a customer journey it might be possible to do this through rapid prototyping and co-creation; for others this might be too costly or time-consuming, or simply not feasible. To complicate matters a bit more, not all customers might react to stimuli in the same way. You will have to accommodate this in the design of the experience you will offer to them. This will require a smart combination of methods, tools and techniques from this chapter and the previous one, as well as iterations during the overall design process, and successfully combining several sub-design processes within the context of this overall process. The next chapter addresses this specific type of design process in more detail.

SUMMARY

Based on reading this chapter, we hope you will understand and remember the following:

- Design is both a science and an art.
- Designing experiences relates to combining tangible and intangible elements, physical characteristics and behaviours, and technical aspects and emotions.
- Descriptive models of design focus on creating a solution concept early on.
- Prescriptive models of design focus on systematically analysing the problem before creating (possible) solutions.
- Both approaches to design represented by these two models have benefits and pitfalls.
- The generic design process consists of the following seven steps:
  o   clarifying objectives;
  o   establishing functions;
  o   setting requirements;

      o   determining characteristics;
      o   generating alternatives;
      o   evaluating alternatives;
      o   improving details.

- For each step, specific methods, tools and techniques could be applied to execute it.
- Picking the most appropriate method, tool or technique for each step depends on the design task at hand.

FOOD FOR THOUGHT

Based on the content of this chapter, the following questions, challenges and topics could serve as interesting starting points for further discussion:

- If you were assigned the task of designing a skyscraper, what overall design approach would you apply and which specific methods, tools and techniques would you apply in the various steps of the process?
- If you would be assigned the task to design a website for an online shop, what overall design approach would you apply and which specific methods, tools and techniques would you apply in the various steps of the process?
- If you feel up to it, why not actually try to (create a rough) design (for) one of these, or both, using the seven design steps and some of the methods, tools and techniques presented in this chapter.

REFERENCES

Cross, N. (1994). *Engineering design methods*. Chichester: John Wiley & Sons.

Mager, B. & Gais, M. (2009). *Service design*. Paderborn: Wilhelm Fink.

Pahl, G. & Beitz, W. (2013). *Engineering design: A systematic approach*. Berlin: Springer Science & Business Media.

Suh, N.P. (2001). *Axiomatic design: Advances and applications*. New York: Oxford University Press.

Stappers, P.J., Sleeswijk Visser, F. & Keller, I. (2003). Mapping the experiential context of product use: Generative techniques beyond questions and observations. In H. Aoki (Ed.), *Sixth Asian Design International Conference* (pp. 1–8). Tsukuba: University of Tsukuba.

SUGGESTED FURTHER READING

For more details on some of the methods, tools and techniques discussed in this chapter, please refer to the following sources:

Boeijen, A.V., Daalhuizen, J., Zijlstra, J. & Schoor, R.V.D. (2013). *Delft design guide: Design methods.* Amsterdam: BIS Publishers.

Cross, N. (1994). *Engineering design methods* (2nd ed.). Chichester: John Wiley & Sons.

Hanington, B. & Martin, B. (2012). *Universal methods of design: 100 ways to research complex problems, develop innovative ideas, and design effective solutions.* Beverly, MA: Rockport Publishers.

Sanders, E.B.N. & Stappers, P.J. (2013). *Convivial toolbox: Generative design research for the fuzzy front end.* Amsterdam: BIS Publishers.

4 A comprehensive approach to experience design

INTRODUCTION

The previous chapter has described the generic steps of a design process, while highlighting various approaches, methods, tools and techniques that could be incorporated in this process. Ultimately, whether the objective is to design a coffee machine or barista café, a rollercoaster or a theme park, a website or a web shop, the same basic steps could be applied. However, the ultimate design – the outcome of the design process – will of course be different, as will the complexity of this design. Moreover, the specific methods, tools and techniques to be used in the various steps of the design process will likely be different for different types of design tasks, as will the way in which they need to be applied.

This chapter focuses on designing experiences. It describes a comprehensive yet hands-on approach to designing them based on the seven generic steps presented and discussed in Chapter 3. This description highlights the particular characteristics of a design process specifically dedicated to designing an experience. It shows how this process can accommodate for designing different types of experiences. It also explains how you could design one overall experience to be staged for all of your customers, even though some of them may prefer and even go through different customer journeys than others. Finally, it illustrates how this approach can account for different customers reacting differently to the same clues and stimuli incorporated in this overall experience.

The approach presented in this chapter incorporates personas as the starting point for the design process and as the common thread running through all steps of this process. Furthermore, this approach follows the fish trap logic. First, the main objective is established: what type of experience is going to be designed? This represents the topological level. The characteristics of this experience – the typological level – are then based on the needs, wishes, preferences and peculiarities of the (potential) customers – represented by personas – for whom this experience is going to be staged. Finally, this information is then used at the morphological level to flesh out the overall experience as a sequence or collection of particular touch points to be included in the ultimate design.

The remainder of this chapter first elaborates on each of the seven steps that need to be completed in designing an experience. For each step, the particular reference points to be accounted for in completing it are established. These reference points are linked to specific methods, tools and techniques that could prove useful for this step in the design process. Finally, how to apply them is illustrated – step-by-step – through a case study: designing a dining in the dark experience staged by a restaurant specifically founded to do so.

The final section of this chapter then applies the same approach to a more complex design challenge: a two-day gaming convention. This case study shows how to apply the comprehensive design approach presented in this chapter, but now for designing an overall experience incorporating very different customer journeys for the different groups of customers who consume it.

STEP 1: CLARIFYING OBJECTIVES

The first step in the design process focuses on answering the question: what is the purpose of what we are going to design? Within the context of designing an experience, this amounts to creating clarity regarding the specific kind of experience to be designed. To be able to control and manage the process of designing this experience, it is crucial to create a clear overview of all relevant objectives linked to the ambition of staging it. These objectives not only relate to the type of experience to be staged but also the people – the specific customer target groups – to whom it will be offered and the business(es) and/or professional(s) who will be staging it. Are we designing a peak experience for existing, loyal customers to ensure that they remain loyal or a transformative experience for a market segment we have not targeted so far in an effort to increase our profits? Is our objective to design a multi-day event or a show that lasts a few hours, and is profit a requirement or would breaking even suffice? Do we want to organise a music festival that attracts various types of visitors with different tastes in music or are we specifically aiming at people of a certain age group who were born loving soul music and clearly deserve to have an experience staged especially for them?

The outcome of this step of the design process should be: (1) a detailed (set of) persona(s) representing the (potential) customers to whom the experience to be designed will be offered, (2) a clear description of what this experience should do or be for these (potential) customers, and (3) a clear description of what this experience should do or be for the experience provider. To create an overview of all relevant objectives and the hierarchical relationships between these objectives, it could be very useful to bring them together in an objectives tree.

This overview should make it perfectly clear to all involved – the design team, management, investors, commissioners, and so on – what the purpose of the design is without indicating – at this stage – the specific elements to be incorporated. Instead, this overview provides clarity on the experience outcomes that the design needs to be able to create. In fish trap terms, the main objective – the trunk of the objectives tree – needs to be set at topological level and the sub-objectives at typological level.

To ensure a focus on outcomes instead of (sub-)solutions in this step of the design process, it might be wise to formulate them in a specific way. With respect to objectives directly related to what the experience will do or be for customers, the following types of descriptions could prove helpful:

- Persona x will remember . . . after visiting us.
- Persona x will feel . . . after visiting us.
- If persona x is asked about . . . he/she will think about us.
- Persona x will tell his/her friends about our experience in terms like . . . .
- Persona x understands . . . better after being with us.
- Persona x will change . . . after leaving us.

With respect to objectives directly related to what the experience will do or be for us, the provider, the following types of descriptions could prove helpful:

- Our experience should help customers understand . . . .
- Our experience has to be remembered for . . . .
- Our experience creates opportunities for . . . .
- Our experience should change customers' views with respect to . . . .

Dining in the dark – the objectives

The Royal National Institute for Blind People (RNIB) supports people who suffer from sight loss. RNIB is about to launch a new fundraising campaign. One of the initiatives within the context of this campaign is to gather more attention for their cause and for the problems blind people encounter in the labour market by launching a dining in the dark restaurant. The RNIB hopes the restaurant will attract enough guests to make a (small) profit and continue operating based on a self-sustaining business model after the campaign has ended. They aim to attract two specific types of guests but, obviously, other types of guests are also more than welcome to visit the restaurant, especially after the first few months.

The first type of guest specifically targeted by this restaurant is journalists, bloggers, vloggers and other (social) media-active influencers. The persona representing this target group is named Pipa.

Pipa is a popular journalist who writes about labour market trends and social entrepreneurship but also (reviews of) trendy restaurants in local and national media. Curiosity is what drives Pipa in almost everything she does. She eats out a lot, both for business and pleasure, and is a conscious eater in terms of health and food ethics.

The second type of guest specifically targeted is entrepreneurs, recruiters and HR professionals who might be persuaded to employ people with sight loss. The persona representing this target group is named Richard.

Richard works for a medium-sized company. He frequently dines out for business. Recruitment is difficult in his line of business as a lot of other companies are looking for similar talent. His particular company is struggling to adapt to new legislation which forces companies like Richard's to hire people with a so-called 'distance to the labour market'. In other words, this legislation aims to create jobs for people who have so far found it difficult to land a job. Richard and his company understand the purpose and logic of this new legislation – they are even sympathetic to the general idea – but they have, for instance, never hired someone with sight loss and would not know how to deal with a blind employee.

Together with the experience design team, RNIB has formulated the following experience objectives for the organisation and for these two personas:

- After dining in the dark, Pipa will feel/be sympathetic towards RNIB and the people they represent.
- After dining in the dark, Pipa will have enough anecdotes and information to publish in various media about the experience itself *and* its purpose.
- Pipa will have fun during the experience.
- Pipa will be amazed during (and after) the experience by the enormous influence of (the absence of) sight on what someone feels, smells, tastes and hears.
- After dining in the dark, Richard will feel/be sympathetic towards RNIB and the people they represent.
- After dining in the dark, Richard will have a better understanding of how people with sight loss perceive the world, how they (can) adapt to (new) situations, and how they could be facilitated to perform (various types of) jobs.
- Richard will have fun during the experience and will talk enthusiastically about it to family, friends and colleagues.
- Dining in the dark proves to be an overall experience that creates positive memories for all guests.
- The experience leads to publicity for the restaurant and (social) media coverage for the campaign.
- The experience inspires employees to create jobs for people with sight loss.
- The dining in the dark restaurant provides jobs for people with sight loss and provides them with an opportunity to acquire skills that help them to be successful in the job market.

STEP 2: ESTABLISHING FUNCTIONS

Once the objectives have been established and it is clear what the experience should do and be to all relevant stakeholders, it is important to create a full understanding of the functions this experience needs to fulfil to reach these objectives. These functions will need to be fulfilled by the (combinations of) touch points that are incorporated in the experience to be designed and, thus, the ultimate customer journey(s) to be offered to customers, irrespective of the specific details of these touch points generated in step 5 of the design process. It is crucial to think in terms of functions instead of solutions at this stage of the process, to ensure that it results in solutions that truly match the objectives instead of solutions that seem 'beautiful' at first 'sight' but do not actually fulfil the specific needs and wishes of the customers and provider involved.

Most functions will be made up of several sub-functions in which the service aspects for that particular function are highlighted. Some of these (sub-)functions will be process related, which means that they need to be fulfilled at a particular time or in a particular order. For instance, people will need to be able to buy a theatre ticket in advance before it can be checked at the entrance of an auditorium. Most experiences will also (have to) fulfil (sub-)functions related to customers' physiological, psychological and social needs as well as safety. These various types of (sub-)functions could very well be intertwined. For instance, security checks and checking tickets fulfil process functions but are also sub-functions of fulfilling the safety need of customers. How these functions are fulfilled, in turn, relates to psychological and social needs of customers. If security staff make absolutely sure that no dangerous items will enter a theatre by turning all visitors' bags upside down without asking permission, this might fulfil the need for safety but probably not the need for being treated with respect and promoting a good atmosphere.

As for designing products and services, this step in the design process for experiences could benefit from applying reverse engineering to learn from the functions included in the design of existing experiences. Oftentimes, reviewing and analysing existing experiences can create helpful checklists to ensure that all required functions will be fulfilled by the ultimate design. Similarly, applying the function analysis method and system mapping could prove useful at this stage of the process – the first can create understanding with respect to how various functions and sub-functions are interrelated, whereas the latter is especially useful for experiences that will perform very different functions for different customers.

Something that deserves extra attention in this step of the design process for experiences – in comparison to designing products and services – is how the functions that need to be fulfilled and the order in which this needs to be done relate to the so-called overall experience of customers. In other words, how do these functions relate to the overall storyline and the dramatic structure of the customer journey(s) to be offered to them? Analysing (the impact of) these links requires revisiting the objectives. How are some of the (sub-)objectives linked to a need to create specific peaks and lows in the dramatic structure of the ultimate customer journey(s)? Particular objectives might require particular functions to be fulfilled in a way that excites or delights customers so that positive memories are created, whereas others simply need to be fulfilled to avoid dissatisfaction but fulfilling them in a specific way would never lead to increased satisfaction. Therefore, particularly for designing experiences, it is important at this stage of the design process to explicitly refer to the experience outcome objectives linked to the brand/company staging the experience and the personas representing customer target groups – as set out in step 1 – in establishing all (sub-)functions to be fulfilled.

CASE STUDY 4.1 **SANTA GETS A NEW OFFICE**

Vincent Neveu, Xander Lub and Moniek Hover

Lapland (in Finland) is known for its scenic and pure landscape where people can take part in many recreational activities such as hiking, snow-scooter riding, skiing and more. In 1984, the Finnish Tourist Board, together with regional businesses and authorities, began to market the city of Rovaniemi (Lapland) as 'the home of Santa Claus'. Now, many years after this, Santa Claus has become a major tourist feature in Lapland, where tourists can visit the 'real' Santa all year-round in Santa Claus Office. With this success, however, came challenges. With the ever-increasing number of tourists, the city of Rovaniemi and Santa Claus Office faced difficulties holding onto their core values of 'authenticity', 'giving and caring', 'constant presence', 'surprising and creative', which all together bring the 'Christmas story to life'. This is why a team of researchers was asked to develop a new narrative concept and storyline for Santa Claus Office.

As a starting point, existing stories and experiences were collected from visitors to enlighten and inspire the new narrative design. Besides that, observations and interviews with various key stakeholders were carried out to develop a consistent storyline and customer journey for the physical facilities. Based on these findings, five proto-concepts were developed through a number of creative sessions. Then, these proto-concepts were combined into one core narrative concept in an ideation session with the key stakeholders of Santa Claus Office.

The narrative concept was named 'Santa Time'. This concept was created because of its ability to tell a story with different layers, in line with Rovaniemi's core values and the way in which customers may connect with these values. 'Authenticity' is reflected in authentic childhood times and memories. Quality (Christmas) time with family and loved ones relates to 'giving and caring'. The unique moment in time when visitors meet Santa in person connects with the value of 'constant presence'. Finally, the new concept refers to Santa as a magical timekeeper who is able to slow down and speed up the clock in order to deliver presents all over the world in a short time span, which is reflected in the value of 'surprising and creative'.

This narrative was further translated into a storyline around the visitor journey. In almost every story (whether orally or in written form, in film or in any other medium) a basic (dramatic) structure can be recognised. A five-step dramatic structure model was used to redesign the future customer journey at Santa's Office. The visitor journey suggests progression of the guest in a loose plot of space and builds story tension, leading from 'Anticipation Time' (F&B waiting space as a set-up) to an immersive multisensory journey ('Special Time at a Special Place' as the motoric moment) to 'Play Time' (Elves' toy factory as a turning point) to 'Santa's Moment' (meeting Santa as the climax), and 'Sharing Time' (as a resolution) where visitors can share their experience with loved ones through postcards, photos and presents.

The new narrative concept and the storylines have been positively received and the redesign of Santa's Office in Rovaniemi is currently in progress. Maybe when Rovaniemi is your next destination, try to see whether you are able to find these elements.

Sources

Hover, M. (2013). *De Efteling als Verteller van Sprookjes.* (Dissertation). Kaatsheuvel: Efteling Publishing.

Lub, X.D., Hover, M.H., Tuominen, P.P., Neveu, V. & Marée, G. (2017). *Santa gets a new office: A case-study in using storytelling and service design to redesign a brand anchor.* Presented at Tourism and Hospitality Summit, Orlando, December.

Philips, A. (2012). *A creator's guide to transmedia storytelling.* New York: McGraw Hill.

For example, telling the story of Snow White without a stepmother, dwarfs, poisoned apple and a prince is not an interesting story. Each of these characters has a role to play in it. For the audience to appreciate and remember this story, you need to make sure that the audience understands and feels (through empathy) that Snow White is innocent, pure and kind, the dwarfs are gentle and caring, the stepmother self-centred and evil, the apple a lethal weapon, and the prince someone who cannot help but fall hopelessly in love. He should not be portrayed as someone who is just looking for a fun night. To be able to truly communicate the essence of this story to the audience and make them remember it, you need to be able to tell it in a way that creates all kinds of tensions, resulting in dramatic arcs and an overall dramatic structure. The same applies to other experiences, regardless of whether they are staged in a city centre, a restaurant or at an event.

Dining in the dark – the functions and the dramatic structure

The dining in the dark experience will be staged within the setting of a restaurant and, therefore, many of the functions that have to be fulfilled in a regular restaurant also have to be fulfilled for this one. However, there is one particular function that needs to be added to this list, which relates to the ambition of RNIB to raise awareness about the problems people with sight loss encounter on the labour market. The resulting list of main functions to be fulfilled is the following:

- Taking reservations.
- Welcoming guests and showing them to their table – the arrival phase.
- Provision of food and drinks, which includes sub-functions such as taking orders, serving and clearing tables.
- Preparing food and drinks, which includes sub-functions such as preparing and pouring drinks, and preparing and plating food.
- Raising awareness for the RNIB cause.
- Lavatory visits.
- Payment, which includes sub-functions such as presenting the bill and guests actually paying the appropriate amount – sometimes in cash and sometimes by card.
- Saying goodbye to guests and escorting them to the door – the leaving phase.

Obviously, the function of raising awareness of the RNIB cause deserves some extra attention at this stage of the design process. Pipa needs to be inspired to write about her experience – and, obviously, it would really help if she were inspired to write *positively* about the restaurant and RNIB's cause. This means that the experience needs to provide her with the right and enough input, such as specific examples. Therefore, creating the right storyline for Pipa's overall experience would benefit from some of the other functions (also) being fulfilled in a way that allows her to not only experience some of the problems blind people encounter but also become aware of some of the solutions that could assist them in coping with these problems. As for Richard, RNIB would like him to leave the restaurant with a positive feeling about and attitude towards possibly hiring people with sight loss. Therefore, his overall experience needs to be a pleasant one but it would help if some of the other functions would (also) be fulfilled in a way that would allow him to learn about the life and work of visually impaired people, how jobs could be created which suit them – without that being an enormous challenge, and that people with sight loss can actually perform (a number of) jobs adequately. All this implies that we need to keep these aspects in mind when we actually start generating touch point and customer journey alternatives (at a later stage of the design process). These touch-point alternatives should include dramatic arcs that allow for creating a dramatic structure for the overall experience that would send Pipa and Richard on their way with just the right emotions and memories (starting to form in their minds).

STEP 3: SETTING REQUIREMENTS

Before we can move on to establishing (key) characteristics of the ultimate design and actually designing the way in which all functions will be fulfilled, we first need to focus on setting and understanding the requirements this design will need to meet. Three types of requirements relevant to experiences can be distinguished: (1) user requirements, (2) technical requirements, and (3) managerial/organisational requirements.

User requirements can be expressed both qualitatively and quantitatively. Some of these requirements can relate to specific numbers, such as the resources – you could think of time and money – customers are likely to be willing to spend on consuming the experience. Other – qualitative – requirements relate to their expectations with respect to the experience and their (personal) customer journey or particular products and/or services that should be included.

Technical requirements need to be identified and quantified. They could relate to aspects such as the space, time and resources available to create/construct the experience and for staging it but also to specific safety and quality standards that need to be met.

Managerial/organisational requirements can usually be quantified and relate to aspects such as minimum and maximum capacity, targets with respect to cash flow and margins, the number of repeat visits, and the number of recommendations on review sites. Chapter 5 will explore the actual management of staging experiences in more detail but it is important to address specific requirements linked to these types of managerial/organisational objectives at this stage of the design process, so that reaching them will not turn out to be a mission impossible.

In some (specific) cases, a fourth set of requirements, so-called brand requirements, could also be relevant to address in this step of the process. Brand requirements are usually linked to particular physical facets of what spaces or uniforms should look like/incorporate in terms of colours, logos, and so on, but can also relate to specific personality, culture and relationship aspects of the brand that need to be accounted for.

Dining in the dark – the requirements

For the dining in the dark experience, specific user, technical and organisational requirements can be distinguished, also in relation to aspects discussed in the previous section with respect to ensuring that Pipa and Richard leave the premises of the restaurant with the right mind-set. The following requirements to be met by the ultimate design could be set:

- Pipa needs to feel that food and drinks are tasty and healthy.
- Pipa needs to be convinced that the way the restaurant operates does not create unnecessary food/drink waste or other unnecessary negative environmental impacts.
- The restaurant setting should allow Pipa to talk to staff and ask them questions about sight loss and the implications for finding/performing a job.
- Richard needs to feel that food and drinks are tasty and remarkable/interesting/exciting.
- The restaurant setting should allow Richard to learn about (successfully) performing a job with sight loss.

- The restaurant setting should allow Richard to learn about facilitating people with sight loss in doing their/a job.
- The restaurant needs to be self-sustaining (in the longer term).
- An initial investment of €500,000 could be covered by RNIB.
- The restaurant (mostly) needs to employ people with sight loss.
- Guests and staff need to be safe at all times.
- The experience needs to create positive reinforcement of RNIB's cause and brand in public opinion, possibly also measured in terms of specific minimum proceeds of the fundraising campaign.

Obviously, some of these requirements are still rather generic and the design process for the dining in the dark experience could therefore benefit from applying a more detailed performance specification analysis and the Kano method in this step of the process. These details are omitted here to save space and not to burden the reader with too many details that do not necessarily contribute to conveying the overall train of thought on which the design approach presented in this chapter is based.

STEP 4: DETERMINING CHARACTERISTICS

Through completing the first three steps of the design process, the playing field for creating appropriate solutions has now been established. The design team should now have clarity on what type of solutions would be acceptable and preferred, and what type of solutions would not. They can now start thinking about the characteristics of design alternatives to be generated in step 5 of the process. To assist in generating viable, interesting and appealing designs – both from a customer and provider perspective, this step focuses on determining those characteristics. As discussed in the previous chapter, the key to this step is to translate the information gathered so far into actual (key) characteristics of the experience to be designed, so that the design team understands what they need to focus on in generating alternative designs.

The best way to create an overview of the relationships between customers' needs and wishes and the provider's needs and wishes on the one hand and the characteristics of a successful experience on the other is to link them in a House of Quality or a Kelly Repertory Grid. Our suggestion – as authors of this book – is to apply the first when it comes to designing experiences because it allows for the establishment of a more detailed and direct link with the ultimate customer journey(s) to be offered to customers and the touch points that need to be created for doing so.

The starting point for creating an initial House of Quality (HoQ) is formed by the needs and wishes at customer journey level for the targeted customers – the personas established in the first step – and the provider. Obviously, these needs and wishes are closely related to the objectives and requirements established earlier in the design process. All relevant needs and wishes are listed on the left-hand side – the first column – of the HoQ. It is important to ensure that these needs and wishes are described at the right level of detail; otherwise you might end up with a seemingly endless list and therefore unmanageable HoQ. For example, at a customer journey level it would be acceptable to include the need for lavatory visits but it would be a bit silly to focus on details such as cleanliness of the ladies room, specific ways of washing and drying your hands, and the possibility of checking and adjusting your makeup. These kinds of details would clog the overview you are trying to create with this HoQ.

In the upper part of the HoQ – the top row – all design characteristics that need or can be used to create the ultimate customer journey(s) to be offered to customers should be listed. Chapter 1 has introduced the Brady and Cronin model of perceived service quality and this model could be incorporated in a HoQ applied for designing experiences. By listing all relevant variables established by Brady and Cronin (2001) in the top row of the HoQ, the logic of their approach can be utilised to design the ultimate experience to be staged. This allows for a holistic but straightforward approach to designing an experience that accounts for the physical, social and personal contexts that will determine the quality of the experience as perceived by customers – as suggested by Falk and Dierking (1992) and discussed in Chapter 2.

These variables relate to three types of characteristics: (1) interaction with staff, (2) the physical environment, and (3) the outcomes – the actual products, services and processes used for staging the experience, as well as the personal contexts of the customers involved. The first category of variables relates to attitude, behaviour and expertise of staff interacting with customers. The second category of variables relates to design of the physical environment in which the experience is staged, the ambient conditions and social factors – the social context. The third category relates to waiting times, tangibles and valence – the personal context. It is important to note that social factors can both relate to the physical environment and to outcomes. Furthermore, each of these nine variables is affected by the same three key factors: (1) perceived reliability, (2) perceived responsiveness, and (3) perceived empathy.

The latter implies that the ultimate design of the experience needs to include clues – at customer journey or touch-point level – that provide evidence of reliability, responsiveness and empathy. These clues are quite similar to the humanic, mechanic and functional clues (Berry et al., 2006) discussed in Chapter 2. Which specific clues, related to which specific characteristics, should be included or are the most important to include in the ultimate design can be determined through creating a HoQ at a customer journey level but sometimes this may also require creating a HoQ at a touch-point level, for instance if fulfilling particular functions implies that particular touch points need to be/become the highlight of the overall experience. In those situations, it might not be enough to create a HoQ at a customer journey level with Brady and Cronin's nine variables in the top row. You might also need to create a HoQ for specific touch points and sometimes you might need to incorporate the three key factors that affect these variables in doing so, thus

FIGURE 4.1 Brady and Cronin's perceived (service) quality model

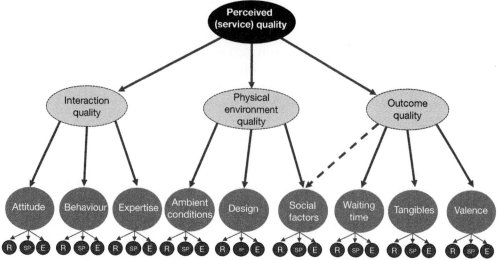

Adapted from: Brady, M.K. & Cronin Jr, J.J. (2001). Some new thoughts on conceptualizing perceived service quality: a hierarchical approach. *Journal of Marketing*, 65(3), 34-49.

leading to a list of up to 27 characteristics in the top row. In other words, depending on the specific type of experience to be designed, the specific objectives to be reached and the specific functions to be fulfilled, this step in the design process can relate to creating one overall HoQ with nine characteristics to consider but it could also relate to creating several (layers of) HoQs with different levels of detail.

After listing all relevant needs and wishes in the first column and listing all relevant characteristics in the top row, you then need to indicate the predicted/expected impact of specific characteristics on (satisfying) specific needs and wishes in the corresponding cell in the HoQ. For most HoQs, you would use the numbers 0, 3, 6 and 9 to represent this impact, with 0 indicating no impact and 9 the highest impact. Subsequently, these numbers are used to calculate the priority scores for the characteristics in the top row. To do this, you first need to determine the importance of the various needs and wishes on a ten-point scale. This could be done by asking (potential) customers but also through discussing this with the design team, based on the personas and objectives established earlier in the design process and sometimes even through a comparison with existing experiences provided by your competitors. Multiplying all impact scores in the cells that relate to a specific characteristic with the importance score of the need and/or wish that corresponds with the same cell and then adding up the outcomes of these multiplications results in the priority score per design characteristic.

All of this may sound rather complicated and time-consuming. And, to be honest, sometimes it is, especially for extensive experiences based on a wide range of very different touch points that allow for offering very different customer journeys to different customer target groups. However, ultimately, the train of thought to be applied for creating a HoQ is always the same. The steps you need to take and the logic you need to apply to ensure that they provide you with useful information are not different for a rather abstract HoQ with a short list of needs and wishes and a limited number of design characteristics to consider than for a very detailed HoQ with an extensive list of needs and wishes and a high number of design characteristics to consider. And, more importantly, you are very likely to be rewarded for spending the time required to create these HoQs in this step of the design process because the chances of ending up with an ultimate design that truly accommodates meeting or even exceeding the expectations of customers will increase significantly if you do.

To illustrate the steps and logic involved with creating them, consider the example of designing an extensive experience – for instance a theme park – based on medieval city life. One of the functions of the overall experience is to provide dinner for visitors and fulfilling this function could provide an interesting opportunity to create a specific dramatic arc within the overall dramatic structure. Given that dinner usually represents one of the final touch points in your customers' journey (of a given day spent at your premises) makes this a perfect time to create a peak experience or memorable encounter linked to the overall storyline of the overall experience that you stage for them. Therefore, it might be wise to create a separate (more detailed) HoQ for this touch point – the function providing dinner will be fulfilled by a specific touch point; a restaurant – alongside the HoQ at a customer journey level. The first three steps in the design process might have shown that customers would prefer a seated à la carte dinner with their families. Obviously, it would be wise to account for this preference in the design of the restaurant. As for any touch point, this restaurant relates to a particular type of interaction between your customers and your staff, taking place within a particular physical environment and creating particular outcomes.

FIGURE 4.2 A House of Quality for a medieval-city-life-themed restaurant

Medieval dinner experience	Design characteristics								Importance
	Interaction			Physical environment			Outcome		
Needs and wishes	Attitude	Behaviour	Expertise	Ambient	Design	Social factors	Tangibles	Waiting times	
Seated family dinner	3 3*7	3 3*7	0 0*7	0 0*7	9 9*7	3 3*7	0 0*7	0 0*5	7
À la carte	6 6*6	6 6*6	3 3*6	0 0*6	0 0*6	0 0*6	9 9*6	6 6*6	6
Medieval	6 6*9	6 6*9	0 0*9	6 6*9	9 9*6	0 0*9	9 9*9	0 0*9	9
Priority scores	111	111	18	54	117	21	135	36	

The HoQ created for this touch point in Figure 4.2 therefore incorporates these characteristics in the top rows – the valence variable is purposely left out because for this particular experience it is probably not possible to purposely influence the personal circumstances of (all of) your customers. The first column lists three of the needs/wishes that this touch point needs to address: having a seated family dinner, having an à la carte dinner, and creating (a peak in) the overall medieval theme of the overall experience. The numbers in the cells in the middle of this HoQ indicate the impact specific characteristics are likely to have on satisfying these needs/wishes. For instance, the design team might have established that the need to create (a peak in) the medieval theme of the overall experience will likely be impacted most by the design of the physical environment and the specific food and drinks – the tangibles – served in the restaurant. Within the context of the overall experience staged for customers and the dramatic structure of this experience, this third need/wish is considered to be the most important to satisfy and, therefore, has been assigned the highest importance score in the last column of this HoQ. Based on all scores included in the cells in the middle and the last column, the priority scores for all characteristics can now be calculated. In this example, the priority scores show the design team that in generating alternatives for this touch point in the next step of the design process it is advisable to pay special attention to food and drinks and the design of the physical aspects of the restaurant but also (!) to attitude and behaviour of staff. Obviously, this information might also prove very useful in the sixth step of the design process; evaluating design alternatives.

It is important to note, once more, that after completing this fourth step in the design process no decisions have been made (yet) with respect to whether this dinner should take place in a castle or tavern setting, nor have decisions been made (yet) about the types of food and drinks to be served, how to serve them and what seating arrangements will be incorporated in the ultimate design. The priority scores created in this step do, however, guide the (creative) process in step 5 and the evaluation process in step 6.

This particular HoQ is just one example of the various different (types of) HoQs that could be created in the determining characteristics step of the design process. The website accompanying this book contains some more examples, also examples of sets of HoQs representing different layers (of detail) in one and the same design process.

Dining in the dark – the key characteristics

For the dining in the dark experience, it would be crucial to first create a HoQ for the overall experience. Based on the first three steps in the design process, it has become clear that this experience needs to satisfy quite a number of different needs and wishes. For instance, Pipa and Richard need to enjoy the experience, the food and drinks, but also learn about life and work with sight loss. For Pipa the experience should help her write articles, whereas for Richard it should

FIGURE 4.3 The House of Quality for the dining in the dark experience

Dining in the dark experience — Design characteristics

(Each cell shows the relationship rating / weighted score.)

Needs and wishes	Interaction			Physical environment			Outcome		Importance
	Attitude	Behaviour	Expertise	Ambience	Design	Social factors	Tangibles	Waiting times	
Understanding life with sight loss	3 / 24	3 / 24	9 / 72	9 / 72	3 / 24	3 / 24	6 / 48	0	8
Understanding work with sight loss	3 / 27	3 / 27	9 / 81	6 / 54	0	0	3 / 27	0	9
Safety	6 / 54	3 / 27	6 / 54	3 / 27	6 / 54	0	0	0	9
Pipa – social fun	3 / 15	3 / 15	3 / 15	3 / 15	6 / 30	6 / 30	0	0	5
Pipa – sensory fun	3 / 24	3 / 24	6 / 48	9 / 72	3 / 24	0	9 / 72	3 / 24	8
Pipa – stories	6 / 48	6 / 48	6 / 48	9 / 72	6 / 48	0	9 / 72	0	8
Richard – discuss	6 / 42	6 / 42	6 / 42	3 / 21	3 / 21	6 / 42	6 / 42	0	7
Richard – food	0	0	0	6 / 30	0	0	9 / 45	3 / 15	5
Richard – work	6 / 48	6 / 48	6 / 48	3 / 24	9 / 72	9 / 72	0	0	8
Priority scores	282	255	408	387	273	168	306	39	

highlight the challenges *and* opportunities related to hiring visually impaired staff. The design team is also very aware that guests will only be open to the experience staged for them if they feel they are safe and in good hands. Like with any HoQ, these needs/wishes need to be listed in the first column, as shown in Figure 4.3.

With respect to this specific experience, it is important to note that both Pipa and Richard have a need for information but the type of information they need is different, as they have different purposes for this information. They need to gather this information during/through the experience staged for them but the specific solutions and/or touch points to be created for each of them might very well be different.

However, just like in the medieval restaurant example, the process of completing the HoQ is fairly straightforward. After establishing the impact scores, the importance scores for each of the needs/wishes listed in the first column need to be established. In the HoQ displayed in Figure 4.3, Pipa's needs have received a slightly higher importance score than Richard's. In the end, realising RNIB's cause is probably more dependent on the articles that Pipa writes than on Richard's experience. Ultimately, through calculating the priority scores for all design characteristics, this HoQ shows that staff expertise is the biggest priority, as well as ambient conditions and tangibles – the latter obviously relates to the food and drinks served in this restaurant. In this particular example, ambient conditions and tangibles are closely related because for specific parts of the experience guests and staff can only rely on touch, smell, sound and taste in experiencing the ultimate design. It is also important to realise that the high priority score for tangibles is not so much the result of the need/wish of Richard for high-quality food but rather of the crucial role of these tangibles in creating fun and stories for Pipa, as well as the key role these tangibles play in creating an understanding about life with sight loss. Therefore, it might be advisable to create (an extra layer of) more detailed HoQs for the functions of preparing the food and drinks and providing specific information about life and work with sight loss to (individual) guests. You might notice that the latter has not been included in the original list of functions established in step 2 of the design process described in this case study. However, now that we have arrived at step 4, the crucial role of this function in realising the objectives set in step 1 is becoming increasingly clear. Therefore, this might be the perfect time for a so-called iteration in the design process and refinement of the list of functions in step 2. Once again, these specific details of the actual process – as it would be executed in real life – are left out here to save space and to not bother you – the reader – with too many details that do not necessarily contribute to conveying the overall train of thought of the design approach presented in this chapter.

STEP 5: GENERATING ALTERNATIVES

This is the step in the design process when and where actual touch points, customer journeys and overall design alternatives are generated. Iteration will play a crucial role at this stage of the process because you will be moving back and forth between the levels of individual touch points, customer journeys that can be offered based on those touch points, and the overall design incorporating those touch points and customer journeys. What's more, you will keep a constant eye on the priority scores generated in the previous step in doing so, while accounting for the requirements set in step 3.

The design team needs to collect information on known (characteristics of) touch points and possibly create (partly or completely) new ones for each of the functions that need to be fulfilled by the customer journey(s) offered to customers. This might involve a so-called creative process and this process might benefit from brainstorming on multiple touch points at the same time, trying to translate touch points offered by competitors or in different industries to your specific context, user interviews, actual co-creation with end users, and so on. Generative techniques such as rapid prototyping, role playing, story boarding and mood boarding could prove useful for specific touch points or customer journeys, whereas others might require a more systematic or algorithmic approach. There is a vast body of (popular and scientific) literature and other sources of information available to inspire/ assist/guide you and your fellow members of the design team in this stage of the process, some of which have been mentioned in the references section of the previous chapter.

Regardless of which specific methods, tools and techniques you end up using for exploring existing and generating new ideas, it is usually wise to bring all of those ideas together in a morphological chart. Within the context of designing experiences, morphological charting can assist in generating customer journey alternatives. These alternatives should account for the priority scores determined in step 4, as well as the requirements set in step 3 and the objectives set in step 1. Through listing all functions to be fulfilled during a customer journey in the left column of the chart, displaying all touch-point alternatives that have been generated in the row next to each function and then picking one of the alternatives from each row, specific customer journey alternatives can be generated. However, there are some complicating factors to consider. For instance, different customers might very well go through the various touch points incorporated in your ultimate design in a different order and some might not even go through all of them – not everyone in a theme park dares to ride all rollercoasters; some might go for the scariest one first, while others need to build some confidence by first going for some less intimidating attractions. Also, some touch points might fulfil several functions, while some functions might actually need multiple touch points to be fulfilled. Finally, it is important to realise that different touch-point alternatives incorporate different dramatic arcs – and the specific arc created by them for different personas might also be different – and thus the choice for including or excluding a particular touch point in the ultimate design influences the dramatic structure of the overall experience staged for customers, even if all customers go through the same customer journey. Therefore, as with creating the HoQs in the previous step of the process, this step in the design process might actually involve creating a number of (layers of) morphological charts. Simultaneously, it might not always be necessary or make sense to create a separate morphological chart for all the different customer journeys that could be created by incorporating a different order and collection of touch points and thus all of the different customer journeys that, in theory, different customers could go through. At some point, common sense should override the ambition to cover all possible options. The same applies to when and where specific functions can and need to be fulfilled for different personas. Ultimately, the aim of the design team should not be to make every touch point an exciter just in case a specific customer decides to only go through that specific touch point. To create an appropriate dramatic structure for the overall experience for most customers, you need highs and lows, not just highs.

Therefore, a reasonable compromise is to start with creating a morphological chart for the overall experience offered to (all) customers based on a time-based sequence of the functions as established in step 2 in the left column of the chart. Most of these functions can be clustered based on whether they need to be fulfilled prior to, during or after the core experience. For a theatre show, the first would relate to buying tickets online, the second to the actual evening of the show, and the third to a satisfaction survey sent to visitors by email a few days after the show. Functions that need to be fulfilled but are not bound to a particular time or have a more generic nature are put in a separate category: miscellaneous. Now that the sequence is clear, the rows next to each function can be filled with touch-point alternatives. It might be wise to start with those functions that need to create peaks in the dramatic structure or specific touch points that could create those peaks. By regularly revisiting the priority scores and requirements from the previous steps, you know which design characteristics should be included or you should focus on at touch point or customer journey level to ensure that (the most important) needs and wishes are satisfied. Obviously, you also regularly check whether the resulting dramatic structure that would be created by combing specific touch points for specific personas would live up to the objectives set out in step 1. If it is your (or the commissioner's) objective to incorporate a few peaks in the overall experience to be staged, the morphological chart is not complete if combining touch-point alternatives included in this chart will not result in multiple peaks. Similarly, your morphological chart is also not ready for generating design alternatives yet if it does not allow for creating customer journeys – by selecting touch-point alternatives included in the chart – that would equal an extended or transformational experience, if one of those options were your ambition. In doing these checks, do keep in mind that some touch points or particular staff members or physical environments might very well fulfil more than one function and can thus be included in the chart more than once and for several functions.

Once all relevant touch-point alternatives have been clustered at function level, you can now start combining them into customer journey alternatives. The goal at this stage is to create two or three alternative journeys for each persona addressed in this design process that match the objectives and requirements set earlier. Usually, one of these objectives is linked to the dramatic structure of the experience to be staged. If it is not possible to create logical, coherent and appealing customer journeys by selecting touch-point alternatives from the morphological chart, you might very well have to revisit the early stages of this step and generate more. You might even have to go back to earlier steps in the design process. For instance, combining some of the (priorities regarding) characteristics determined in the previous step might not go together with some of the requirements set in step 3. In those circumstances, you might have to require a bigger budget or accept that specific needs and wishes simply cannot be satisfied with the resources available to you.

Keep in mind that, if needed, extra touch points could be generated to allow for creating the desired contrasts within the dramatic structure of these customer journeys. For instance, you could choose to have customers walk for a few minutes to create a relaxing moment after a specific peak and before the next peak in their customer journey. Such an additional touch point could be created by physically moving the touch points linked to those peaks to different locations. Another reason to add a touch point could be to create a small peak in between functions that need to be fulfilled because fulfilling these – not so exciting – functions without something in between would result in a low that lasts too long. Adding a surprise here and there, now and then, can also help in repairing dramatic structures that would otherwise be faulty. Disney does this by having characters show up and hug you while you are waiting – for too long – to board specific (popular) attractions.

As indicated earlier, you also need to account for the fact that specific touch points might create different dramatic arcs for different personas. If the overall experience is designed for multiple personas, this might be a reason to rethink these touch points or add alternative touch points that specifically fit these personas and allow for creating the right peaks and lows for all different customers.

Once viable customer journey alternatives have been created, the next stage in the process is to check and see how these alternatives could be combined to create overall design alternatives. Can specific journey alternatives be combined or even create synergies or do certain journey alternatives exclude each other? For instance, can the choice for a specific type of restaurant in a holiday resort for one persona be combined with a different type of restaurant to accommodate for the needs and wishes of another persona? Is there enough budget and space to do so, or would we have to go back to the generating touch-point alternatives stage to create a restaurant that could meet the needs and wishes of both personas? This final stage of this step in the design process is all about checking for and generating overall design alternatives for the overall experience to be staged that could reach all objectives, fulfil all functions, meet all requirements and satisfy the needs and wishes of all personas. If it turns out that such design alternatives cannot be generated, you need to revisit some of the earlier stages in this step or some of the earlier steps in the design process. As indicated before, iteration is a natural part of just about any design process.

Dining in the dark – getting to design alternatives

Once again, all of this may sound rather complicated and time-consuming – the authors of this book are quite willing to apologise for that if that makes you feel better. However, you might find out that – as is the case for many things – explaining this step in the process could very well turn out to be more complicated than actually executing it. By now, having arrived at step 5, you are well and truly immersed in the process of designing 'your' experience and a number of the attention points and suggestions incorporated in this explanation are more likely to make you say 'yes, of course, duh!' or even 'obviously, we need to include x because that's what [fill in name of one of your personas] really wants' than 'how on earth. . .?' or 'I give up!' To illustrate this, the example of dining in the dark shows that completing this step in the process is actually not that complicated based on all the work that has already been done.

The RNIB wants to generate attention for their cause by informing the general public about life and work with sight loss and informing potential employers about ways to create jobs for visually impaired people. This very short summary of their objectives tells us that the ultimate experience to be staged by the restaurant to be designed should be a transformative experience. It should lead to learning and actions by a number of parties: guests telling others about their experience and the cause, companies creating job opportunities, people donating money to RNIB, and so on. The dramatic structure that would fit such an experience would need several peaks, with an attention grabber early on but also slowly but surely building up to the biggest peak near the end of the experience. The experience as a whole should provide guests like Pipa and Richard with the information they need and the motivation to act on that information. Therefore, particular affective peaks should instil memories in them that will benefit RNIB's cause. With this overall objective in mind, touch-point alternatives that could fulfil the functions established in step 2 can now be generated. The morphological chart shown in Figure 4.4 displays (the names of) some of the alternatives that could be generated. Obviously, these names do not (yet) provide details on the specific characteristics of these touch-point alternatives and the dramatic arc they are expected to create for each persona. In real life, this morphological chart would therefore be accompanied by a document/file/source showing these details.

To illustrate the kind of details included in such a document/file/source, consider the three alternatives for the (sub-)function 'appetiser'. After guests have arrived at the restaurant and have left their coats in the cloakroom, they are not necessarily at their table yet, or even already ordered something. The choice that has to be made now is how to introduce guests to the core of the experience they have chosen to consume. At this early stage of the overall experience, before the core of the experience when and where guests actually get to experience eating without being able to see anything, it would be wise to create a first peak – the attention grabber – in unveiling some of the issues of life and work with sight loss.

FIGURE 4.4 The morphological chart for the dining in the dark experience

Functions		Touch point alternatives name		
Pre-experience	Reservations	Phone ▲▲	Website/ app ●○	email
	Preparing guests	No dress code ▲●	Dress code	
Experience	Arriving	Group welcome – light ○ ▲	Individual welcome – light ● ▲	Welcome in the dark
	Appetiser	Intro dining in the dark presentation ○ ▲	Find your spot – lights off	Meet your waiter ▲ ●
	Starter	How is your soup? ▲	Finger food ● ▲	What's in your salad? ○
	Main course	What am I eating? ▲ ●	Have you finished? ○ ▲	Blindfold–peek-a-boo
	Digestive	Coffee and tea	Interview your waiter ● ▲ ○	Backstage tour ▲
	Leaving + payment	Guided through the dark ▲ ● ○	Lights on ▲	Night vision goggles ▲
	Miscellaneous – Menu	Fixed menu ▲	À la carte ○ ▲	Surprise ●
	Miscellaneous – Lavatory visit	Do you need help with that?	Guided visit ▲ ▲ ● ○	Flashlight
Post-experience	Soliciting diner evaluation	Pro-active online ○ ●	Passive ▲	Pro-active personal ▲

○ ● = Pipa journey alternatives   ▲ ▲ = Richard journey alternatives

The first alternative is to provide guests with a welcome drink and then a presentation (e.g. a short movie that is shown on a screen) in a bar that introduces them to what dining in the dark is like and some background information of the people who will be serving them. Only then are guests guided to their table in the dark restaurant. This will help establish an explicit link between the restaurant and RNIB's cause in the minds of guests.

The second alternative is to immediately take guests to their table after arriving and hanging their coats, where they are presented with a welcome drink before the lights are turned off. This will create the shock of 'going blind', being disoriented and having to adjust to using senses other than sight.

The third alternative is to have the particular waiter assigned to particular guests that evening to meet them in the bar. This waiter then tells these guests about his personal background and explains what the evening will be like and, for instance, how to ask for (his/her) assistance in the dark. He or she takes time to answer questions before guiding the guests to their table through the restaurant that is already dark by asking them to put their hands on his shoulder. This alternative focuses on establishing a relationship between the staff member and guests and building trust between them, as well as on stimulating anticipation of what will happen next.

These three ways of operating represent three examples of the types of touch-point alternatives that could be generated in this step. For each function, specific alternatives are generated and included in the morphological chart. Now, guest journey alternatives need to be generated based on this chart. For Pipa, two guest journey alternatives have been indicated in Figure 4.4. For Richard, two possible journeys have also been incorporated. For some functions, the same touch points could be chosen for both Pipa and Richard, for instance because they both have a preference for either a personal introduction or a presentation and the opportunity to gather more personal information from staff through an interview or a backstage tour. However, whereas Richard is keen to know what he will be eating, Pipa is more curious about the actual experience of eating in the dark than what exactly she will be eating. Therefore, the touch points included in their customer journey alternatives for the function of eating are different. In constructing the customer journey alternatives for both Pipa and Richard, the designers have accounted for the fact that the main course and digestive together should create the type of peak or climax needed for a transformative experience. The alternatives also need to ensure that by that time Pipa and Richard have been able to gather enough information to appreciate some of the life and work challenges faced by people with sight loss and feel sympathetic towards their waiter.

The final stage of this step needs to generate overall design alternatives. These design alternatives incorporate all touch points that will actually be created and thus will be available to shape the actual customer journeys of Pipa and Richard, including the dramatic structure associated with them. In creating these design alternatives, you look for possibilities to combine the customer journey alternatives for both personas into one overall design but you might be forced to make choices between touch-point alternatives preferred by Pipa and touch-point alternatives preferred by Richard. For instance, the restaurant will probably either have a dress code or not — it would be silly to force some guests to stick to a dress code and have others choose whatever outfit makes them feel comfortable. Similarly, the restaurant will likely either welcome all guests individually or organise a group welcome. However, for some functions, it might very well be possible to create multiple touch points. For instance, guests could choose to go on a backstage tour or have a one-on-one talk with their waiter. Maybe you could even offer guests both alternatives. Similar to any other experience, choices made at this stage of step 5 of the design process need to account for all the information gathered in the previous steps. For the dining in the dark experience, this could result in selecting the two design alternatives shown in Figures 4.5 and 4.6, each creating a particular dramatic structure for Pipa and for Richard.

FIGURE 4.5 First design alternative for the dining in the dark experience

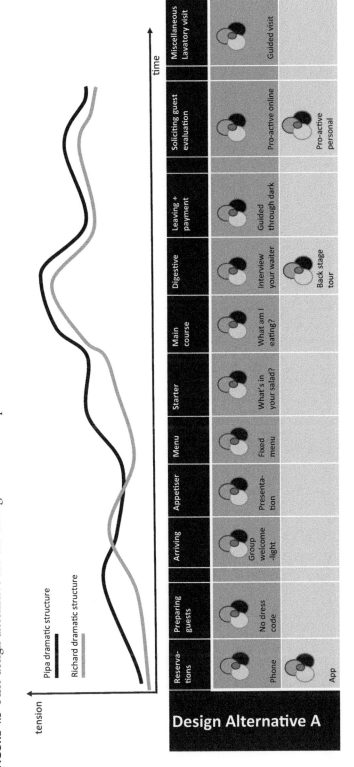

FIGURE 4.6 Second design alternative for the dining in the dark experience

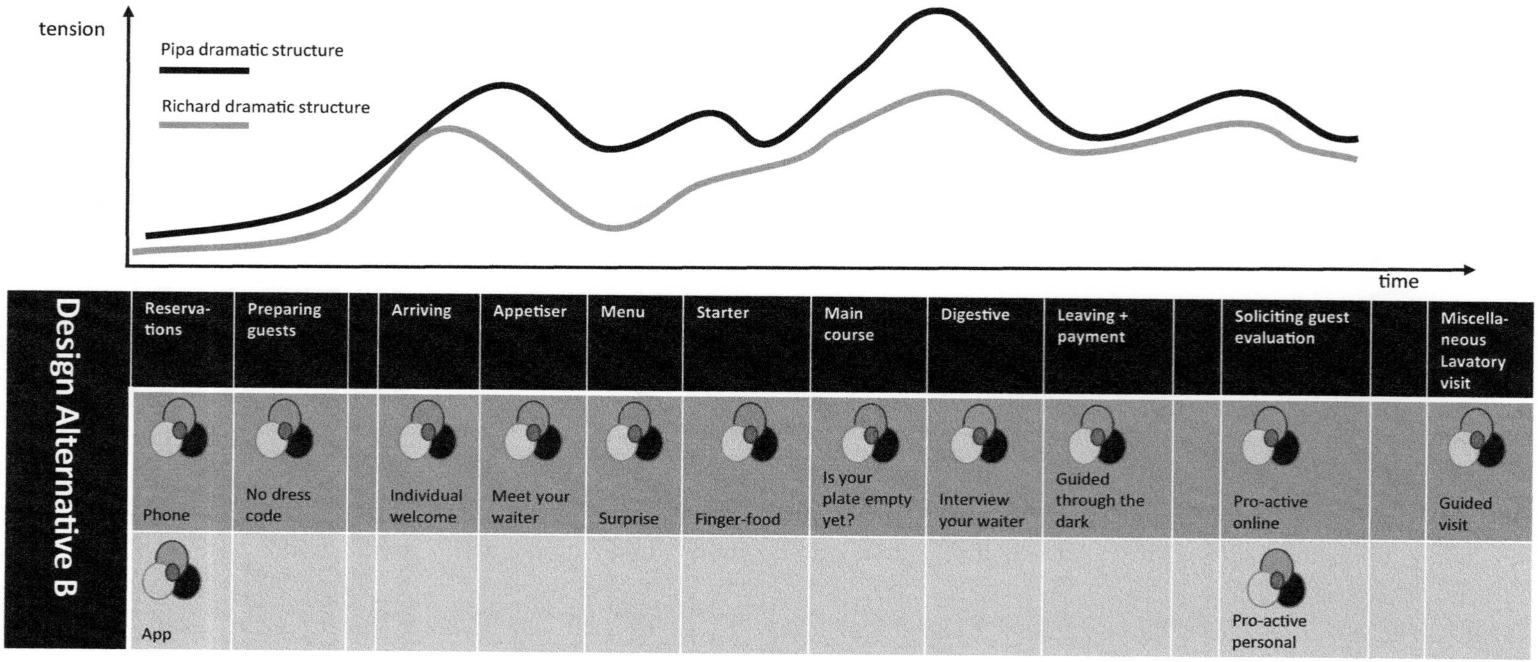

tension

time

Pipa dramatic structure
Richard dramatic structure

Reserva-tions	Preparing guests	Arriving	Appetiser	Menu	Starter	Main course	Digestive	Leaving + payment	Soliciting guest evaluation	Miscella-neous Lavatory visit
Phone	No dress code	Individual welcome	Meet your waiter	Surprise	Finger-food	Is your plate empty yet?	Interview your waiter	Guided through the dark	Pro-active online	Guided visit
App									Pro-active personal	

Design Alternative B

STEP 6: EVALUATING ALTERNATIVES

This step focuses on deciding which design alternative will actually be created and staged for 'real' customers. Coming to an informed decision usually involves comparing these alternatives based on a number of criteria. These criteria can be derived from the objectives formulated in step 1 and the requirements set in step 3, but can also directly be linked to specific customer preferences. The latter could for instance be incorporated in the evaluation of design alternatives by means of stated preference studies based on the sub-solutions incorporated in these alternatives or having actual (potential) customers test prototypes of (parts of) these designs. As discussed earlier, creating an actual physical prototype of some experiences might not be possible – how would you prototype a fly-drive holiday? – but storytelling techniques, artist's impressions, animations and digital mock-ups could very well provide opportunities to gather customer feedback.

Performing a multi-criteria analysis is an obvious route to follow for most (complex) experiences, especially to address all the various criteria involved in making up your mind with respect to the design to be realised. Chapter 3 has already explained the basics of conducting such an analysis. However, with respect to aspects such as expected margins, investments required, and operating and maintenance costs involved with actually staging the experience, gathering all relevant information can be extremely time-consuming and complicated in 'real' life. Predicting revenues based on predicting customer demand is at best still a prediction and not a fact. Simultaneously, these numbers are not just needed for a multi-criteria analysis but also for decisions with respect to how and whom to fund, all that is needed to get from the stage of a design (on paper or digital) to an experience staged for 'real' people. These numbers might very well determine who will be the actual 'owner' of the experience to be staged, the business model to be applied for staging it, and so on. This book purposely does not cover these kinds of (more generic) legal and financial matters for two reasons: (1) it would be a distraction from what this book is all about – designing, staging and managing *experiences*, and (2) there already is a vast body of literature and other sources of information available to the readers of this book to address these issues.

Dining in the dark – decision time

However, for our dining in the dark experience, we still need to arrive at a decision with respect to which design alternative will actually be realised. As for any multi-criteria analysis, the first step would be to establish all relevant criteria for this decision and listing them in the left column of the matrix created for each alternative. This matrix also shows the weights assigned to these criteria. Subsequently, for each design alternative a (performance) score is determined for each criterion. For each criterion, this score is multiplied by the weight and the resulting scores are added for each design alternative. The alternative with the highest total score is deemed to represent the best design.

FIGURE 4.7 The multi criteria matrices for the two design alternatives

Dining in the dark experience alternative A			
Criterion	Weight	Score	Weight × score
Profitability	7	7	49
RNIB investment	7	7	49
Capacity	6	9	54
Richard experience	9	8	72
Pipa experience	10	7	70
		Total	294

Dining in the dark experience alternative B			
Criterion	Weight	Score	Weight × score
Profitability	7	9	63
RNIB investment	7	6	42
Capacity	6	7	42
Richard preference	9	8	72
Pipa experience	10	9	90
		Total	309

The matrices for the two design alternatives created for the dining in the dark experience could very well look like the ones shown in Figure 4.7. In this example, design alternative B scores best, mostly because the ultimate experience for Pipa would be near optimal – considering her specific needs and wishes – and the restaurant would be more profitable. Ultimately, this increases the chances of the restaurant serving RNIB's cause both in the short term – during the fundraising campaign – and in the long term – also after the campaign has ended. Therefore, based on the steps completed so far, choosing this design alternative very much looks like the smart choice.

STEP 7: IMPROVING DETAILS

Based on the previous steps, it is now clear which design alternative will be pursued. However, this experience is not operational yet – it is not yet staged for actual customers. The design of this experience still needs to be worked out in detail and oftentimes specific physical environments need to be created, which could very well involve building or construction work. This final step of the design process focuses on improving details of the design before and during the period between choosing a specific design and the point in time the provider can actually start staging the experience, but it could also be argued to continue after that. As Chapter 3 has explained, this step is all about optimising the design without changing its essential characteristics. For physical elements, this could involve applying value engineering for instance to reduce (operational) costs or the investments needed to construct the physical environment but also to further improve (evidencing of) the experience. For improving the details of the processes that need to be executed in staging it, tools such as spaghetti diagrams can assist in improving effectiveness or productiveness of processes and staff but also reducing the (amount of) resources they require – obviously, all this is done without fundamentally changing the interactions with customers and thus the overall experience staged for them.

Improving details could also be the stage of the process to get all numbers straight. How many customers can specific processes handle, and could this be increased? Should specific services be outsourced? What are the consequences of these types of decisions for the operating costs? Maybe you could check whether specific synergies could be created that have not been factored into the design yet. One of the reference points for this step is to also repeatedly review the balance between steps 1 and 6 of the design process; if changing specific details implies that the alternative chosen in step 6 is no longer the most logical or only way to reach the objectives set in step 1, this might point to the need for (yet) another iteration in the overall design process. Similarly, if specific details need to be improved but doing so cannot be done within the context of decisions made in previous steps, this also suggests that iteration is in order. Perhaps those details could be improved by relaxing one of the requirements set in step 3 or changing the details of one of the touch-point alternatives generated and picked in step 6. Obviously, this step in the process should not force or urge you to start all over – if it does, this would mean you have made some fundamental errors in previous steps – but it might very well assist in carefully reviewing some of the decisions made earlier and fine-tune them to allow for making the ultimate design even better.

It is important to note though that some specific details that could be improved might only become apparent after staging the experience has started. It might turn out that (specific) customers react differently to specific clues and stimuli than expected. Once staging the experience has started, staff members will get used to performing their roles and tasks in the experience and this might enable them to pick up on specific details that could be done better or smarter. This stage of the improving details step is addressed in more detail in the next chapter.

Dining in the dark – 'eye' for detail

For the dining in the dark experience, design alternative B has been chosen as the one to be staged for real. However, it is not operational yet. The basic physical spaces needed are known, as are the main interactions between waiters and guests, the type of food and drinks to be prepared and served, and so on. However, in this step of the process, specific details of the design could still be improved.

For instance, although the design incorporates booking through an app, we might find out that also creating the opportunity to make reservations by phone – as preferred by Richard – is actually possible without increasing costs too much or disturbing the other processes that need to be executed. Other details that we might focus on relate to the layout of the restaurant to ensure that our (blind) waiters can move around easily and safely. Are we going to use trays or carts to move food and drinks from the kitchen to guests' tables? The choice for one of those affects details of the layout, as well as the optimal routing to the restrooms, and so on.

Finally, clear guidelines for staff need to be created and they will need to be trained, for instance with respect to safety and emergency procedures. These are just a few of the details that will need to be worked out before the restaurant is ready for the grand opening.

DESIGNING MORE COMPLEX EXPERIENCES

However, before moving on to actually staging and managing experiences in the next chapter, it might be wise to not get bogged down in the details of the dining in the dark example. Instead, this final section focuses on another example to show how the comprehensive approach to designing experiences presented in this chapter could be applied to designing more complex experiences. This second case study describes the steps in the design process – and how they could be executed successfully – for a two-day gaming event hosting a number of very different types of customers – without going into too much detail but still showing the key reference points to account for in completing such a design task. One of the reasons why the design for this experience is more complex than the design for dining in the dark is that participants in this event have – and will definitely take – a lot more freedom in creating their own individual customer journeys based on the full range of touch points offered by the event organisers. However, as this case study will show, this does certainly not mean that their individual experiences cannot be designed (purposely and concurrently)!

Clarifying the objectives

HighTECH gaming brings together game designers, hardware engineers and professional gamers in cutting-edge events. Member companies that specialise in new games and game concepts fund the HighTECH gaming organisation. They now want to organise a new (annual) event called UXtream in the Kintex Convention Centre in Seoul, South Korea. This event should stimulate collaboration between and innovation by software and hardware developers linked to creating optimal gaming experiences. The two-day event should attract about 1,000 visitors and the design team for this event has established that it should target two specific types of visitors, for which they have developed personas.

The first persona is Steve. He is a member of the research and development team at a major hardware-engineering company. He visits UXtream together with some of his team members and for several reasons. The main reason is to demonstrate and sell the newest technologies his company offers and find partners to develop games and applications that could apply them. Steve also wants to get an idea of the (types of) innovations offered by some of their competitors and be inspired by some of the leading figures in the gaming industry. Finally, he wants to catch up with some old friends he has studied and worked with in the past. Steve was born and raised in the US but has lived and worked in Seoul for more than ten years now. He will commute to the event.

The second persona is Hannah. Hannah works for one of the major game studios in Australia. Her job is to liaise with hardware engineers and introduce their latest technologies to the studio, while also sharing her company's views on the next step in 4D gaming experiences with engineers who could and would need to develop associated hardware solutions. She visits UXtream to network with some of the hardware partners they already work with, to order new equipment and to see what is new. She also wants to showcase a prototype of their newest game on (a) stage together with a hardware partner and two professional e-players at the event. Hannah would like to stay in a hotel close to the Kintext Convention Centre, so that she can plan some meetings in the evening, but is also curious about the city of Seoul.

The design team has formulated the following key objectives for Steve:

- Steve will feel UXtream has helped him demonstrate and sell hardware.
- Steve will feel UXtream has informed him about innovations of competitors.
- UXtream will have inspired Steve and will have stimulated him to reflect on future developments.
- Steve will remember UXtream as being fun and a great opportunity to catch up with friends.

The design team has formulated the following key objectives for Hannah:

- Hannah will feel UXtream has helped her to do business.
- UXtream will have inspired Hannah with respect to future developments.
- UXtream will be remembered by Hannah as a great platform to share knowledge and insights with (potential) partners.
- Hannah will feel UXtream has facilitated her and her studio in building a reputation.

Finally, the design team has formulated the following key objectives for HighTECH gaming:

- Our event will stimulate cooperation and inspire visitors who represent the best game design and hardware-engineering companies (in the world).
- Our event is seen as a great opportunity to network and do business.
- The UXtream experience positions HighTECH gaming as *the* organisation inspiring collaboration and innovation in this industry.

Establishing the functions

The following list displays some typical functions linked to organising an event like UXtream that the design team will have to consider:

- Hosting hardware and software companies *and* their equipment.
- Providing or arranging accommodation for visitors.
- Providing visitors with information and planning of (various touch points of) the event.
- Providing food and drinks at the event.
- Providing business meeting opportunities – in time and space.
- Staging showcases and inspiration sessions.
- Providing opportunities for networking, social events and side programmes – in time and space.

Setting the requirements

The overall experience to be staged through organising UXtream will need to meet a number of requirements to be considered a success. As far as HighTECH gaming is concerned, the event needs to attract a minimum of 800 visitors representing at least 30 hardware-engineering companies and 60 game studios. They also want HighTECH gaming members to be happy about the business they were able to do through UXtream. Obviously, to reach the objectives set in the first step of the process, both HighTECH gaming members and all other visitors should feel the event is well organised and should allow visitors to do what they came to do – which can be very different for different visitors, as shown in the previous two steps of this case study. The design team has also set specific requirements with respect to budget, space available in the convention centre, and so on.

Determining the (key) characteristics

As in the dining in the dark example, this step in the process focuses on linking user needs to design characteristics. However, for UXtream, completing this step is a bit more complicated because fulfilling the needs and wishes of Hannah actually requires some different touch points from those fulfilling Steve's needs and wishes.

Figure 4.8 shows the HoQ that the design team has created for the overall experience staged for (all) visitors – the HoQ at the highest abstraction level. By zooming in on some of the needs and wishes included in this HoQ, the logic they applied in constructing it can be illustrated.

Optimal facilitation of company booths is one of the needs of HighTECH gaming – the provider of the UXtream experience. For them, the success of the event very much depends on the opportunities given to visitors, and thus the companies they represent, to demonstrate and explain their companies' technologies.

FIGURE 4.8 The highest-level House of Quality for UXtream

UXtream extended experience	Design attributes								
	Interaction			Physical environment			Outcome		
Needs and wishes	Attitude	Behaviour	Expertise	Ambient	Design	Social factors	Tangibles	Waiting time	Valence
Provide inspiration				6	9	9	3	6	6
Optimal facilitation of partner booths	9	9	9	6	6	3	9	9	6
Facilitate business meetings	6	6	3	9	6	6	6	3	
Facilitate networking	6	6		6	6	3	6	3	3
Facilitate way finding	6	6	6		9		6		
Steve – booth				9	9	6	9	6	
Steve – relax	3	3	3	3	6	6	6	3	
Steve – deals				6	9				
Steve – social	3	3	3				6	3	
Hannah – meet				6	9	3	3		
Hannah – present	6	6	6	9	9	3	9	9	
Hannah – network	3	3		6	6	9	9	3	
Hannah – deals				6	6	3			
Hannah – hotel	6	6					6	3	3

This requires state-of-the-art facilitation in terms of power, bandwidth, space and lighting but also event staff who anticipate specific wishes and needs of companies and who are able to solve any (technical) problem that might arise swiftly and in a way appreciated by visitors – in other words, staff who provide a high (perceived) interaction quality.

One of Steve's needs is, in fact, related to the HighTECH gaming need; he wants to demonstrate his hardware. However, he also wants to do business and, therefore, he actually needs two types of spaces within his booth: an attractive demonstration space – in terms of ambient conditions, physical design and social factors – and a quiet, private meeting space – once again linking to ambient conditions, physical design and social factors – where he can sit down with clients and negotiate deals. Steve wants his clients to be comfortable and thus expects UXtream to provide drinks and snacks on demand – tangibles and waiting time – and comfortable furniture – design – in that meeting space.

Hannah represents a different type of visitor with different needs and wishes. She needs a place to sleep, eat and meet after opening hours of UXtream. Even though providing them might not be incorporated in UXtream, Hannah's experience will very much be influenced – positively – if and when UXtream staff assists her in finding and booking a suitable hotel or AirBnB – a link to attitude and behaviour of staff. UXtream could provide transportation for commuting between the convention centre and Hannah's accommodation – tangibles, waiting times, valence. Together, these services included in the UXtream experience could ensure that Hannah can focus on what she actually came to do: do business and showcase – valence.

All numbers incorporated in the HoQ shown in Figure 4.8 represent similar trains of thought and links between specific needs and wishes on the one hand and the extent to which fulfilling them is likely to be impacted by specific design characteristics of the overall UXtream experience. Importance scores and priority scores have purposely been left out for this HoQ to not overwhelm you – the reader – with too many details and numbers right here, right now. However, like the dining in the dark example, finalising this HoQ by executing the analyses, discussions and calculations associated with adding them would provide the design team with some clear insights and guidelines with respect to what characteristics to focus on in the next step of the design process. Also similar to dining in the dark, the design team for UXtream could and probably would have to create multiple (layers of) HoQs in this step of the process. For instance, a more detailed HoQ focusing on the specific design characteristics of booths would probably provide them with information that would prove extremely helpful in generating appropriate alternatives for this touch point in the next step. The website accompanying this book contains fully worked out versions of both HoQs – the overall experience and booths. Feel free to have a look at them, if and when you are 'ready'.

Generating touch point, customer journey and design alternatives

One could argue that UXtream represents a so-called extended experience. The overall experience lasts for two days, is immersive and should create a lasting memory linked to specific emotions triggered by memorable encounters and peak experiences taking place during those two days. UXtream should immerse visitors in an inspiring, state-of-the-art gaming technology 'world'. Visitors should experience emotions such as amazement and appreciation but also feel proud to be a member of this community. To ensure that these emotions and feelings are linked to UXtream Seoul, they should at least partly be triggered by the physical environment created for visitors. UXtream Seoul should be seen as *the* 'place' where industry leaders get together to show, sell and compete.

Together with the lessons learnt in the previous step, understanding what creates an extended experience proved important for the design team in this step of designing UXtream. It helped them to create an appropriate morphological chart for the functions to be fulfilled for Steve and Hannah. The design team decided that it would be wise to apply a specific theme for UXtream, which could be communicated through decor and costumes worn by staff but also through food and drinks and having staff adopt some of the habits and language associated with this theme. They decided to focus on two options: Star Wars and gamification. The resulting morphological chart at the level of the overall experience is shown in Figure 4.9.

This morphological chart contains touch-point alternatives for all functions UXtream will fulfil. However, Steve and Hannah do not need all these functions to be fulfilled during their individual customer journeys. For instance, Hannah will make use of (accommodation) booking services, Steve will not. This morphological chart is thus different from the one included in the dining in the dark case study. It shows all touch points that could be selected to be included in the overall experience staged for all visitors. However, people like Steve and Hannah themselves will decide which ones they will actually go through, at what time and in what order. Steve and Hannah decide on when they want to have a meeting, which showcases they want to see, when they will arrive and leave, and so on.

It is the design team's job to make sure that all touch-point alternatives that will be included in the final design will actually allow Steve and Hannah to shape their own individual customer journey in such a way that it fulfils their individual needs and wishes. Obviously, the complicating factor for the team is that specific requirements might make it impossible to include all touch-point alternatives. HighTECH gaming's objectives might also require a specific timing of providing specific touch points over the course of the two days of UXtream to create a specific dramatic structure for visitors. Furthermore, maybe it would not be the most logical and smartest thing to do to combine a Star Wars and gamification theme – for one, Star Wars fans tend to be quite strict when it comes to sticking to the Star Wars storyline!

Therefore, the UXtream design team has first selected specific touch-point alternatives from the morphological chart that together could create some viable customer journey alternatives for Steve and Hannah. They have also selected touch-point alternatives that HighTECH gaming would really like to be included in the ultimate design. These mostly relate to touch points that all visitors go through – such as the entrance and the exit – but also touch points that could be offered to all (types of) visitors simultaneously, for instance by purposely staging them just once a day using the main stage. These touch-point alternatives would allow the organisers to create the right dramatic structure for most visitors, which would assist them in turning UXtream into the extended experience they aim to stage. Other touch-point alternatives that could assist them in doing so could relate to sub-solutions such as pop-up events and themed so-called random acts of kindness – see Chapter 5 for an explanation of the latter. Ultimately, the design team has incorporated all three sets of preferences in the morphological chart, as shown in Figure 4.9.

FIGURE 4.9 A morphological chart for UXtream incorporating two alternatives for a theme

	Functions	Touch-point alternatives			
Pre-experience	Partner invitation	Darth Vader / Yoda message □ ●	Traditional invitation	Personal invitation from industry leader □ △	Roadshow ●
	Ticket booth	Online □	VR/AR-meeting □ ●		
	Booking services	Hotel packages △ □	Meeting ● package □	Social ● programme △ □	F&B booth services □ ●
Experience	Arrival	Gamified welcome	Game □ character host	VR/ AR check-in □ △	
	Setting-up booth	Techn. personal assistant ● □	Do it yourself	Assistance on demand □ ●	
	Booth meetings	Basic chairs, table and buffet □ ●	Luxurious lounge △	Personal droid butler □	On demand ●
	Meetings	Meeting centre ●	Themed meeting spaces	Themed pop-up meeting space on demand ●	Jabbas' Luxurious Lounge △ □
	Networking	Opening reception △ ●	Network breakfast △	Digital networking assistant	Gamified △ gala dinner and awards □ ceremony ●
	Showcase	Theatre and △ stage, fixed schedule ●	Pop-up showcase □	On-demand Mixed reality presentation △	
	Relaxing	Simple backstage lounge	Old school gaming zone □ ●	Home base, private lounge	Themed random acts of kindness

FIGURE 4.9 continued

	Food and drink outlets	Themed F&B outlets ●	Local food trucks △	Themed food and drink ■ ●	Gamified food and drinks △ ■
	Hotel transfer	Modern local provider	Traditional △ local provider	Themed van Rebel vessel ■	Do it yourself
	Exit	No frills ●	Gamified narrow Jedi escape ■	'May the ■ force be with you host' △	
	Social programme	Grand opening by big name △ ■	Seoul tour △	Themed evening party ●	Gamified gala dinner △ ■ ●
Post-experience	After sales contact	Impact and satisfaction survey	AR / VR feedback ● meeting ■	Personal call from HighTECH △	Thank you message ■ from Yoda

△ = Preferred by Hannah	● = Preferred by Steve	■ = Preferred for HighTECH

Subsequently, the design team has created two overall design alternatives to be considered in the next step of the process. In creating these design alternatives, the team has looked for possibilities to combine all preferences linked to creating viable customer journey alternatives for Steve and Hannah, as well as HighTECH gaming's preferences, into one overall design. Obviously, the requirements set earlier forced them to make some choices. For some functions it turned out to be possible to create multiple touch points. For others this would be too costly, require too much space or simply prove ineffective in relation to creating an appropriate dramatic structure for all visitors. These two overall designs are presented in Figures 4.10 and 4.11 by not only indicating which touch-point alternatives are included but also what type of dramatic structure is likely to be created by them for Steve and Hannah.

FIGURE 4.10 First design alternative for UXtream

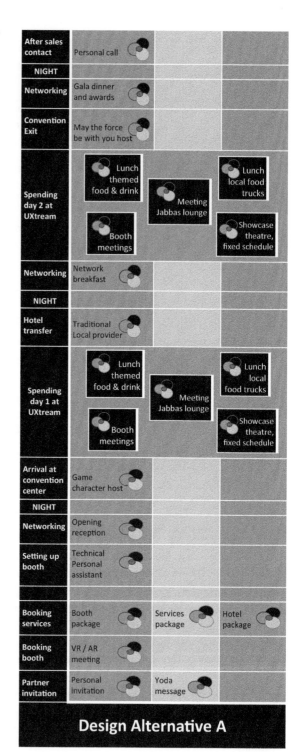

tension

time

— Hannah dramatic structure
— Steve dramatic structure

After sales contact	Personal call		
NIGHT			
Networking	Gala dinner and awards		
Convention Exit	May the force be with you host		
Spending day 2 at UXtream	Lunch themed food & drink / Booth meetings	Meeting Jabbas lounge	Lunch local food trucks / Showcase theatre, fixed schedule
Networking	Network breakfast		
NIGHT			
Hotel transfer	Traditional Local provider		
Spending day 1 at UXtream	Lunch themed food & drink / Booth meetings	Meeting Jabbas lounge	Lunch local food trucks / Showcase theatre, fixed schedule
Arrival at convention center	Game character host		
NIGHT			
Networking	Opening reception		
Setting up booth	Technical Personal assistant		
Booking services	Booth package	Services package	Hotel package
Booking booth	VR / AR meeting		
Partner invitation	Personal invitation	Yoda message	

Design Alternative A

FIGURE 4.11 Second design alternative for UXtream

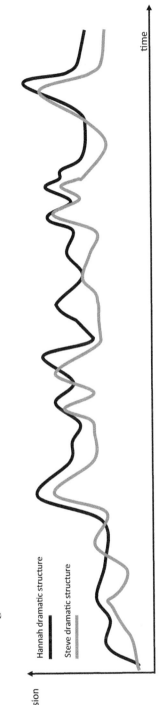

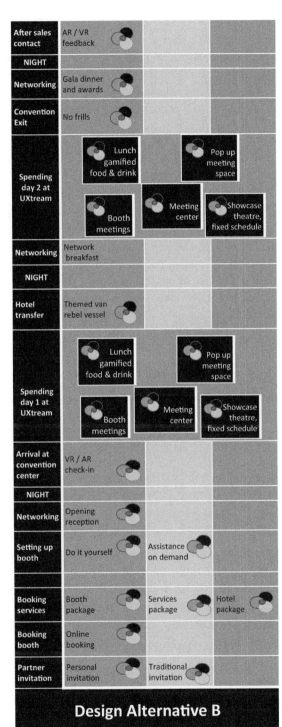

Choosing the best design and improving its details

Similar to the dining in the dark example, the final two steps in the process of designing UXtream focus on choosing the best design and then improving all details that can still be improved. The multi-criteria analysis matrices that the design team has created are shown on the website accompanying this book. Also similar to the previous case study, these final two steps could very well point to a need for iteration and returning to earlier steps to address specific aspects, such as the range set for a specific requirement or the way a specific key characteristic of the overall design has been worked out in a particular touch-point alternative, that – with a little tweaking – could accommodate for an even better experience to be staged.

These details are omitted here. By now, the way in which the comprehensive approach to experience design presented in this chapter could assist in designing various types of experiences should be clear to you. The two case studies together with the explanations provided for each of the seven steps in this process have portrayed its overall train of thought and some specific reference points that deserve your attention in applying it. It is now time to move on to actually staging the experiences that have been designed, and managing the processes involved. This is the topic of the next chapter.

SUMMARY

Based on reading this chapter, we hope you will understand and remember the following:

- The overall train of thought of the comprehensive approach to experience design presented in this chapter.
- How personas can be used as the starting point and common thread running through all steps of a design process aimed at designing an experience.
- The main differences in the design process for designing an experience that incorporates more or less the same customer journey for all customers and the design process for designing an experience that incorporates a collection of touch points that allows different customers to go through different customer journeys.
- The key roles of dramatic arcs and dramatic structures in designing successful experiences.

FOOD FOR THOUGHT

Based on the content of this chapter, the following questions, challenges and topics could serve as interesting starting points for further discussion:

- Create the Houses of Quality for some of the touch points incorporated in the ultimate design of the dining in the dark restaurant.

- Create the Houses of Quality for some of the touch points incorporated in the ultimate design of the UXtream gaming convention.

- Come up with at least three touch-point alternatives not yet included in the morphological chart for the dining in the dark restaurant.

- Come up with at least three touch-point alternatives not yet included in the morphological chart for the UXtream gaming convention.

- Would you make different choices for the remainder of the design process for the dining in the dark restaurant based on these new touch-point alternatives? Explain and, if necessary, adjust the relevant outcomes of all relevant design steps.

- Would you make different choices for the remainder of the design process for the dining in the dark restaurant based on these new touch-point alternatives? Explain and, if necessary, adjust the relevant outcomes of all relevant design steps.

- Would you make different choices for the remainder of the design process for the UXtream gaming convention based on these new touch-point alternatives? Explain and, if necessary, adjust the relevant outcomes of all relevant design steps.

REFERENCES

Brady, M.K. & Cronin Jr, J.J. (2001). Some new thoughts on conceptualizing perceived service quality: A hierarchical approach. *Journal of Marketing*, 65(3), 34–49.

Berry, L.L., Wall, E.A. & Carbone, L.P. (2006). Service clues and customer assessment of the service experience: Lessons from marketing. *The Academy of Management Perspectives*, 20(2), 43–57.

Falk, J.H. & Dierking, L. (1992). *The museum experience*. Ann Arbor: Whalesback Books.

5 Staging and managing experiences

INTRODUCTION

Chapter 4 has shown how to combine the social sciences and design science perspectives in designing experiences. However, designing experiences is only the first step towards actually staging them. Once the specifics of the experience you want to offer to your customers are known, you need to make sure that it is staged in a way that matches the design. Ensuring that experiences are staged the way they need to be staged is referred to as (customer) experience management.

Experience management involves correctly applying insights, principles, methods, tools and techniques from disciplines such as quality management, process management, leadership, and selection and training within the context of staging experiences. However, for specific experiences, such as extended experiences that are staged at various locations and involve a number of different businesses and (independent) professionals, it can also relate to stakeholder management, supply-chain management, network management, negotiating, setting up contracts, and so on. A typical example would be a fly-drive holiday offered to (potential) customers by a travel agency. Whereas the travel agency represents the party actually selling the experience to customers, staging the experience involves a number of other parties. Ultimately, one single fly-drive holiday could require a contribution from three airports – because the driving part of the trip is a one-way route, two airlines that operate the respective flights, two different car rental companies, a number of hotels and resorts as well as restaurants located along the route, various museums, a few theatres, two zoos, three theme parks, five wildlife reserves, and many, many more parties. A number of these parties will be businesses or professionals from other sectors than the travel sector. In fact, some of them would normally not be considered to be part of events, tourism and hospitality. This highlights that staging experiences is not limited to these specific industries and that the importance of experiences can be witnessed in many other industries as well. What is more, also as a result of the rise of the experience economy, boundaries between industries could be argued to be disappearing or at least thinning – a topic addressed in more detail in the next chapter. The consequences of this blurring of industries for designing, staging and managing experiences, such as an increased focus on topics such as stakeholder management, are addressed in the subsequent chapters.

This chapter first focuses on the basics of experience management: what basic requirements need to be fulfilled to ensure that touch points which together shape a customer journey match the specifics laid down in the design of that customer journey? This means that this chapter addresses the operational and tactical level of experience management – the strategic level is addressed in the remainder of the book. The discussion presented here is based on the assumption that a single provider – one company or a group of professionals joining forces – stages the experience to be managed. This allows for highlighting the specific operational and tactical processes, decisions, dilemmas and complications involved with actualising touch points – and thus the customer journeys that they shape – in line with how they have been designed.

One could argue that, strictly speaking, some of these decisions, dilemmas and complications actually need to be dealt with in the final stage of the design process: improving details. In reality, there is no such thing as a precise dividing line between the last phase of designing and the first phase of staging/managing experiences. This is especially true for (parts of) experiences designed through applying a more heuristic approach to design, for instance by using rapid prototyping or co-creation techniques. However, also if a systematic or even axiomatic approach was used to create the design, the proof of the pudding is still in the eating! In other words, the first steps of staging a new experience will almost always reveal some details that still require attention or processes that need fine-tuning. Regardless of whether you call this the final stage of design or the first stage of implementation, it involves taking a close and critical look at the on-stage and back-stage processes involved in all touch points that shape the customer journey. Could those processes be executed more effectively or efficiently? Are they executed the right way every time and in a way that is consistent for all touch points? How can we ensure that this will also be the case for a prolonged period of time? Those are the types of questions addressed in the next section. The types of methods, tools and techniques that can be applied to do so are very similar to the ones applied in the improving details stage of the design process: service blueprints, Standard Operating Procedures and flow charts.

Once this final check on the details of the processes involved is completed, we can switch our attention to actually managing the physical and social contexts – and sometimes even, to some extent, the personal contexts – of all touch points in a customer journey, thereby guaranteeing that those touch points (continue to) fulfil their function in that journey according to specification. The three sections that focus on this topic are linked to the same three categories of performance variables that were used to design those touch points – interaction quality, physical environment quality and outcome quality (Brady and Cronin, 2001).

The chapter concludes with a section that discusses some generic aspects of quality management that are also relevant to experience management – such as laws, regulations, contracts and agreements, but this section also includes a warning to not fall into the trap of management as a goal instead of a means; otherwise you might end up with a service instead of an experience.

PROCESS QUALITY

Applying the design approach presented in the previous chapter should have ensured that the design of the experience has been based on the specific needs and wishes of the specific customers who (are expected to) consume it. However, as highlighted by the ServQual model (Parasuraman et al., 1988) discussed in Chapter 1, correctly translating customers' needs and wishes into an experience design is no guarantee (yet) that the experience will be staged in line with customers' expectations. Sometimes this difference between how customers perceive the (quality of the) experience staged for them and what they expected can be explained by faulty marketing communication – you should never promise more or something else than what you are actually going to present to paying customers. Yet, it could also be the result of an incorrect translation of the design into specifications for the various processes involved in making the touch points of the customer journey(s) come to life. Finally, even if the specifications for those processes are correct, this does not automatically ensure that they will be executed according to specification. Most experiences represent complicated and delicate 'machines', in which employees, physical spaces and artefacts, technology and customers come together in a co-creative process aimed at meeting or even exceeding the expectations of those same customers.

Experience blueprinting

In order to be able to ensure that this 'machine' performs according to specification, it is essential to always have a clear overview of all the customer actions and organisational reactions involved in staging an experience. As discussed in Chapter 1, a technique that can prove very useful in creating such an overview is service blueprinting. If and when this technique is applied to experiences, the resulting experience blueprint shows exactly what processes – both on-stage and back-stage – are involved in staging the experience for customers. It shows when and where customers and the experience provider interact, the communication channels used for doing so, how the processes involved are organised, and – if applicable – what physical evidence of this interaction is provided to the customer. Essentially, the experience blueprint shows the chronological sequence of activities a customer will engage in and the sequence of activities staff and systems of the experience provider engage in on their end. As such, an experience blueprint can provide management – and all other staff – with an overview of all the processes and information that need to be coordinated to actually stage the experience. However, most experiences are shaped by multiple touch points, with each individual touch point incorporating multiple processes. Including detailed information on each of these processes in one overall blueprint would lead to such a huge blueprint that doing so usually is infeasible or at least impractical. Whereas an experience blueprint can be very useful for keeping track of the bigger picture, focusing on the details of individual processes requires application of other tools and techniques.

Scripts, Standard Operating Procedures and flow charts

Making sure that experiences are staged the right way every time implies making sure that both on-stage and back-stage processes are executed the right way every time. A process is generally defined as a specific ordering of activities across time and space with a beginning, an end, and clearly defined inputs and outputs. Especially for repeating processes that are executed by people, so-called scripts and Standard Operating Procedures (SOPs) can be very useful in formalising these processes and thus assist in ensuring that they are executed according to specification. Scripts focus on what staff should say or do within each step of the process that involves direct interaction with customers. Standardisation of these interactions through scripting them helps to ensure consistency and uniformity of the interactions with guests by different staff members, location and time. SOPs can relate to those same interactions but also to processes that do not involve direct interaction with customers – the back-stage processes. Generally, SOPs not only include one-dimensional scripts but also specific options available to staff to customise the interaction with a customer based on the specific needs and wishes of that customer. From a managerial perspective, the added value of including these options in a SOP is in making both standard and customised processes more or less predictable and thus manageable. In other words, scripts and SOPs are important tools in ensuring (perceived) quality of the staged experience in terms of reliability and responsiveness – two of the ServQual factors included in the Brady and Cronin (2001) framework, which is incorporated in the design approach presented in Chapter 4 to identify key characteristics of touch points. Simultaneously, SOPs also make the time spent on specific processes more or less predictable, which is key to managing one of the variables included in the Brady and Cronin framework: waiting times. As such, these tools can prove vital in making sure that processes are executed according to the specifications that follow from the original design for the experience to be staged, and thus that touch points actually perform the functions they need to perform in the overall customer journey(s).

SOPs usually not only include scripts and descriptions but also flow charts. A flow chart is a diagram that represents a process. There are many different kinds of flow charts but most of them include two key items: (1) process steps – or activities – that need to be executed to complete the process, and (2) decisions. Steps are usually displayed as rectangles and decisions as diamonds. To illustrate the logic and added value of flow charts, consider the welcoming process at a fine-dining restaurant. The steps in this process include activities such as a couple arriving at the reception desk, the couple waiting their turn, the couple being greeted by the host, the host asking a member of staff to take the couple's coats to the cloakroom, and the host taking the couple to their table. Especially if this restaurant employs more than one host and more than one member of staff to take clients' coats to the cloakroom, or if the restaurant is part of a chain of restaurants, it can be very

FIGURE 5.1 The flow chart for the welcoming process in a fine-dining restaurant

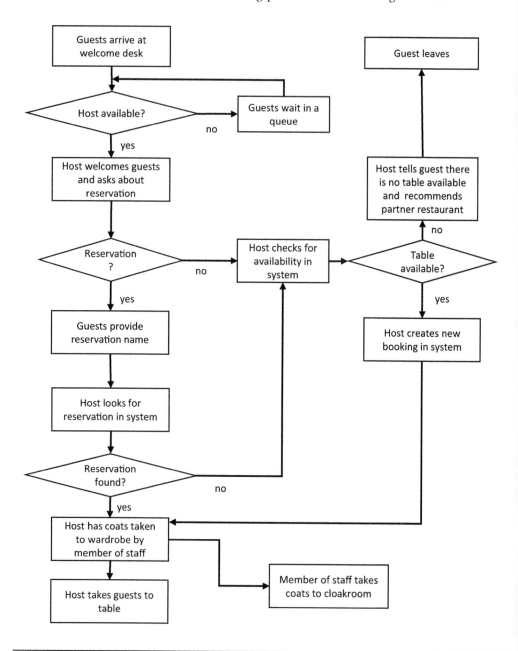

useful to display this process in a flow chart to be able to manage the reliability and responsiveness of the steps in the process. A flow chart could also prove helpful in analysing the process with respect to possible waiting times. In fact, flow charts can assist in identifying all kinds of weaknesses and inefficiencies, as well as opportunities for further improvements, in the processes involved in staging an experience. As such, flow charts can not only be used to ensure that experiences are staged in line with the design but also to continue working on improving details while already staging the experience. As discussed earlier, it is not at all uncommon for this final phase of the design process to continue after the design process has formally been completed.

For the fine-dining restaurant example, the flow chart could look like the one depicted in Figure 5.1. This flow chart could assist in training new staff and coaching/managing current staff members with respect to the restaurant's welcoming process. It can also assist in highlighting the consequences of unexpected circumstances or ways to use specific variations in steps to be executed to adapt the process to those circumstances. For instance, if the forecast for a specific evening indicates that the restaurant will not be very busy, maybe it is wise to let the additional member of staff stay home and make the host responsible for taking coats to the cloakroom after she has accompanied the guests to their table. Obviously, this would represent a simple way to save some money without deteriorating the overall experience for guests. One could even argue that on very quiet nights the host should simply forget about the original flow chart and focus on welcoming guests and taking them to their preferred table. However, this requires employees who are able and willing to do so, and thus influences the criteria to be applied in selection and training. Simultaneously, selection and training need to address that simply going with the flow is not always possible or allowed, for instance in the event of emergencies and evacuation. In those circumstances, it is actually crucial that all staff members know the relevant flow charts by heart and will not deviate from them.

INTERACTION QUALITY

The previous section highlighted the importance of applying specific tools and techniques as well as selection and training within the context of process management. Ultimately, however, successfully managing the staging of experiences requires much more than what is traditionally considered to represent the domain of process management; it requires actually managing the physical and social contexts of all touch points in the customer journey(s). Managing these contexts relates to more than consistency and predictable adaptability of specific processes. As indicated in Chapters 1 and 4, the quality of staged experiences as perceived by customers is determined by the reliability, responsiveness and empathy levels of nine variables, which can be grouped into three categories: interaction quality, physical environment quality and outcome quality (Brady and Cronin, 2001).

This section addresses the first of these three categories: interaction quality. Interaction quality of specific touch points within the overall customer journey(s) can have a significant impact on how customers perceive the overall quality of the experience staged for them, both in a positive and a negative way. This is especially true for experiences that are 'interaction heavy', such as many experiences staged within events, tourism and hospitality. A grumpy waiter can definitely ruin your dinner. A friendly, laid-back waiter with a sense of humour who knows exactly when to take your orders and, more importantly, when not to, because he might interrupt while you were reciting that poem you memorised to impress your future girlfriend – or at least, she could be if dinner goes well – could be crucial in making it a night to remember for the right reasons. In fact, the specific combination of particular behaviour accompanied by the right attitude and required expertise displayed by one of your staff members could be what creates a memorable encounter for one of your customers – who then writes glowingly about the experience you staged for him on a review site!

For some experiences, employees not only need to know and understand what they are supposed to do, in what way and in what order to make processes run smoothly, efficiently and adapted to the needs and wishes of the customer. Sometimes they also need to know and understand how their actions are linked or contribute to the symbolism, overall storyline and dramatic structure of the experience. Food being served by footmen at a ball in Cinderella's castle should not feel the same as food being served by Maids to Hobbits at the Inn of the Prancing Pony. Staff members involved not only need to be capable of performing specific tasks but they also need to understand what character they are 'playing' within the story and why their costumes look the way they do. A staff member needs to realise which part of the story is being communicated by performing a specific task and which behaviour, attitude and expertise is required to make the way he or she performs that task fit in with his or her own character and the other characters – some of which are 'played' by customers.

Those same three variables linked to interaction quality – behaviour, attitude and expertise – are clearly crucial in turning rock-climbing lessons into a transformative experience, a disappointment, or worse. The same would apply to a guided tour of a museum. In other words, behaviour, attitude and expertise of employees play a crucial role in the ultimate success of a range of experiences. That is why these variables not only need to be addressed in designing experiences but also in management of staging them. Consequently, experience management requires a lot of attention and effort with respect to recruiting, instructing, training, coaching and evaluating the employees involved.

Job design

However, before you can recruit, instruct, train, coach and evaluate people with respect to performing specific tasks within the context of staging experiences, you need to have clarity on what exactly it is that you expect them to do. Managing experiences not only requires proper execution of specific jobs, but also proper design of those jobs. Formally, the term 'job' can be defined as the aggregation of tasks, duties and responsibilities, which as a whole are regarded as a regular assignment for an individual employee. Job design thus relates to specifying jobs with respect to content and methods to be used and relationships with other jobs in order to satisfy technological as well as social and personal requirements of the job holder (Buchanan, 1979). Designing jobs can be done at an individual level but also at a team level. The latter is especially relevant if and when the team can only achieve its goals by working together or if and when, throughout the working day or working week, the responsibilities of a majority of team members shift from one task to another.

For job design within the context of experience management, there is a fine line between designing a job that leads to productivity and quality on the one hand and designing a job that leads to inefficiency on the other. This is the direct result of the inseparability and perishability characteristics of experiences and is particularly relevant for tasks that involve direct interaction with customers. If a staff member is facing too many customers at the same time, quality might become a problem. If a staff member is not facing any customers at some times and cannot switch to another task when that happens, this is clearly inefficient. Especially for staging experiences that are 'interaction heavy', such as those offered by restaurants, hotels, theme parks, theatres and so on, this can mean the difference between satisfied and dissatisfied customers – because they had to wait or queue for a long time – but also between a healthy profit and going bankrupt. Therefore, getting both the qualities and quantities of job design right is essential. Obviously, the latter is closely linked to both the way the experience was designed in the first place – as discussed in Chapter 4 – and to managing outcome quality with respect to waiting times, which is addressed in more detail in the section dedicated to outcome quality.

However, job characteristics not only relate to output or capacity. It is also important to design jobs that are interesting enough for staff to enjoy doing them without putting too much pressure on them. Some tasks that need to be executed in events, tourism and hospitality are of a highly repetitive nature, for instance serving coffee and cleaning hotel rooms or checking entry tickets and preparing French fries. Whereas repetition can help staff to get better at executing specific tasks (effectively and efficiently), it can also lead to boredom and physical strain. To prevent this from happening, job design needs to account for variety within the aggregation of tasks, duties and responsibilities that shape a job. One way to accomplish this is to ensure that roles and (repetitive) tasks change between team members throughout a working day or week. This approach not only increases performance and motivation of individual team members. It can also have a positive effect on the team as a whole by creating a cooperative atmosphere and a sense of shared responsibility for team performance. Other options for improving job design relate to issues such as safety, ensuring that staff members have enough time to rest and relax during a working day, and creating enough opportunities for satisfying so-called social needs. In fact, the full range of needs included in Maslow's hierarchy of needs (1943), as discussed in Chapter 2, could serve as a helpful checklist for job design.

For instance, esteem and self-actualisation needs relate to accounting for task significance in job design. Ensuring task significance could mean making sure that the relevance of a specific job or task is known to people within and outside the organisation, as well as to the staff member(s) performing this job or task. For many employees, it is important to feel they are contributing to a greater good, such as realising the mission of the organisation or the wellbeing of customers. Once again, satisfying these needs through job design has the added benefit of leading to employees who are satisfied and motivated to do their job well.

Selection and recruitment

Once a job has been properly designed, it is important to select and recruit the right people to do them. Especially within the context of staging and managing experiences, it is crucial to have people performing tasks for which they have the right behavioural, attitudinal and expertise characteristics. For instance, for theme parks, conveying a specific story to visitors could represent a crucial element of the overall experience staged for them. For some of these parks, storytelling has therefore become an integral part of all aspects of the organisation. For example, the Land of Ever was a Dutch theme park that really took the main story, on which the overall experience for visitors was based, to a 'next level'. The Land of Ever represented a medieval country where kids ruled the nation, and where knights, witches and giants lived. The border patrol (ticket officers) would introduce every visitor to the local customs, rules and rituals, including the EverGreet and EverGoodbye – the way of saying hello and goodbye in the Land of Ever. Parents would be instructed to listen to their children. The seat of power was located in a pink castle; most of the inhabitants lived in and around this castle and very much liked the Governor. However, some inhabitants, who lived near the DeepDarkWoods, were looking to overthrow him. The organisation behind the Land of Ever tried to create a cross media concept with their characters and stories. As well as the theme park they created TV shows, books, games, theatre productions, and so on. In their effort to be as consistent as possible in communicating the story, they also created their own bits of language, rituals and expressions, which were present everywhere, also back-stage. Suppliers would be greeted with the EverGreet, and any phone call would end with the EverGoodbye. The story logic was also applied to job titles and department names: the operations manager was the Secretary of Domestic Affairs, the marketing communication department was named Ministry of Foreign Affairs. The reasoning behind all this was not just to have fun; those working for this organisation always needed to be aware of the role they had to play in truly making this story come alive as a crucial element of successfully staging the overall experience. A successful application for a job with this organisation thus involved proving that you could play this role with credibility and tenacity, which basically turned the job application process into an audition. This example clearly highlights the relevance of choosing the right man/woman for the job within the context of managing (the staging of) experiences. It is obvious that not everyone can cope with being the Secretary of Domestic Affairs in the Land of Ever. Similarly, not all of us are cut out to wear a 'silly' costume and smile while patiently addressing children – in Land of Ever language – who would really like to go on that thrilling rollercoaster ride but take quite some time to actually step into the cart because they are also a bit frightened.

Making sure that you can select and recruit the right people for staging an experience requires translating a job design into a job specification. A job specification generally consists of two elements: a description of the job and the selection criteria. A job description includes items such as the job title, work location, tasks, duties and responsibilities involved in doing that job, the team or department that the job holder will be part of, a description of the people, tools and materials that person will be working with, working conditions such as number of hours, shifts, salary and hazards, training and development possibilities, and relationships with other jobs within the wider organisation. Job descriptions are not only useful for external recruitment but can also assist in lining up talent within the organisation for switching jobs and assessing currently available and required sets of skills for teams and departments.

The selection criteria in the job specification include criteria such as the (minimum) level and type of (successfully completed) education or training (also from a legal perspective), experience level, competencies (addressed in terms of skills, attitude and knowledge), ability to deal with specific levels and types of physical and mental strain, and attitude and personal characteristics. Obviously, all of these criteria are based on what is needed to do the job well and to fit into the team, the department or organisation.

It is important to realise that a job specification is not (yet) the same as a vacancy. A vacancy would usually also include information about the organisation, its mission, vision and culture, as well as type and duration of the contract. A vacancy does also not necessarily include all details laid down in the job description and selection criteria.

A specific job could become available when it is newly created – for instance, if and when an existing company is going to stage a new (type of) experience – or when the person who used to do the job is leaving. In the case of an existing job, team or department managers and the human resource department generally first review their options. Do we need to fill the position? Do we advertise internally, externally, or is someone up for promotion or looking for a new position? If the choice is made to open it up for (external) applications, the proper communication channels, such as media or websites, need to be selected to communicate the vacancy to interested candidates. Also, a recruitment team needs to be established. Usually you would like to have a manager or supervisor on the panel, as well as someone from human resources, but maybe also a future team member. Sometimes it can be practical and beneficial to make selection of the best candidate the responsibility of the team the future employee will be working with, especially if the job has been designed to include alternating tasks within the team. Obviously, it is important to involve this recruitment team in establishing the selection criteria or at the very least discuss these criteria with them to ensure that everybody involved is on the same level with respect to what type of candidates would be suitable for the job and how to choose between equally qualified candidates. Methods, tools and techniques that could assist in doing so range from reviewing application letters and/or videos to interviewing candidates, checking their references, or having them engage in role play, undergo a formal assessment or join the team for a trial day.

Within this context, it is important to note that companies operating in events, tourism and hospitality have a bit of a reputation of having 'warm body syndrome'. Some of them have been known to select the cheapest workforce based on applying one criterion only: candidates seem to have a functioning body that should be able to do (the physical aspects of) the job. Obviously, based on the discussions so far regarding what is needed to successfully design, stage and manage experiences, also in events, tourism and hospitality and maybe even especially in these industries, this is hardly the way to ensure having empathetic, responsive and reliable staff with the right behaviour, attitude and expertise. Any business or professional aiming to attract and hold on to (paying) customers should know better by now.

Teamwork

As discussed earlier, creating teams and alternating roles and tasks within teams can be useful in mitigating the negative effects of repetitive tasks and can contribute to overall performance and job satisfaction. In fact, team performance and job satisfaction are often very much interrelated. This also means that if staff members are unhappy with their role within a team, feel that they are over- or under-qualified for the tasks they need to perform within that team, or feel they are not supported sufficiently, this can negatively influence team performance significantly. In turn, this could have a negative effect on job satisfaction of colleagues and on the experience staged for customers. Therefore, managing a team needs to focus on ensuring that everybody in the team makes a positive contribution to team performance. Aspects such as creating an open atmosphere in which team members provide each other feedback, help each other, and feel free to also point out issues that for instance a supervisor can and needs to resolve can prove crucial in getting the best out of the team. Some organisations also instate or foster specific rituals that support an atmosphere of joint responsibility and willingness to continuously improve (details). An example of such a ritual would be a so-called stand-up session of 15 minutes each day. These sessions are part of the daily routine and are very similar to the way sports teams get together before or after a game – a so-called huddle. The idea of stand-up sessions is to have the team reflect on what went really well the day before and what could have gone better, and then have the team use that input to formulate improvement points or plans. Within the specific context of staging experiences, this would for instance allow for discussing what types of behaviour had a positive or negative effect on the experiences of specific types of customers or what expertise could assist in further improving them. During such sessions, management could also share data of the previous period with respect to the way customers have rated/reviewed their experiences, but also productivity, revenues, budgets, forecasts, up-coming special events, and so on. This and similar approaches bear resemblance to the so-called Lean Management concept and could result in a number of specific benefits:

1. The team learns to reflect on team performance and focus on continuous improvement based on feeling competent, autonomous and valued.
2. Experienced staff members get the opportunity to share tips with and transfer expertise to other team members, whereas less experienced staff members get a better understanding of what is expected of them and how to do that.
3. Management and supervisors do not have to point out improvement points in a top-down way and can transfer key learning moments to other teams and departments, while also taking in and giving feedback on specific request of the team, for instance with respect to tools, equipment or budgets.
4. Management and supervisors can observe and stimulate the development of the team and all individuals in it, while getting a clear picture of specific talents and competencies (or lack thereof) of team members.

Overall, working in teams has many benefits in terms of flexibility, variety and fun. However, it is still very important to also understand and establish who is responsible for (executing or supporting the execution of) specific tasks; otherwise you run the risk of nobody feeling responsible and tasks not being executed at all, at the wrong time, or in the wrong way. RASCIQ offers a practical approach to mapping roles of people involved in specific touch points, events or projects. This approach can be particularly useful when multiple suppliers or a big team are involved. In a RASCIQ matrix, tasks that need to be executed for a touch point, event or project are listed in the first column and the top row lists the people, departments and/or companies involved. The matrix is then filled by assigning roles to specific people, departments or companies for each task. The following roles are distinguished:

•   Responsible: this is usually the party assigned to execute a particular task.
•   Accountable: the party legally responsible for the (successful execution of the) task.
•   Supporting: the party who assists the Responsible in executing a task.
•   Consulted: the party whose opinion is sought with respect to a particular task.
•   Informed: the party who needs to be informed about decisions, changes or outcomes regarding a particular task.
•   Quality review: the party responsible for meeting quality requirements.

For a restaurant, a typical RASCIQ matrix would look like the one displayed in Figure 5.2.

FIGURE 5.2 An example of a RASCIQ matrix for a restaurant

	Owner	Restaurant manager	Host	Waiter	Chef	Kitchen assistant
Financial management	A	R			C	
HRM	A	R			C	
Create menu	A	C	I	I	R	I
Ensure food safety	A	Q			R	I
Welcome guests		Q	R	S		
Take and bring orders		Q	S	R	I	
Prepare food					R	S
Clean kitchen					Q	R

Leadership

Ultimately, in any organisation, specific people make specific key decisions. Regardless of whether an organisation applies a traditional hierarchical structure or is more democratic, some decisions have an enormous impact on the overall success of the organisation. Those involved in making them need to show leadership. Leadership is not necessarily the same as managing; it relates to clarity on things like the (shared) vision of the organisation, its targets and the way it wants to achieve those targets. Leadership is a crucial element of experience management. An organisation cannot successfully stage peak, extended or transformative experiences if those making the key decisions do not truly believe in the added value of experiences in comparison to simply selling a product or service. Those people also need to understand what is needed to design, stage and manage those experiences, to allow them to make the right decisions. They need to realise that more efficient is not always more effective from an experience perspective and thus also not always better for the organisation. Sometimes, experiences require processes that take longer and require more resources than would be needed if you only focus on delivering a specific product or service to a customer. Specific touch points might seem superfluous from an efficiency perspective but can be crucial to communicating a specific storyline or preserving a specific dramatic structure. Leadership needs to get that. However, leadership is not the exclusive right of managers and management teams. Good managers understand that and create the opportunities for staff members with good ideas, specific expertise and high motivation to join them in making the vision come alive. Leadership with respect to creating a shared vision, and development of teams and the experiences they stage, relies on ensuring that professionals, specialists, innovators and supervisors are all moving in the same direction. Obviously, not every staff member will be able to contribute to the organisation in the same way. Some need more room to explore and experiment, while others will do well based on clear instructions.

The RASCIQ matrix displayed in Figure 5.2 provides a clear example of how roles of people in organisations differ but also how they all rely on each other. The restaurant owner needs a good chef and manager for the restaurant to be a success, but also a good host, waiters and kitchen assistants. However, the roles of the chef and manager are very different from those of waiters and kitchen assistants. The owner is more likely to argue with the chef about the type of food the restaurant is going to serve to customers than with kitchen assistants. Simultaneously, the host and waiters can probably provide the owner and manager with a better perspective on the specific needs and wishes of specific customer segments than the chef and kitchen assistant can, while the kitchen assistant can provide valuable input to the chef, manager and owner with respect to efficiency aspects of the layout of the kitchen. All roles need input from other roles to perform tasks successfully and to jointly stage successful experiences. Leadership implies ensuring that everybody not only knows what role they need to play in the team or organisation but also that they are motivated to do so and go the extra mile if needed. Especially in (small) operational teams staging experiences, leadership and management often come together in master-apprentice type relationships between individual team members as an appropriate way of organising these aspects. In the restaurant example, this could involve the chef and the kitchen assistant but also experienced and less experienced waiters.

All this means that job design, selection and recruitment, teamwork and leadership need to come together in good experience management. The way you approach these challenges determines whether the right people, with the right behaviour, attitude and expertise, will be interacting with your customers at the right reliability, responsiveness and empathy levels. Jointly they determine whether interaction quality, and some aspects of physical environment quality and outcome quality for that matter, live up to or even exceed the expectations of customers.

PHYSICAL ENVIRONMENT QUALITY

Obviously, the behaviour, attitude and expertise of staff are not the only factors influencing the perceived quality of experiences. Experience management also needs to carefully address the physical environment in which experiences are staged. Especially for the types of experiences staged in events, tourism and hospitality, the physical environment can significantly impact how customers will perceive the quality of the experience you stage for them. In the design phase, a number of characteristics of the physical environment have already been established. Design decisions influence the level of immersion that can be accomplished in staging the experience and influence the possibilities to communicate a coherent storyline through linking separate touch points through symbolism incorporated in artefacts, decor, packaging and more. This means that ensuring these decisions are realised during the staging of the experience is an important element of experience management. Obviously, for experiences within the context of, for instance, nature or city tourism, designers have less control over what customers will see, touch, smell and hear. Nevertheless, also for these experiences, the physical environment plays a crucial role in the quality of experiences as perceived by customers and thus also requires management (of aspects that can be controlled) while staging them.

In general, managing the physical environment quality tends to be quite technical in nature. A lot of the activities involved revolve around maintenance and cleaning in and around touch points. The aim of these activities is to keep the physical environment in shape so that it continues to match specifications laid down in the design of the experience. Sometimes this is easier said then done, especially for touch points that are part of experiences that are staged for and open to customers (close to) 365 days a year, such as many restaurants, hotels, theme parks, zoos, cinemas and museums. With respect to cleaning, housekeeping and waste management, most activities involved are based on daily routines that are scheduled to take place at times of the day (or night) when customers are not present. For some activities, such as clearing tables and emptying litterbins, this is not an option. However, these activities still need to and often can be executed in a way that will not disturb customers too much and will not negatively influence their experience. For maintenance this can be quite different. Maintenance might actually require certain touch points to be closed for customers, sometimes even for quite some time. Whereas routine maintenance can generally be planned on quiet days in low season, unexpected maintenance and repairs due to breakdowns can have a significant (negative) effect on the experiences of quite a few customers. In these cases, expectation management and clear communication play a crucial role in minimising the damage done. Customers are usually quite understanding in force majeure situations and the way they perceive the overall quality of the experience can also be influenced positively by offering them alternatives or compensation. However, do not expect them to forgive you if they feel they have been misled or treated differently from other customers. In other words, managing expectations through being transparent and informing customers in time, preferably before they decide on engaging in the experience(s) you are offering, is an important element of experience management and key to preventing disappointed and disgruntled customers.

Understanding the potential impact of problems and incidents is a key element in ensuring appropriate organisational responses to them. If and when more than one incident occurs simultaneously, this becomes even more important. Some organisations, also in events, tourism and hospitality, create impact matrices and train their staff to assess incidents based on their impact and coordinate organisational responses. Basically, an impact matrix – an example of which is shown in Figure 5.3 – assigns a specific priority to an incident based on the assessment of two elements: (1) the impact on customers, and (2) the number of customers affected. The more perilous an incident and the more customers are affected by it, the bigger and faster the

FIGURE 5.3 An example of an impact matrix

Impact matrix	Gravity of incident for customer (experience)			
	Catastrophic	Critical	Marginal	Negligible
> 1000 customers	Extreme	Extreme	High	Medium
101 < 1000 customers	Extreme	Extreme	High	Medium
2 < 100 customers	Extreme	High	Medium	Low
1 customer	Extreme	High	Low	Low

Impact level	Action?	Alert emergency team	Inform manager a.s.a.p.	Log incident
Extreme	Take immediate action	V	V	V
High	Handle a.s.a.p.		V	V
Medium	Handle if possible			V
low	Ignore			V

response should be. Falling and breaking an arm in a zoo is very unfortunate and painful for that person, and he or she will clearly require attention from medical staff. However, there is really no need to alarm other visitors and such an incident does not necessarily have to affect many other customers. However, if that person fell as a result of panicking because he saw a tiger escape from its cage, this is obviously a perfectly good reason to fully evacuate the zoo and start emergency procedures. Similarly, repairing the most popular rollercoaster in a theme park clearly would have to take precedence over repairing one of the three merry-go-rounds in the same park, even if the tears of that little girl who really wanted to ride that specific pink pony in the broken merry-go-round might make it difficult to stand firm.

Physical design

Obviously, dealing with incidents and repairing physical components of touch points are important elements of ensuring an appropriate physical environment quality. Many of these activities are guided by specific routines and procedures, and regulations. These activities are important for keeping the design of the experience in shape. However, there is more to management of the physical environment than that. Experience management with respect to one of the three variables of physical environment quality, i.e. physical design, relates to management of all tangible elements of all touch points within the customer journey(s). Managing the physical design variable implies making sure that these tangible elements are in good shape

FIGURE 5.4 An example of a restaurant layout

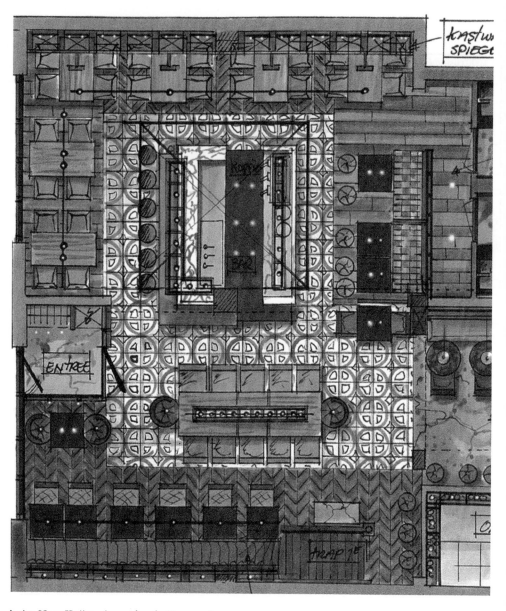

Artist: Hans Kuijten (www.hanskuijten.com)

and ready for being used in staging experiences for customers. These tangible elements can be rollercoasters and animal cages but also decor, props, furniture, tableware, and so on.

To create an appropriate and consistent level of quality regarding physical design can require introducing routines and stimulating team discipline with respect to

FIGURE 5.5 An example of an artist's impression of a restaurant

Artist: Hans Kuijten (www.hanskuijten.com)

making sure that furniture, tableware, decorations, props, and so on are all in the right place at the right time. Similarly, routines and discipline could be crucial in assuring an appropriate and consistent level of cleaning. Obviously, some of the aspects discussed in the previous section could prove helpful here as well, such as creating a sense of joint responsibility in a team and ensuring that staff members are qualified and motivated to get the job done. To assist staff members in doing so, it might be useful to also provide them with floor plans, photos and drawings of different set-ups for furniture, equipment, decor, props and more that are part of the touch point, but also to create and share cleaning schedules and instructions. You might not need them every day, but a good management information system could ensure that documents like these are available when needed. They can also prove helpful as a guideline for team members, as a reference point for giving each other feedback and continuous improvement, and as a starting point for new team members to get acquainted with quality standards and routines relevant to that touch point. Finally, this type of information could be crucial in planning the activities to be executed by different team members and supervisors – it makes no sense to check the cleanliness of a hotel room before it has been cleaned.

As discussed earlier, sometimes those responsible for maintenance and repairs need to step in to repair damages, fix glitches and prevent wear and tear. It is wise to ensure close cooperation between these departments and staff directly involved in staging parts of the experience at various touch points. They can report those glitches and damages and look for signs of wear and tear. Once again, a management information system could be helpful, for instance by showing logbooks with entries from team members with respect to those aspects. Some of the tools discussed in the previous section, such as joint stand-up sessions with different departments, could also assist in creating a culture within the organisation that sees ensuring appropriate (realised) quality of the physical design as a shared responsibility of all employees, regardless of whether they work on-stage or back-stage.

Ambient conditions

Similar to the (realised) quality of the physical design, ambient conditions are to a large extent determined by decisions made in the design of experiences. Ambient conditions relate to aspects such as temperature, sound, smell and air quality. In buildings, most of these aspects are controlled through all kinds of technical installations, such as air conditioning, audio equipment and heating. If these aspects have been addressed correctly in the design phase, managing them during staging experiences is a matter of cleaning, maintenance and repair of these installations. Therefore, many of the same reference points discussed earlier in this section also apply to this variable linked to physical environment quality.

Obviously, managing ambient conditions can be quite a challenge if an experience is staged outdoors. Sometimes it is possible to adjust elements of the experience you are offering based on weather predictions but usually you will just have to accept whatever the weather gods have decided. However, it is wise to create contingency plans for extreme conditions. Such a plan could, for instance, relate to handing out extra water and sunscreen or spraying crowds with water and creating extra room in the shade during a festival if and when temperatures are really high. Similarly, you could put measures in place for windy or rainy conditions. With respect to the latter, these might not always have to be executed though – for some reason, some people visiting specific (music) festivals seem to rate their experience higher if the festival terrain resembles a swamp!

CASE STUDY 5.1 **EVALUATING VISITOR EXPERIENCE AT A MOUNTAIN ATTRACTION: THE NORDKETTE MOUNTAIN IN TYROL, AUSTRIA**

Ady Milman and Anita Zehrer

The year-round Nordkette mountain attraction overlooks the City of Innsbruck, the valley of the river Inn, and the surrounding mountain ranges. The journey from the city centre's Congress Station to the final mountain cable car station takes about 25 minutes. The first stop, reached by a funicular, car and public transportation, is the Hungerburg station (elevation 857 metres). Modern cable cars transport visitors to the subsequent stations: the Seegrube at an elevation of 1,905 metres and the Hafelekar at an elevation of 2,256 metres. The two mountain stations offer excellent panoramic views and an array of summer and winter outdoor activities.

Data were collected from 600 visitors at the attraction's four stations during a period of four months that allowed observations of both winter and summer experiences. The observers kept detailed field notes, including reflections on day-to-day informal encounters and personal experiences. The attraction's settings, facilities, and visitors were photographed and sorted according to the experiences observed.

The study concluded that the visitor experience involved a blend of events made of material and human elements. Material elements included accessibility infrastructure to the attraction's main entrance (a staircase, an escalator, or an elevator), a funicular and cable cars, pictorial and electronic display boards, outdoor terraces with tables and benches, lounge chairs, restaurants, a gift shop, bathrooms, and so on. Human elements consisted of people observed on the mountain attraction, primarily visitors and employees.

The observations revealed the following highlights: (1) upon arrival, visitors were confused about their expected experience; (2) visitors exhibited curiosity, anticipation, excitement and wanted to travel up the mountain as soon as possible; (3) there was a lack of verbal and non-verbal communication between the visitors, as well as between the visitors and employees; (4) visitors were involved in a variety of active and passive activities like hiking, snowboarding, sunbathing, socialising, dining or shopping; (5) the majority of the experiential consumption activities focused beyond the mountain itself, primarily viewing the surrounding landscape and photography, and (6) the observations indicated that visitors's expectations did not live up to the attraction's material and human elements – i.e. lack of clear cable car timetables, single-language signage, or the staff members' lack of hospitality.

The results were presented to the attraction's management, and recommended developing a stronger focus on the actual attraction rather than away from the attraction, and hence connecting customers more to the brand, increasing their length of stay, and enhancing revenue. More specifically, the following recommendations were suggested and implemented: (1) installation of large electronic display screens that showed the weather conditions on the mountain; (2) augmenting the food services and merchandise experience; and (3) promoting the experience's co-creation by improving the encounter between visitors and the attraction's human and material elements. These included the installation of multi-lingual signs, cable car timetable display screens, restaurant renovation, the installation of an outdoor bar, and customer-service training for employees. Management confirmed that attendance increased following these improvements.

Based on: A. Milman & A. Zehrer (2017). Exploring visitor experience at a mountain attraction: The Nordkette mountain in Tirol, Austria. *Journal of Vacation Marketing*. DOI: 10.1177/1356766717691805.

Social factors

Managing social factors relates to managing the impact of other people – such as other customers – on the quality of the experience as perceived by customers. A simple example would be a masked ball. This will only really feel like a masked ball if most of the guests – and staff for that matter – dress for the occasion. Within this context, managing social factors thus involves communicating the storyline and associated rules and norms to (potential) guests before they enter the venue.

Usually, however, the storyline of an experience has already been communicated through advertising, the website and social media. Potential customers may also already be aware of it through word of mouth or mouse. Finally, if the experience is staged more than once, customers might be repeat customers and know what to expect, and what is expected of them. For some types of experiences, it also helps if a customer has already consumed a similar experience. If you have been to an open-air music festival before, you probably know what to expect if and when you visit another festival – and that rain can actually be a good thing from a social factor perspective because it creates some sort of positive 'we're in this together and we're not gonna let the rain get to us' vibe. The same applies to five-star hotels, escape rooms, and so on. In fact, customers who have a pretty clear idea of the experience that will be staged for them are usually quite willing to 'play along' by adjusting their behaviour or in the way they dress. Doing so is in their best interest because it enhances their experience. Consequently, some rules and norms can remain implicit and do not have to be written down or put into a contract.

Nevertheless, sometimes it is wise to draft so-called house rules. These house rules could for instance state what is expected of customers to ensure that they do not ruin the experience for other customers or that customers and staff are not put at risk. They include the absolute do's and don'ts such as whether open fires are allowed or not, whether playing music is allowed or not, what time it should be quiet, whether you should wear a jacket or rain gear, or a tie, and how you dispose of garbage. Sometimes managing social factors can imply only allowing people who stick to the rules to join or stay at (the venue of) an experience. This in turn implies that staff should be aware of what is expected of them with respect to communicating and enforcing these rules. The reference points with respect to selecting, instructing and coaching staff highlighted earlier are therefore also relevant for managing social factors.

OUTCOME QUALITY

As indicated in the Brady and Cronin framework and the explanation in Chapter 4, the social factors variable is not only linked to physical environment quality but also to outcome quality. Therefore, it is also the first variable discussed in this section.

Social factors

Within the context of outcome quality, managing social factors relates to managing the effect of queues, waiting times, availability of seats, and so on, but also to the effect of how other customers are treated. With respect to the latter, it is easy to imagine that you will perceive the quality of an experience higher if all people around you are smiling as a result of how they are treated by staff and lower if a number of people are complaining and are clearly unhappy. You are not very likely to enjoy a romantic dinner in a restaurant if customers at the table next to you are raucously voicing their dissatisfaction about a waiter who is rude to them. However, this aspect can also relate to whether or not customers are treated equally. Waiting in line for more than an hour for a rollercoaster ride is long but acceptable if everybody has to wait. However, if some customers are allowed to jump the queue because they apparently know the staff member on the boarding deck, this might upset other customers. If a child were allowed to jump the queue because he hurt himself, most people would probably accept that and actually appreciate the staff member caring enough to do so. Obviously, some of these actions by staff could be managed through clear instructions and coaching. Others might rely on staff members daring to not follow procedures if and when appropriate. This is where managing social factors depends on making sure you have selected staff with the right behaviour, attitude and expertise, and created an environment in which they feel motivated, and free and safe enough, to make judgment calls when necessary.

Waiting times

Obviously, waiting times are closely linked to social factors because the number and behaviour of (other) customers significantly impacts their length and how they will be perceived. However, waiting times are also to a large extent determined by the design of the experience. In fact, sometimes, waiting times and queues represent purposely-designed elements of a specific touch point. In a restaurant, most people would not like their main course to be served within seconds of finishing their starter. In a theme park, a specific queue can be part of the dramatic structure by building up suspension and anticipation for the next touch point. The environment in which people wait for that next touch point could be used to communicate parts of the overall storyline of the experience. Simultaneously, waiting time could be used to communicate the type of rules and norms discussed in the previous section.

However, most queues and waiting times are the result of having more demand than capacity. In the design phase, specific decisions have been made with respect to waiting time characteristics of touch points based on their possible added value within the overall experience but also based on expected demand and (costs involved with creating additional) capacity. For some contexts, such as supermarkets, fast-food restaurants and hospitals, it is not unusual for the provider to have made a conscious decision to create a design that will result in customers having to wait because preventing these waiting times would imply that staff members would sometimes have to wait for customers. From a cost perspective, this is a logical decision because it costs money to have staff waiting for customers and having customers wait for an available staff member does not. Obviously, however, waiting for a specialist in a hospital represents a very different situation from waiting for a staff member to check your ticket before you enter a zoo or a theatre, especially if the birds of prey show or play is about to start. In other words, managing waiting times needs to consider a number of aspects both from a consumer perspective and from an experience provider perspective. This is why most service management books, such as the well-known book entitled *Service Management* by Fitzsimmons and Fitzsimmons (2004), include at least a full chapter on queuing strategies.

Whatever the reason for having to wait, not all waiting feels the same. Maister (1984) has established eight basic principles that influence a customer's perception of waiting:

1. Unoccupied time feels longer than occupied time.
2. Pre-process waiting feels longer than in-process waiting.
3. Anxiety makes waiting feel longer.
4. Uncertainty about waiting time makes waiting feel longer.
5. Unexplained waiting feels longer than explained waiting.
6. Unfair waiting feels longer than fair waiting.
7. The more valuable the service or experience is to the customer, the longer he/she is willing to wait.
8. Waiting alone feels longer than waiting with other people.

Both in designing and managing experiences, these principles could serve as reference points for ensuring that they are staged in ways that positively influence customers' perceptions of possible waiting times and queues. Simultaneously, experience management also needs to ensure that actual waiting times match the parameters set in the design. One way to accomplish this is demand management. Demand management focuses on influencing the period/day/time customers choose to engage in a particular (part of an) experience as a way to ensure that demand is not (too much) higher than capacity. The main tools that experience managers have available to them are pricing and availability but these need to be applied carefully and in combination with demand forecasting. Many experiences in events, tourism and hospitality have huge fluctuations in demand due to the influence of holidays, weather conditions, seasonal aspects, and so on. Price and availability could influence demand to some extent, for instance by raising prices in busy times (like hotels and airlines do) or offering special deals for quiet times – such as a discount for an early or late dinner in a restaurant. You could also set a maximum for the number of tickets to be sold but in these events you need to make sure that you communicate it in time and clearly to prevent disappointed or disgruntled customers. In contrast, you could also extend opening hours to spread the demand over a longer period. All of these measures can be used to influence demand but usually they do not completely neutralise demand fluctuations.

In those situations, experience management needs to focus on (adapting) capacity. The objective of capacity management is to ensure that customers do not have to wait longer than anticipated without operating costs getting out of hand. This requires calculating how the flow of people and goods can remain optimal throughout customer journeys and can support the ultimate customer experience. Capacity management is especially relevant for processes that need to deal with high fluctuations in demand, such as security and ticket checks at (the entrance of) experience venues, food outlets and queues for rollercoasters in theme parks, but also needs to address issues such as the number of lavatories, showers, power sockets, and water taps at an event like an outdoor music festival.

Consider a festival that attracts 20,000 people as an example. One of the key aspects in capacity management for such a festival is to create a (reliable) prediction of the number of people showing up at the entrance of the festival grounds at specific times, for instance, for every 15 minute period. All visitors will have to go through a security check, which takes 45 seconds for three sub-processes: 10 seconds for checking the ticket, 15 seconds for checking bags, and 20 seconds for frisking. If the aim is to make sure that visitors do not have to queue before the actual security check for more than 5 minutes, you can calculate how many parallel security (sub) processes would have to be in place. Obviously, the more parallel processes there are, the more gates and security staff you will need. With only one security check process in place, with one staff member executing all three sub-processes and all visitors showing up at the same time, letting everybody into the festival grounds would take 20,000 times 45 seconds, which amounts to 250 hours. By the time the last visitor enters the festival grounds, the festival would be well and truly over. Therefore, you will need parallel processes and sub-processes, and thus more staff members. By combining the duration of specific sub-processes with the arrival times of visitors, you can calculate exactly how many staff members for ticket checking, bag checking and frisking you would need to ensure that the maximum or average waiting time – two very different reference points that lead to different numbers – you would need. Similarly, you can use calculations to decide on the number of lavatories that need to be installed. For all of these calculations, you also need to account for the costs involved; more staff members or more lavatories means higher costs. Obviously, most of these decisions should really be part of the design process and during the actual staging of the experience you can probably only make slight adjustments to specific touch points, if and when needed. In other words, whereas capacity management is a crucial element of experience management, the opportunities for adjusting capacity during staging the experience need to be accounted for in the design phase.

For example, if you only install five ticket offices at the entrance of a zoo, this limits your options to increase the capacity of your entrance on busy days compared to having eight ticket offices. Simultaneously, installing eight offices is pointless if you do not have enough staff members available to execute the actual process of selling tickets. Therefore, whereas the physical environment needs to be addressed in the design phase, during staging you still need to apply capacity management with respect to having enough staff available at the right time at the right place. That is why experience management also involves some form of labour forecasting and planning. Based on forecasted number of visitors, the productivity standards established in job design, and through using calculations and tools such as flowcharting, you can predict how many staff members are needed per shift for each touch point. These predictions need to be accounted for in scheduling but also in planning breaks, holidays, meetings and training sessions.

Tangibles

Social factors, waiting times and queues are not the only variables that could require management in guaranteeing outcome quality. In some cases, part of the experience staged is to provide customers with tangibles. Tangibles could relate to food and drink but also to merchandise, give-aways, and so on. Obviously, for tangibles such as food you need to ensure that it is tasty and that plates served to different customers look similar. With respect to the latter, the previous sub-sections have already highlighted the importance of treating customers fairly and equally.

If tangibles are designed and prepared or handed out in a specific way, they could be a key element to staging memorable encounters or peak experiences. They can also form an integral part of the story communicated by the experience or the brand behind it. Some tangibles can also contribute to the immersive character of the experience by activating customers. Think of unrolling a giant banner by the crowd attending a Liverpool match at Anfield while they sing 'You'll never walk alone' or handing out glow in the dark bracelets or blinking lights at a dance event. Bracelets and lights not only enhance the experience but also offer customers something tangible to remember it by.

Obviously, arranging the production, preparation and delivery of tangibles involves capacity management and a number of the reference points discussed in the previous sub-section also apply here. Further, tangibles need to look, taste, feel and smell the same every time or be adaptable to customer needs and wishes. Sometimes, preparation and/or handing them out need to be scripted or offer staff opportunities to surprise customers or exceed their expectations. The latter could be illustrated by the example of Dutch/French airline company KLM. In 2010, they staged a campaign to highlight their focus on customer care. They installed a specific team of people at their home airport Schiphol in Amsterdam, the Netherlands. The task of this team was to screen social media messages of frequent flying KLM passengers and react to their messages by organising so-called little acts of kindness linked to their trip. For instance, a passenger flying to New York, who wrote a Facebook post about how he was looking forward to his trip but also feeling sad about missing his favourite team play, was approached at the gate with a travel guide in which New York bars were highlighted where he could watch the game. Obviously, KLM was not just interested in making this particular passenger happy; they also made sure their little act of kindness was seen online by millions of people.

BEYOND THE LINE OF VISIBILITY

So far, this chapter has discussed experience management by directly linking it to improving details and the three categories of variables that together shape experience quality as perceived by customers. This final section puts experience management within a broader context: some of the responsibilities of management that are not explicitly linked to staging experiences instead of selling products or services.

Laws, regulations, norms and certifications

Some laws and regulations apply to all businesses and professionals, regardless of whether they stage experiences or sell products or services. Typical examples would be Health Safety and Environment regulations in relation to work and work environment, and Hazard Analysis Critical Control Points (HACCP) in relation to working with food. Further, over the years, all kinds of standards, norms and certification schemes have been established to ensure that departments, suppliers and other stakeholders know their responsibilities and how to fulfil them. Most countries, but also institutions such as the European Union, have their own standardisation bodies, which publish guidelines, rules and norms for all kinds of things. Well-known examples are ISO and BSI norms. Most of these guidelines, rules and norms can be used to assess whether your customers' and employees' safety is assured and who is liable in case of accidents. Obviously, any business or professional staging experiences will have to address all of these aspects if and when they apply to the way they stage them.

Management contracts, Service Level Agreements and PDCA cycles

In many companies, part of the responsibility of management is also to assess the performance of specific teams, departments and business units. For commercial departments, this could relate to sales, margins and revenues. For service departments or suppliers, performance is usually measured based on different criteria than just financial ones. A typical way of dealing with these criteria is to agree on so-called management contracts or Service Level Agreements (SLAs) that include performance indicators and scores on these indicators that the department or supplier needs to deliver. For instance, a company could agree with a supplier of copiers that their machines need to be up and running 99% of the time and that in case of problems a mechanic will arrive within 60 minutes. Such an agreement often is accompanied by a bonus or penalty system based on actual scores. Customer-oriented service departments could be made accountable for scores with respect to customer satisfaction, for instance 80% of customers need to rate the service with a 7 or higher. Agreements for these departments could also include scores with respect to availability of products, time needed to respond to complaints, and so on.

Managers of those teams, departments and suppliers will try to reach the targets agreed upon in those contracts and agreements. Most managers are inclined to do this through organising so-called quality cycles in their operations following (a specific version of) the PDCA cycle: Plan, Do, Check, Act. The planning step relates to setting targets that are included in the management contract or SLA. The acting step then relates to day-to-day operations, which is followed by the check step to measure actual performance and compare it to the targets. Depending on the outcome, this could lead to interventions in the act step, for instance aimed at improving operations in order to be able to meet the targets.

A warning!

As discussed earlier in this chapter, improving (the details of) operations is a key element of experience management. Without doubt, it is crucial to not only focus on possible improvements during the design process but also while staging experiences. Doing so, and organising this effectively and efficiently, is a key aspect of experience management. There are a number of management methods, tools, techniques and even philosophies available to managers and other staff involved to assist them. Some of those have been discussed in this chapter, such as flowcharting, spaghetti diagrams, Lean Management, management contracts and PDCA cycles. Anyone responsible for managing the staging of experiences should take full advantage of them, as well as (operations) management literature discussing them in more detail. The same applies to other management methods, tools, techniques and philosophies addressed in both scientific and popular science literature. Reviewing (the details of) all of them is well beyond the scope of this chapter.

However, applying them needs to be done wisely. You have to be very careful that key performance indicators, such as those included in a management contract or SLA, are formulated in terms that fit with staging experiences and allow for meeting or even exceeding the expectations of your (potential) customers. You need to ensure that making processes more efficient does not reduce their ability to excite customers. Short-term financial results are great but they should never come at the expense of the dramatic structure of customer journeys. If Lean Management is useful, use it! If you feel Lean is so yesterday and Agile is the way to go, go! *But*, whatever you do, do it in a customer-oriented way that accounts for what those customers feel, want, dream about and aspire to. Otherwise, before you know it, you have turned your organisation into one that provides standard(ised) products and services instead of the types of customised experiences that allow you to survive in today's and tomorrow's experience-focused and ever-so-competitive marketplace.

SUMMARY

Based on reading this chapter, we hope you will understand and remember the following:

- There is no firm boundary between the final step of the design process for experiences – improving details – and the first stages of actually staging and managing experiences.
- The relevance of blueprints, scripts, Standard Operating Procedures and flow charts in managing the staging of experiences.
- How ensuring appropriate interaction quality – as perceived by customers – links to aspects such as job design, selection and recruitment, teamwork and leadership.
- The crucial role of managing the (quality of the) physical environment, through addressing physical design, ambient conditions and social factors, for the ultimate quality of the experience staged for customers, and how they perceive this quality.
- The crucial role of managing the (quality of) outcomes, through addressing social factors, tangibles and waiting times, for the ultimate quality of the experience staged for customers, and how they perceive this quality.
- The relevance of generic management methods, tools, techniques and philosophies for managing the staging of experiences but also the dangers involved in applying them in a non-customer-oriented way.

FOOD FOR THOUGHT

Based on the content of this chapter, the following questions, challenges and topics could serve as interesting starting points for further discussion:

- Discuss relevant aspects to address in staging the two experiences designed in the previous chapter. In this discussion, you could answer questions such as:
  - o   How would you train staff?
  - o   What are the most important aspects of the physical design to account for in managing the staging of this experience?
  - o   What are the most important aspects of the social factors to account for in managing the staging of this experience? Is this different for ensuring the appropriate physical environment quality than for ensuring the appropriate outcome quality?
  - o   Which generic management methods, tools, techniques or philosophies would be especially useful to apply for managing the staging of the experience?

REFERENCES

Brady, M.K. & Cronin Jr, J.J. (2001). Some new thoughts on conceptualizing perceived service quality: A hierarchical approach. *Journal of marketing*, 65(3), 34–49.

Buchanan, D. (1979). *The development of job design theories and techniques.* Aldershot: Saxon House.

Fitzsimmons, J. & Fitzsimmons, M. (2004). *Service management.* New York: Irwin.

Maister, D.H. (1984). *The psychology of waiting lines.* Boston, MA: Harvard Business School.

Maslow, A.H. (1943). A theory of human motivation. *Psychological Review*, 50(4), 370.

Parasuraman, A., Zeithaml, V.A. & Berry, L.L. (1988). Servqual: A multiple-item scale for measuring consumer perception. *Journal of Retailing*, 64(1), 12.

PART II

SUSTAINABLE DEVELOPMENT AND THE ROLE OF BUSINESSES AND PROFESSIONALS

6 Sustainable development and blurring boundaries

INTRODUCTION

This chapter provides an important turning point within the overall storyline presented in this book. The first part of this book has described how the rise of the experience economy impacts businesses and professionals. To be successful in today's and tomorrow's marketplace, they need to understand their (potential) customers and adjust their value propositions accordingly. Successful value propositions are more and more based on staging customised experiences for (individual or groups of) customers.

This is not the only challenge facing those businesses and professionals though. This chapter addresses a second main challenge that all of them (will) need to address: sustainable development. The United Nations' World Commission on Environment and Development (UNWCED) defined sustainable development as: 'development that meets the needs of the present without compromising the ability of future generations to meet their own needs' (1987, Chapter 2, item 1). Even though this is the most widely accepted definition of the concept of sustainable development, one could argue that it is also rather vague. What does 'meeting the needs of the present' actually mean? Do these needs refer to the same type of needs discussed in the previous chapters? And why does this definition put so much emphasis on the relation between the needs of the present generation and the needs of future generations? To answer these questions and to understand the impact of these answers on businesses and professionals offering experiences to their customers, the first section of this chapter explores the concept of sustainable development in more detail. It explains why the United Nations felt the need to define it and why it is more and more becoming one of the main challenges facing not just businesses and professionals but all of us.

The second section of this chapter then focuses on the relevance of sustainable development for events, tourism and hospitality. It explains how these industries not only have contributed to the emergence of the problems addressed by this concept but also how they can play a crucial role in solving them. In fact, any business or professional who focuses on staging experiences could contribute to sustainable development if the way these experiences are designed, staged and managed incorporates sustainable development principles. Some of these principles are actually closely related to both the reasons for the rise of and critical success factors for successfully operating within the experience economy. Together, these two key developments in our society – the rise of the experience economy and the urgent need to make a societal transition towards sustainable development – have already changed and will continue to change industries such as events, tourism and hospitality but also other industries. In fact, in combination with technological progress and some of the other developments discussed in Chapter 2, such as the on-going process of individualisation of our societies, the rise of the experience economy and sustainable development contribute to the blurring of boundaries between industries. This is the topic of the third and final section of this chapter. It explains and illustrates the increasing fluidity of the business world. It also sets the stage for discussing the consequences of all of these developments for the business technologies and business models to be applied by businesses and professionals that aim to remain/be successful beyond the right here and right now – the topic of Chapter 7.

THE CONCEPT OF SUSTAINABLE DEVELOPMENT

Global climate change is one of the biggest and scariest problems our world is faced with. Most of us are probably familiar with the shocking pictures of emaciated polar bears that are finding it increasingly difficult to survive because of sea ice melting earlier in spring and forming later in autumn. Another example of the effects and impact of climate change – although not everybody seems to realise this yet – is the increasing number and especially the increasing intensity of hurricanes. Hurricanes need high sea surface temperatures to develop. Higher ocean temperatures as a result of global warming therefore increase the chances of weather disturbances, such as thunderstorms, to develop into hurricanes as well as the chances of these hurricanes to develop into storms of the highest category. However, climate change is not the only problem linked to the concept of sustainable development. In fact, sustainable development entails addressing a number of complicated and often interrelated problems. To better understand the concept of sustainable development, it is wise to first explore these problems, and especially the way they are all linked to each other, in more detail.

Sustainability and unsustainability

The term sustainability is derived from the Latin word *sustinere*, which in turn is made up of *sub* – meaning: under – and *tenere* – meaning: hold. In English, to sustain can mean to maintain, to support, or to endure. By adding 'ability' to 'sustain', the term sustainability then logically refers to the ability to support, to maintain or to endure. In other words, taken literally, something sustainable is something that endures for a long time – something that does not wear out quickly. A car that continues to work for years and years without ever breaking down could be called a sustainable car. A company that makes huge profits, year in year out, apparently applies a sustainable business model. However, over the years we have come to interpret the term sustainability differently. More and more, it is used in relation to the ability of us, humans, to survive on our planet. Interestingly, this means that a car that simply will not stop functioning is now actually often referred to as being unsustainable because it uses a lot more petrol than its modern–day equivalents. Similarly, a company that makes huge profits will not always be considered sustainable: it all depends on whether or not that company damages the environment in doing so and how they treat their employees.

The reason that we now put so much emphasis on those types of aspects in deciding which items or people deserve to be labelled 'sustainable' is as simple as it is sobering: our ability as humans to survive on our planet Earth is under threat. This is the direct result of the way we, humans, have arranged our world. In his book *Fundamentals of Sustainable Development* (2017), Roorda describes a number of flaws in this system. One of these flaws relates to our food chain and, more specifically, the amount of meat we eat and the way this chain is organised. Animals that are used for the production of meat consume vegetables, such as grass, maize and soya. This animal feed used to be grown locally and many farmers would have a mixed farm: producing animal feed and producing meat. Today, this situation has changed dramatically. Many countries, such as Vietnam and a number of countries in Western Europe, actually import most of the animal feed needed for meat production from other countries, such as Brazil. The consequences of this rearrangement of the food chain are nothing less than catastrophic. The nutrients in the soil used to grow this animal feed are basically transported from the supplying countries to the meat production countries, and ultimately end up in the soil in the latter countries through the manure of cattle, pigs, and so on. This leads to increasing levels of nitrate in groundwater and surface water, algae in lakes and rivers, acidification of water and ground, and, ultimately, a decrease in biodiversity, lower-quality drinking water and acid rain in those countries. Simultaneously, the supplying countries are left with a shortage of nutrients in the ground, which in turn leads to less fertile soil and erosion. To make matters worse, animal feed producers are consequently forced to move their activities to new pieces of land, which results in further loss of natural systems such as rainforests. To top it off, animal feed production often takes place in countries where the local population already has a hard time producing enough food for themselves and the booming animal feed industry further reduces the land available to them to do so.

The example of our meat production system incorporates a number of interrelated problems. In fact, the list of problems linked to this system in real life is even longer. Meat production requires enormous amounts of water, while water shortage is a big problem in some parts of our world. Meat production leads to methane being released into the atmosphere through the gases produced by livestock, and methane is a very powerful greenhouse gas – a gas that contributes to global climate change. Further greenhouse gases, such as huge amounts of CO_2, are released into the atmosphere as a result of transporting animal feed from one country to another and then transporting the meat to yet another country. All this becomes more poignant when you realise that meat is actually a very inefficient source of proteins. We, humans, do need proteins to survive. However, meat – and the same applies to dairy – basically represents a very inefficient way of converting proteins in vegetables into animal proteins. For every kilogram of animal protein, a cow needs to eat 10 kilograms of vegetable proteins. As Roorda (2017) explains, this means that you need 3 to 6 hectares of agricultural land to produce 20 kilograms of animal protein a year. We do not have the luxury of wasting land; there is actually a shortage of land!

The amount of land that people or countries need to fulfil their needs is called their ecological footprint. You need land to produce your food, such as meat. However, land is also needed for producing other types of food, to live on, for generating electricity, for producing the products and services that we consume, for processing our waste, for absorbing the greenhouse gases that we emit, and so on. The amount of land needed to do so is your ecological footprint. Today, we, humans, already use more resources than the Earth can provide in the long run. If you combine the way we have arranged our world to fulfil our needs with the predicted growth of our world's population, we would actually need roughly two Earths by 2030! In other words, we are drastically overexploiting our planet and this is already causing serious problems now and will cause even bigger problems in the future. These problems range from rising temperatures and extreme weather conditions leading to flooding, droughts, wildfires and changing landscapes to acidification of our land and water, pollution and deforestation seriously undermining the functioning of our planet's ecosystems. In turn, the latter can lead to biodiversity loss and direct health problems but also to problems with our ability to produce enough food for our world's population. Finally, all of these problems contribute, in some way or another, to poverty, armed conflict, acts of terrorism and migratory flows.

Sociologist Richard Sennett (2008) describes this situation as Pandora's Casket. As a human race, we have become so good at extracting and exploiting the resources that our planet provides to fulfil our needs that we might actually end up destroying ourselves in doing so. However, he is far from the only or first one to highlight this problem. In his paper on the relation between foresight – trying to predict the future – and sustainable development, Destatte (2010) illustrates this by referring to French mathematician, economist and philosopher Antoine Cournot (1801–1877), who stated in 1861 (!) that

> natural wealth, which is the greatest asset in civilised society, is gradually being used up and is being consumed at a faster rate than civilisation and industry are making progress [thereby risking] human fate of perishing suddenly by some great cataclysm or slowly by using up all of the material resources that nature has placed at its disposition.
>
> (Destatte 2010, p. 1576).

FIGURE 6.1 Our current situation – Pandora's casket?

Artist: Anabella Meijer (www.kanai.nl)

About a hundred years later, the so-called Club of Rome came to a similar conclusion. This 'club' was founded in 1968 and consists of people from the fields of academia, civil society, diplomacy and industry from around the world. They describe themselves as 'a group of world citizens, sharing a common concern for the future of humanity'. In 1972, they published their famous and influential report entitled *The Limits to Growth*, in which they conclude that continued (exponential) growth of the world's population, food production, pollution and the use of non-renewable energy sources – such as oil, gas and coal – will lead to disaster. The exact words they use to describe this disaster are 'a rather sudden and uncontrollable decline in [. . .] population' (Meadows et al., 1972, p. 183). Not a pretty picture is it? Especially, if you realise that more than four decades have now passed since this report was first published and a number of the elaborate predictions included in it have so far proven to be ominously accurate. It is beyond the scope of this section to discuss the full details of these predictions, or all of the flaws in the fabric of the system we have created to fulfil our needs. If you want to know more details, please refer to the numerous (scientific and popular science) papers, books, websites, social media accounts and documentaries out there that portray the full story. For now, it should be clear that it is not an exaggeration to state that our society is currently on an unsustainable course and adjusting this course is an urgent challenge all of us are faced with.

Sustainable development

So, does all this mean that we are doomed? No, certainly not! Over the years, we, humans, have already proved that we can accomplish great things. We can solve complicated problems and develop new products and technologies that can assist in doing so. In fact, in some areas, we have made significant progress already.

A well-known example is the so-called hole in our ozone layer. We used to apply specific gases in aerosol cans – the ones used for hair spray and deodorant – and appliances such as fridges that resulted in harming the Earth's ozone layer. The ozone layer protects us from ultraviolet radiation, which can cause skin cancer and eye problems. However, after realising that these gases were thinning this layer and actually creating holes in it, a vast majority of all countries in the world got together and agreed to stop producing and using most of these gases – the agreement was the Montreal Protocol signed in 1989. Today, through updates of this protocol, more countries joining it, and inclusion of some remaining ozone layer thinning gases in the Paris Agreement on climate change in 2015, almost none of these gases are used in new products. Even though the negative effects of using them in the past will be noticeable in the state of the ozone layer for many, many years to come, it looks like we have reacted in time to prevent the hole getting even bigger. As things stand now, and if we stick to the agreements made, the ozone layer might recover its 'normal state' within 50 to 100 years.

Other examples of progress made relate to issues such as health and poverty. A number of diseases have been eradicated. Even though there are still many people in our world who live in absolute poverty, the percentage of the world's population living in poverty has decreased significantly over the course of the last few decades. In other words, if we really put our minds to it, and we are willing to make the necessary changes in the way we have arranged our world and the way we fulfil our needs, it seems there is every chance that we can adjust the course of our societies to a more sustainable one. Simultaneously, a number of the issues discussed earlier remain (mostly) unresolved up to the present day. The state of most ecosystems is still deteriorating, biodiversity is still declining, temperatures are still rising, pollution is still increasing, and many, many people still have to live their lives in circumstances that can only be described as inhuman.

Turning this around and creating a society that is able to successfully deal with all issues that threaten our survival (in the long run) is called sustainable development. As indicated earlier, sustainable development is defined as: 'development that meets the needs of the present without compromising the ability of future generations to meet their own needs' (UNWCED, 1987, Chapter 2, item 1).

It is extremely important to note that the Brundtland Commission – as the United Nations' World Commission on Environment and Development is often referred to because former Prime Minister of Norway Gro Harlem Brundtland chaired it – added some crucial explanations to this definition that are often forgotten or misinterpreted by people referring to it. The commission explained that there are two key concepts linked to the definition: (1) the concept of needs, and (2) the concept of limitations. With respect to meeting the needs of current and future generations, sustainable development relates to development that ensures that the needs of *all* people are fulfilled, not just those of privileged people. Within this context, the concept of needs refers to more than just basic needs such as food, shelter and safety. It also refers to 'legitimate aspirations [of all people] for an improved quality of life' (UNWCED, 1987, Chapter 2, item 4). In other words, if we relate this to the types of human needs distinguished by Maslow (1943), discussed in Chapter 2, sustainable development implies ensuring that all people, regardless of where they live or their upbringing, family views and local community characteristics, have the chance to fulfil all types of needs distinguished in Maslow's hierarchy of needs. These needs relate to food and safety but also to education, belonging and self-development. Oftentimes, people reduce – or actually: misuse – the Brundtland definition to mean ensuring that more and more people can live decent lives, and interpret decent as having basic needs such as food and shelter being fulfilled. To put it bluntly, these people are wrong! Sustainable development relates to the same types of needs for all people. Who are we, living in rich countries and brought up in favourable circumstances, to decide that other people, living in poor regions or brought up in unfavourable circumstances, do not need education, intimacy, self-esteem and respect? Who are we to decide that it is acceptable for us to eat meat, while others need to survive on rice and water? Who are we to decide that we need iPhones but access to the Internet is a luxury that is not an integral part of a decent life? Sustainable development is not development that distinguishes between (groups of) people and treats them differently. The definition of sustainable development refers to generations, not to specific groups of people. In other words, sustainable development incorporates a normative component to ensure that we create a world in which *all* people have a chance to fulfil *all* of their needs.

The second key concept linked to sustainable development – the concept of limitations – relates to the ability of our planet to continue to support fulfilling those needs. Sustainable development needs to ensure that the way we have arranged our world to fulfil our needs is sustainable. We cannot overexploit natural resources because this will make it impossible for future generations to fulfil their needs. In other words, we need to ensure that temperatures do not rise too much, ecosystems are preserved, biodiversity is not reduced too much, materials that we need do not run out, the air that we breathe does not become too polluted, and so on. The way we fulfil our needs today, tomorrow and all days after tomorrow needs to be based on using the Earth's natural resources in a smart way: in a way that preserves our planet's ability to support us in fulfilling our needs.

Together, these two concepts imply that sustainable development is much more than simply balancing the interests of *p*eople, *p*lanet and *p*rofit – the well-known three pillars or Ps of sustainable development – in the decisions we make. Sustainable development incorporates a normative but also a systemic dimension. The way we

FIGURE 6.2 The two key concepts linked to sustainable development

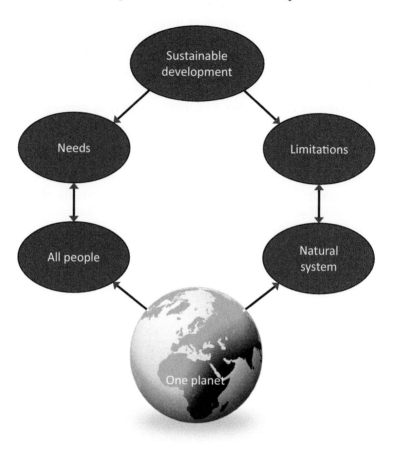

have arranged our world to fulfil our needs really needs to change dramatically. This involves a lot more than recycling some materials or saving energy by not forgetting to switch off lights and appliances. It involves drastic changes to the way we make decisions – our political system, how we distribute wealth – our economic system, how we account for the needs of all people – our social system, how we produce the tangible and intangible products that support us in fulfilling our needs – our production system, the technologies we apply for that – our technological system, and more (Destatte, 2010). In other words, we need to develop an alternative for our current socio-economic system – an alternative that is based on equality, inclusiveness and a responsible and sustainable way of interacting with our natural environment (Loorbach, 2014; Melissen, 2016; Melissen and Moratis, 2016). This is definitely quite a challenge but not impossible. However, to ensure that the negative effects of our current socio-economic system do not get out of hand, we need to act fast. Our planet is sending us a very clear signal: get your act together!

SUSTAINABILITY AND EVENTS, TOURISM AND HOSPITALITY

You might wonder why a book focusing on designing, staging and managing customer experiences in events, tourism and hospitality features such an elaborate discussion on the concept of sustainable development. The simple fact is that any business or professional needs to deal with this societal challenge – those operating in events, tourism and hospitality are no exception to this rule. This is not the only reason though. If you take a closer look at the specific relation between these industries and the (currently unsustainable) course of our societies, it becomes clear that events, tourism and hospitality could play a crucial role in realising sustainable development.

Contribution to unsustainability

Over the years, events, tourism and hospitality have contributed significantly to (some of) the problems discussed in the previous section. For example, events can put quite a strain on local resources such as water and energy but can also generate significant amounts of waste and cause pollution. Imagine a large music festival that attracts 100,000 visitors or more over the course of a few days. All of these visitors need to travel to the festival grounds and return back home afterwards. If public transport is not available because of the location that was chosen for the music festival, this means that most visitors will have to travel by car and this leads to significant emissions of greenhouse gases. Some of these festivals are well known around the world and also attract visitors from other countries. The same goes for artists performing at those festivals. Obviously, this means that a number of them will travel by aeroplane. This increases the greenhouse gas emissions associated with the festival considerably. Visitors that stay over at multi-day festivals also need a place to sleep, which is often organised in the form of a temporary camping site. The impact on the natural environment in which this camping site is located – and oftentimes festivals are actually purposely staged in rural areas – is not difficult to imagine. Consider the impact tens of thousands of partying people have on local flora and fauna in terms of noise, treading down plants, waste, and so on.

Obviously, at the festival itself, these visitors want to see and hear great performances – they want something special and exciting because they paid a lot of money to be there! Therefore, the installations for light and sound on the multiple stages in the festival grounds are nothing like your home cinema set or stereo system; these are brutal machines that use enormous amounts of energy and that were transported to the festival grounds in enormous lorries. To top it off, any self-respecting festival needs a fireworks display at the end of the day and one that really blows your mind at the end of the final day. This means additional greenhouse gas emissions associated with transporting the light and sound systems and the energy used during performances but also extensive air pollution that comes with fireworks. Fireworks lead to metal particles, toxins, chemicals and smoke in the air. Many of those substances are harmful to people, plants and animals, not only through direct contact with them through smoke and haze caused by the fireworks but also through the particles that eventually fall to the ground and pollute the soil and both ground and surface water. If you add to that the emissions, pollution and destruction caused by mining the raw materials needed for fireworks and producing the ultimate product in factories, it becomes rather clear that as festive as a fireworks display might be, it is not exactly a feast for our planet.

Obviously, these are just a few of the environmental impacts associated with events. These are also just the consequences associated with this specific type of event. Some events involve and impact even more people and last a lot longer. Consider, for example, mega-sports events like the Olympic Games or the football World Cup. These involve years of preparation, oftentimes extensive construction work and sometimes even creating completely new cities. The environmental but also the social impact of such events can be massive. Over the years, even though almost all of these events were advertised as 'the greenest ever' and 'promoting the local economy', a number of them have actually resulted in huge damage to local ecosystems, pollution, enormous debts for regions involved and negative effects for local people – some of whom were even forced to move to make way for sports facilities and accommodation for athletes. Most of us have probably read the news reports on how (migrant) workers have been (and still are?) treated during construction works for the Qatar 2022 football World Cup or the detrimental effects of the Sotchi Winter Olympics on local ecosystems and people. In other words, even though events are temporary, their contribution to the unsustainable course of our societies can be significant and long lasting or even permanent.

Tourism can have similar negative impacts. Just consider the possible negative effects of (increasing numbers of) tourists visiting pristine natural destinations across the globe. Roads have been constructed cutting through wilderness. Hotels and resorts have sprung up in areas that formed the last undisturbed habitats of rare species of animals. However, the negative effects of tourism are not limited to remote exotic locations. One of the biggest impacts of tourism, especially mass tourism – which relates to the vast majority of holidaymakers, is linked to greenhouse gas emissions associated with travelling. Most tourists travel to their holiday destination either by car or aeroplane. With more and more people in our world being able to afford flying, air travel has already increased considerably and will continue to increase rapidly in years to come. Aeroplanes emit particles and gases such as CO_2, hydrocarbons, carbon monoxide, nitrogen oxides, sulphur oxides and lead. All of these substances contribute to pollution and climate change. The impact of these emissions and thus air travel becomes clear if you realise that – based on current predictions of both further growth of air travel and anticipated increased efficiency and innovations in air travel technology – around 2050/2060 emissions from air travel alone (!) would amount to almost all emissions that our societies could afford if we wanted to limit the worldwide average rise in temperature to 2° Celsius (Peeters, 2017), as agreed in the Paris Agreement. In other words, that would leave us just a few decades to reduce all other emissions, such as those associated with factories producing our products, heating our homes, driving our cars, eating meat, and so on, to zero! Given that the chances of realising that are extremely slim at best, this illustrates the gravity of the problem associated with air travel. However, tourism not only leads to environmental problems. It can also result in negative social impacts. A typical example is city tourism. Inhabitants of cities like Venice, Barcelona and Amsterdam no longer think tourism is just a blessing – many of them feel the influx of tourists has turned their city into a theme park and has significantly decreased their quality of life. In some cities this has actually resulted in anti-tourism protests and even violence against tourists.

Hospitality is an integral part of tourism and therefore many of the issues discussed so far also apply to this sector. The hospitality industry can seriously affect the environment, both locally and globally. Construction of hospitality facilities, such as hotels and resorts but also theatres and casinos, requires significant natural resources and can damage (local) ecosystems. However, once a hospitality facility has been completed and 'goes into operation' it continues to consume natural resources. In fact, hospitality accommodations are responsible for more than 20% of greenhouse gas emissions of tourism. The hospitality sector can also have a negative impact from a social perspective. Just imagine the effect of a new hotel on the income of local people operating a bed and breakfast. This particular industry is also not exactly known for treating its employees well in terms of salary, and working hours and conditions. A final issue that definitely deserves mentioning here is food – both what is served and what is wasted. As discussed earlier in this chapter, there is a clear link between (un)sustainability and food. From a sustainable development perspective, we (privileged) humans, need to reconsider our eating habits. For instance, eating huge quantities of meat or fish that is harvested using unsustainable fishing methods damages our natural environment through greenhouse gas emissions, land use, water use, disturbing animal population dynamics and disrupting ecosystems. Furthermore, we are facing a serious and ever-increasing problem with respect to being able to produce enough food for our world's population. Combined, these two aspects make it difficult to understand some of the choices made in (parts of) the hospitality industry regarding dishes on the menu, quantities served and the way leftovers are handled.

In other words, events, tourism and hospitality have, unfortunately, contributed to the unsustainable course of our societies. To be fair though, so have almost all other sectors and industries. It is true that events, tourism and hospitality are currently to a large extent unsustainable. This implies that a number of businesses and professionals in these industries operate in ways that are not (completely) in line with the principles of sustainable development (yet). Does this mean that these businesses and professionals are purposely trying to ruin our world? Does this mean that they do not care about the environment and the interests of those less privileged? Of course not! It means they are struggling to adjust the way they operate. Just like most of us, in our role as consumers, are (still) struggling to adjust our consumption patterns. Most of us still fly. Many of us still eat meat and drive a car. Not all of us have already insulated our house and turned down the thermostat.

FIGURE 6.3 Predicted CO_2 emissions from flying compared with Paris scenarios

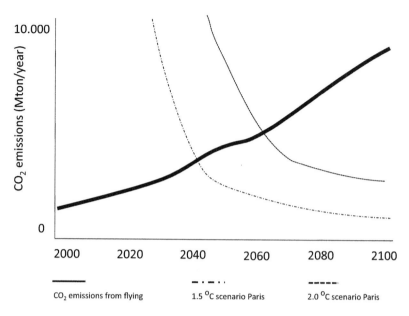

Adapted from: Peeters, P. (2017). *Tourism's impact on climate change and its mitigation challenges: How can tourism become 'climate sustainable'?* (Dissertation). Delft: Delft University of Technology

Not everybody spends significant amounts of time and/or money trying to help the poor. Given that many of us still (prefer to) consume unsustainable products, services and experiences, it is hardly surprising that businesses and professionals (are tempted to) provide them. The question who is to blame for that is both difficult to answer and mostly irrelevant.

The simple fact is that there is no doubt that the events, tourism and hospitality industries, like most industries, need to become more sustainable. There is also no doubt that this is both an urgent and complicated challenge. However, there are also reasons for optimism. In fact, one could even argue that these industries are perfect candidates for leading the way in adjusting the course of our societies to a more sustainable one.

Contribution to sustainable development

There are a number of things one could do to reduce the negative impact of events on both nature and people. In fact, both practitioners and researchers have developed quite a significant number of guidelines, checklists, standards, and so on, to assist in doing so. For instance, a specific ISO standard – ISO 20121 – is now available to assist organisers of events in improving the sustainability of their events. Numerous websites provide practical tips and suggestions to create sustainable events.

Researchers have published papers and books, such as *Sustainable Event Management* by Meegan Jones (2014), that contain a wealth of insights and reference points related to making events more sustainable. In fact, a whole new industry has emerged of companies, professionals and consultants who specialise in assisting event organisers and initiators with respect to sustainability aspects of their events. In other words, quite a lot is already known and can be done to improve events from a sustainable development perspective.

Obviously, a crucial decision with respect to sustainability of an event relates to where it is staged. In selecting the location for the event, minimising environmental and social disruption should serve as a reference point. Sometimes it is not necessary to build new facilities, such as stadiums, and you could actually use existing ones. Multiple events could also be organised at the same location at different times, so that infrastructure does not have to be created every time and disruption of nature is limited to one location. However, even if your event is organised at a temporary festival ground only used for your event, why not (re)use, for instance, stages and decor that have been used at other festivals? As indicated in the previous chapter with respect to management of experiences, such as events, it is not always wise to (re)invent the wheel, especially not from a sustainability perspective.

Other issues that can be addressed in staging more sustainable, or at least less unsustainable, events are transport of visitors, recruitment and training of employees or volunteers, sourcing of products and services needed for staging the event, waste management, consulting and cooperating with local stakeholders such as local residents, and so on. Why not rent electric buses to transport visitors to and from the festival grounds? Similar to ensuring that experiences are staged the way they have been designed, staging events in a sustainable way also relies on the behaviour of employees or volunteers. Therefore, the way you select, recruit, instruct and train them is a crucial element of making your event as sustainable as possible, and a number of the reference points discussed in the previous chapter also apply here. If your event serves or sells food to visitors, you could consider buying local products. When handing out water to visitors at a festival on a hot day, use sustainable and reusable cups instead of plastic bottles. Use environmentally friendly ways of cleaning and cleaning products. Invite local people to your event – and make them feel important and listened to – instead of ignoring them. Create opportunities for local entrepreneurs to benefit (financially) from the additional visitors to their town or city. Depending on the specific location and the specific type of event, there are literally hundreds and hundreds of simple or more advanced steps you could take as event organiser or manager to reduce the negative impact of your event. Listing and reviewing all possible measures and innovations that can reduce the impact of events on the environment and people is beyond the scope of this book. However, by now, it should be clear that there is really no excuse to not address this topic when staging an event. There is a wealth of information already available and even if you need to work out the specifics for your specific circumstances, doing so usually does not involve rocket science; just the willingness to take responsibility.

In essence, the same applies to the hospitality industry. There is a range of certification schemes, awards and labels that are available to hospitality businesses and professionals not only to assist them in tackling sustainability challenges but also to stimulate them in doing so. Research in this area is also quite extensive and describes a number of best practices, as well as appropriate reference points and guidelines. Finally, practitioners have joined forces in various ways to exchange information and jointly set standards with respect to sustainability measures, such as ways to reduce hotels' greenhouse gas emissions. A well-known example is the International Tourism Partnership: a collaboration between some of the world's leading hotel chains. This organisation publishes best practices via a dedicated website – www.greenhotelier.org – and has partnered with KPMG, the World Travel & Tourism Council and 23 global hotel companies in launching the Hotel Carbon Measurement Initiative, which includes a common methodology to measure and communicate greenhouse gas emissions by hotels.

Consequently, the hospitality industry has definitely made some progress in recent years with respect to addressing sustainability both within their day-to-day operations and within the context of so-called Corporate Social Responsibility (CSR) initiatives and programs. Most hotel chains, independent hotels and other types of accommodation have taken measures to reduce their energy and water consumption, often within the context of joining existing or setting up their own certification schemes. More and more hotels, restaurants, casinos, theatres and other types of companies that offer food and drink to customers now (also) serve local and organic produce. Vegetarian or even vegan dishes can now be found on most menus. Furthermore, a number of hospitality companies, such as global hotel chains and well-known fast-food chains, are involved in philanthropy and corporate citizenship initiatives, such as supporting aid programmes for the world's poor and local community development programmes. Even though one could argue that many hospitality companies, especially hotels and restaurants, are still neglecting some specific aspects – such as salary and working conditions of their own employees – and that their efforts so far have mostly been the result of public and/or regulatory pressures – and not so much an indication of an intrinsic motivation to become more sustainable, there is no doubt that the situation has already improved considerably compared to 10 or 20 years ago. The hospitality industry might not yet be the most sustainable industry but it is definitely not as unsustainable as it used to be.

Given that the hospitality industry and a number of events could be considered to form an integral part of tourism, one could argue that the same applies to tourism. A number of the measures and innovations that can be and already have been applied within events and hospitality undoubtedly contribute or have already contributed to making tourism more sustainable. What is more, both researchers and practitioners have dedicated considerable time and effort on discussing and promoting the specific concept of sustainable tourism ever since the 1970s. A crucial element of these discussions has been the potential of tourism to bring economic benefits to destinations and their inhabitants. In fact, 2017 was designated by the United Nations as the International Year for Sustainable Tourism for Development. The idea behind this initiative was that tourism could play a crucial role in promoting economic growth and poverty reduction in specific regions in our world. If organised properly, in theory, it can also promote social inclusiveness, environmentally responsible practices and resource efficiency. Tourism has already lived up to these expectations in specific parts of our world. It has helped specific regions, especially in so-called developing countries, to create new sources of income for local residents. A number of companies involved in tourism have contributed, either directly or indirectly, to improving local infrastructure and basic social services. Without their presence, a number of people would certainly be worse off. Also, specific types of tourism have evolved, such as ecotourism and community-based tourism, that are designed to contribute to preserving local ecosystems and assist in developing local communities. Sometimes, tourism can generate the awareness and financial resources needed to preserve and protect specific ecosystems. A simple example would be tourists that pay to visit a natural park. If the number of tourists is controlled, and thereby the disruption of the local ecosystem, the money they spend could be used to 'fight' poaching but also to create jobs and income for local people. Obviously, these positives do not compensate for the negatives discussed earlier. However, they do show that tourism can have positive effects, for all dimensions of sustainable development, if organised properly – a 'big if', to be fair (Melissen & Koens, 2016).

The complications involved with that 'big if' – not just for tourism but also for other sectors of our socio-economic system – are discussed in more detail in Chapter 7. This section has shown that making events, tourism and hospitality less unsustainable is not necessarily a mission impossible. There is a range of measures, innovations and concepts that could assist in realising this. Together, the economic, social and environmental impact of these industries on our societies is quite significant; they generate a significant portion of many countries' Gross National Product (GNP), the market value of all products, services and experiences produced by all citizens of a country. They employ a significant portion of the working population and impact the lives of even more people, and they consume significant amounts of natural resources. Consequently, if the combined effect of all of these measures, innovations and concepts is that events, tourism and hospitality can continue to generate the same value or more, while improving salaries and working conditions of employees, negatively influences the lives of fewer people, and consumes smaller amounts of natural resources, this is clearly a significant contribution to putting our societies on a more sustainable course. It would certainly adjust that course to a less unsustainable one.

However, this is not the only contribution that these industries could make. In fact, the discussion on the International Year of Sustainable Tourism for Development has already highlighted some ways in which they could not only contribute to reducing unsustainability but also to promoting sustainability. In other words, the actual contribution of events, tourism and hospitality to sustainable development is not limited to reducing the negative impact of these industries. They could also create positive impacts. This section has already shown that businesses and professionals in events, tourism and hospitality are closely linked to local social, economic and environmental systems. However, the (types of) companies that operate in this sector of our economy range from influential and powerful international, globally operating companies to local, independent entrepreneurs who are very much intertwined with local communities (Melissen, 2013). Therefore, regardless of whether you want to pursue sustainable development through a policy-based, top-down approach or through grassroots movements and a bottom-up approach based on local initiatives, businesses and professionals in events, tourism and hospitality can and probably should be involved. Based on their impact on and interrelationship with all levels of our societies they could play a crucial role in furthering sustainable development. As the next chapter will show, all types of professionals, businesses and industries have a role to play but, given their omnipresence in our societies, businesses and professionals in events, tourism and hospitality have a huge potential to have a significant impact and act as a catalyst in this process.

This potential is further increased by the specific characteristics of these industries. First of all, the specific product these industries offer to consumers – regardless of whether you refer to this product as a service or staging an experience – is often based on direct interaction between their employees and their customers. What better opportunity to discuss sustainability issues than through personal communication! Together, these industries could get the sustainability message across to almost all people in our world. Second, they can do so within the context of staging experiences. As discussed in the previous chapters, staging experiences focuses on creating memories, on linking to the needs and wishes of customers, on understanding what they want and what makes them tick. You cannot ask for better circumstances to discuss and address sustainability. This is a chance to address this complicated topic with the benefits of doing so with detailed background information about the customer, by people who have been trained in interacting with customers and selected based on their specific expertise, attitude and behaviour in relation to interacting with customers, in surroundings that have been created to fit the needs, wishes and preferences of those customers. If there was ever a chance to discuss sustainability and really get through to people, this is it!

Furthermore, customers who engage in experiences staged by businesses and professionals in events, tourism and hospitality often do so outside their own home and daily routines. This creates two additional opportunities for these industries to promote sustainable behaviour and sustainable products and services. First of all, you can create circumstances in which customers can test behaviours and products that they do not engage in or use at home and in their 'normal' daily lives. For instance, the best place to make people realise that sustainable food tastes as good as or even better than non-sustainable food is a fine-dining restaurant. The best place to let people experience that a water-saving showerhead is just as effective and comfortable as a regular showerhead is a hotel room. A perfect time and way to let people realise the seriousness of climate change and their own contribution to that problem is probably during a pleasant night to remember in a theatre and through a perfectly timed dark joke by the artist performing that night. Second, you can make use of the positive effects of a specific human characteristic: biophilia. As Griskevicius et al. (2012) explain in their paper on the evolutionary bases for (un)sustainable behaviour, almost all if not all people are endowed with biophilia: an appreciation of and desire for natural environments. Research shows that people who are immersed in beautiful natural surroundings or engage in pleasant outdoor experiences develop more appreciation for our natural environment and are more inclined to engage in sustainable behaviour. A number of experiences staged in events, tourism and hospitality offer a perfect opportunity to 'awaken' that human characteristic and tap into it to promote sustainability.

In other words, there are plenty of possibilities and opportunities for these industries to reduce their own negative impact from a sustainability perspective but also to make a significant positive contribution to furthering sustainable development in general. Probably one of the biggest opportunities for doing so is to stage experiences in such a way that consumers are exposed to sustainable products, services and behaviours in a pleasant and positive way, thus encouraging them to buy, use and engage in them more often, also in their daily lives and at home. If businesses and professionals in events, tourism and hospitality can make this happen, this sector could truly function as a catalyst for sustainable development. The details of what is needed for that, for instance with respect to the design of experiences and business models applied by businesses and professionals staging them, are discussed in more detail in the next few chapters. This chapter concludes with a discussion on the implications of sustainable development, especially in combination with the rise of the experience economy, for traditional boundaries between industries.

SUSTAINABILITY, EXPERIENCES AND FLUIDITY

The previous section has highlighted how staging experiences can contribute to promoting sustainability. However, these two concepts – experiences and sustainable development – are actually linked in more ways.

Experiences as replacement for tangible products

To further illustrate the logical link between the rise of the experience economy and sustainable development, it is important to return to the fundamental difference between unsustainability and sustainability. A key element of the unsustainable course of our societies is the excessive use of natural resources. We, humans, have grown accustomed to satisfying many of our needs and wishes through buying and using tangible products. The production of these products usually requires all kinds of materials, energy and water, and thereby leads to disruption of or damage to ecosystems, pollution, greenhouse gas emissions, and so on. Consequently, one of the obvious routes towards a more sustainable course of our societies is to reduce the number of products that is produced. The question then is: can we, consumers, satisfy our needs and wishes without having to buy these products?

Consider the well-known example of printers and copiers. Almost any business or professional needs access to documents and sometimes multiple people need access to the same document at the same time. Not that long ago, the way to deal with this issue would have been to print and copy documents, so that multiple people would have a paper copy of the same document. Therefore, businesses and professionals bought printers and copiers. Obviously, the reason for buying these appliances was not that these organisations and people wanted to own a printer and copier. For most professionals, it was not a childhood dream to once be the proud owner of a big noisy machine capable of putting ink on paper. They just wanted to have access to documents. Over the years, a new concept was developed: leasing printers and copiers. A business or professional would no longer actually buy a printer or copier but lease it from the manufacturer of printer and copier machines. The printer or copier can still be used for creating paper copies of documents but it remains the property of the producer. From a sustainability perspective, this arrangement comes with a number of advantages. The manufacturer can reuse parts of or complete printers and copiers that have been returned by clients and install them for other clients. The manufacturer can ensure that maintenance is carried out on all machines at intervals that ensure that they last longer, use less ink and energy, and components remain suitable for reuse, refurbishment or recycling at a later stage. Most importantly, as a result, the natural resources needed to ensure that all business and professionals have access to documents can be reduced significantly.

In principle, similar arrangements could be used for all kinds of tangible products. Obviously, some of us really want to own a car – a red shiny one that we wash gently every Saturday and that makes us feel alive and successful! But others simply need a convenient way to get to where they need to go. They do not necessarily have to own a car; they just need access to a car when they need it. These people are perfectly happy to lease a car, or rent one when they need it. These days, it is not uncommon for people to use public transport if and when convenient, and then rent a car if and when a specific destination or timing of an appointment makes using a car necessary. Some people even share a car with their neighbours or relatives. Whatever the exact arrangements that we have already and will come up with, the fact is that the number of cars needed for transporting all of us to wherever we need to go is far less than the number of cars currently owned by people and thus produced by car manufacturers.

Those reading this book who are above the age of 30 remember the days when we would rent a movie at a local video rental shop or even buy one because we would surely watch it again and again. These days we simply go online through our home cinema set and pick one that is available on Netflix. If we want to watch the movie again, no problem! We just watch it again.

In other words, even though we still need transport and we still want to entertain ourselves with a good movie, fulfilling these needs and wishes can be arranged in ways that require fewer tangible products to be produced. Technological developments and getting used to new ways of fulfilling our needs and wishes can further stimulate this process. These days, many of us are perfectly comfortable with having an online version of a document at our disposal and do not always feel the need to print a paper copy, which further decreases the total natural resources needed for fulfilling the need of having access to documents. All this means that a shift from tangible products to intangible products fulfilling our needs and wishes can form an important element of reducing the unsustainability of our societies. However, this does not mean that we are satisfied with just any intangible product. In fact, if anything, we have actually become more critical. We have grown accustomed to getting what we want, when we want it, in a way that is customised to our personal preferences. This process was described in detail in Chapter 1. Consequently, experiences have gradually started to replace tangible products as what we expect from businesses and professionals assisting us in fulfilling our needs and wishes in return for our money.

Therefore, the rise of the experience economy and the challenge of sustainable development have one key element in common: a focus on new ways of fulfilling our needs and wishes. From a sustainable development perspective, an increased focus on intangible products and services and a decreased focus on tangible products and services is clearly a blessing. In fact, if one thing is clear from the discussion in the previous sections, it is that we, humans, cannot continue to fulfil our needs and wishes in the same way we have been doing to date. Somehow, we will have to find ways to create the same or a better quality of life – the latter is definitely true for those less privileged and living in poor regions of our world – that require fewer natural resources. Technology will no doubt have to play a role in realising this. However, an increased focus on using instead of owning and intangible products instead of tangible ones is another obvious route. Therefore, an increased focus on sustainability aspects by customers, competitors and legislators further stimulates those providing products to customers in exchange for money to base those economic transactions on products that require fewer natural resources, such as experiences instead of tangible products. In other words, the rise of the experience economy and the pursuit of sustainable development represent two developments that not only fit with each other but also strengthen and reinforce each other.

Blurring boundaries

These two developments also influence and change the landscape of our economy. They both contribute to changes in and sometimes even the fading of traditional boundaries between industries. Simultaneously, they both lead to new ways in which suppliers and consumers of products interact with each other and stimulate so-called co-creation by these parties.

In Chapter 2, some of the backgrounds to the rise of the experience economy have been discussed, such as the on-going process of individualisation of our society, technological developments, the reduced impact of our upbringing, family views and local community characteristics. All of these changes contribute to the increased importance of the (symbolic) values we associate with consuming specific products. The products that we buy and consume need to assist us in expressing who we are or want to be, to what group we belong or want to belong, to highlighting what we have achieved or want to achieve, and so on. The suppliers of the products we buy and consume not only need to account for this, but also need to assist us in fulfilling those needs and wishes. This has not only changed the characteristics of the products we consume and the way in which we do so – from a focus on tangible and ownership to a focus on intangible and experiencing – but, consequently, also our relationship with the suppliers of those products. We are not going to consume products offered by just any business or professional. Their worldviews, the values that they or their brand represent are important to us and play an important role in our consumption decisions. We are basically entering into some sort of relationship with those suppliers if and when we decide to consume the products they offer. This completely changes the role of these businesses and professionals. The rise of the experience economy implies that they now not only need to ensure that they produce the types of products that we prefer but also deliver them to us in a way that matches our values, our needs and wishes, our specific preferences. In other words, whereas these types of relationships and interaction between supplier and consumer used to be limited to industries such as events, tourism and especially hospitality, they have now become commonplace in many other industries. Some of the principles applied and tangible products associated with these industries are now also applied and offered by retailers, manufacturers, technology companies, and so on. A typical example is a clothing shop, or perhaps a fashion boutique, offering drinks and even serving lunch to customers. Whereas such a shop used to be a place where you would simply walk by clothing racks to spot something nice, try it on, pay and leave, it now often resembles a living room or cosy restaurant where you interact with 'your kind of people' over drinks, while discussing that fantastic new movie *and* what jacket would be perfect for you.

We can see similar changes at all kinds of retailers, department stores and shopping malls but also in other industries, such as banking, sports, and healthcare. A bank is no longer the place to get money. Money is increasingly becoming something that only exists in a virtual world. It is a place where you go to discuss your dreams, your ambitions and your plans for the future with someone that knows and understands you. A gym without childcare facilities and regular get-togethers for members with drinks and (healthy) snacks is just a room with fitness equipment which we already have at home. Modern hospitals are often part of a building complex that also includes shopping facilities, a gym, a cinema, multiple restaurants, and so on. In other words, whereas building host-guest relationships used to be the exclusive territory of events, tourism and hospitality, it is now an integral

CASE STUDY 6.1 **CREATING EXPERIENCES IN DESTINATION SHOPPING CENTRES**

David Strafford and Phil Crowther

Meadowhall, in Yorkshire (United Kingdom), is a vast destination shopping centre, comprising retail, hospitality, leisure, and entertainment. External factors such as online shopping have fuelled a situation whereby shopping centres cannot rely on shopping alone and are increasingly preoccupied with giving customers another reason to visit that goes beyond the ordinary. It is the essence of the Experience Economy; as they increasingly stage many and varied experiences to both attract visitors and also influence them to 'linger for longer' (Europe Real Estate, 2013). The study referred to revealed an increasingly inseparable relationship between the management of shopping centre and experience creation.

During 2015, Meadowhall hosted the 'Gruffalo Experience' – a three-week pop-up experiential children's event. An extensive survey of 1,300 attendees, and in-depth interviews, revealed the potential that such purposefully designed experiences have in shaping consumer behaviour. The results specifically revealed how meeting the children's and parents' experience expectations, at the Gruffalo event, was a strong predictor of visitor re-visitation and advocacy, with visitor intention to share their experience on social media.

Children's excitement, event authenticity, and personalisation linked to the creation of photo opportunities, were the specific factors that the data showed as influencing return visits and advocacy. The quality of the branded experience and the associated drama and interaction with the costumed characters (fox, owl, mouse, snake and, of course, the Gruffalo himself) were influential. Importantly, the experiencescape transcended the specified event space and spilled out into the malls and shops. Retailer, and restaurant, engagement to extend the experience and therefore animate the wider DSC were important features; whether that was finding 'mouse' in the bookstores or 'owl ice-cream' in the food court. Achieving vibrancy, and enlivenment, in the malls, and a co-creative relationship with tenants, were key success factors in the Gruffalo Experience. The experience strategy of shopping centres is to differentiate and augment their customers' journey; henceforth they consider traditional visitor attractions as competition. They seek to be known as a place that stages experiences, like the Gruffalo Experience, so customers choose them. Meadowhall's event and experience strategy is integral to their success as they aspire to achieve short-term outcomes related to sales and advocacy, and also longer-term outcomes linked to inspiring future visits and brand building.

The evidence of the Gruffalo event is of a positive relationship between experience creation and these outcomes, and the challenge for the team at Meadowhall is to craft a continual assortment of many and varied experiences to inject play, enjoyment, and sociality into the shopping centre experience, inspiring enlivenment.

Based on: Europe Real Estate (2013). *Entertainment in shopping centers: Maximising the shopping experience*. Retrieved from http://europe-re.com/entertainment-in-shopping-centers-maximizing-shopping-experience/42425.

requirement for almost any business or professional, regardless of the industry in which they operate. Furthermore, it is becoming more difficult to actually distinguish between separate industries. More and more, boundaries between industries are blurring and new arrangements for producing and delivering products are emerging within the context of an increased focus on offering intangible products and the types of experiences that we, consumers, prefer.

These new arrangements also imply that the boundaries between suppliers and consumers are fading – both with respect to the economic transactions between individual businesses and professionals, and the economic transactions between businesses and professionals on the one hand and individual or groups of consumers on the other. Some of the experiences staged by businesses and professionals require assistance from and products produced and delivered by other businesses and professionals. If cleaning of a theme park is outsourced to a specialised company, the employees of this company need to assist the theme park in maintaining the 'magic' of the storyline that is communicated. They need to adjust their clothing and behaviour accordingly. If a gym serves food and drinks, the supplier of food and drinks needs to be able to react quickly to new trends in healthy food and sports drinks, and expand the range of products they offer based on specific requests of members of the gym. Most experiences offered by an individual business or professional require products and services produced and delivered by other businesses or professionals. Ensuring that the ultimate experience lives up to the expectations of all different groups of consumers, all with their own specific needs, wishes and preferences, requires intensive cooperation between all businesses and professionals involved.

Obviously, this changes the relationship between these businesses and professionals. Whereas their responsibilities used to be limited to producing and delivering specific products and services according to their own specifications, they are now jointly responsible for staging experiences. In other words, they need to engage in co-creation because, ultimately, the only way they can survive in today's increasingly competitive marketplace is to be part of those networks of businesses and professionals that are capable of (continuous improvement in) staging the types of experiences that match the ever-changing needs and wishes of today's consumer.

This changing relationship between individual businesses and professionals – and an increased focus on co-creation – resembles the changing relationship between businesses and professionals staging experiences and the end consumers that engage in those experiences. The relationship between suppliers of experiences and consumers of experiences is also based on co-creation, as discussed in earlier chapters. An experience often involves direct interaction between supplier and consumer and both have a particular role to play in creating the ultimate experience. Therefore, the changes in the economic landscape caused by the rise of the experience economy can be characterised as an increased fluidity of this landscape. Boundaries between industries are blurring but this also applies to boundaries between individual businesses and professionals, and to boundaries between suppliers and consumers.

Interestingly, an increased focus on sustainable development actually reinforces these developments. Individual businesses and professionals who want to produce and deliver sustainable products, services and experiences are dependent on their business partners and suppliers in doing so. You cannot serve sustainable food in a restaurant if your suppliers do not apply sustainability principles for the produce they deliver to you. An important element of serving sustainable food is to use more local and seasonal produce. This requires intensive communication and cooperation with a network of often small local suppliers instead of simply ordering everything you need at internationally operating food wholesalers and distributers. Similarly, guaranteeing the sustainability standards applied in cleaning your theme park implies that intensive communication and cooperation is needed with the company you have hired to do so. Your employees and those of the cleaning company need to work together in making sure that your theme park lives up to the principles of sustainable development.

For some specific sustainability problems, finding a solution can be quite difficult and complex. Sometimes new technologies need to be developed to reduce the negative environmental or social impact of specific products, services and experiences. Reducing the greenhouse gas emissions of our transport system is a typical and probably the biggest challenge within this context. How can we still travel the world and experience nature and different cultures without having to fly in aeroplanes that use kerosene? How can we reduce the number of cars that need to be produced without making it impossible for us to get to our appointments on time? These are examples of challenges that require cooperation between a number of different businesses and professionals but also between different industries. Rising to these challenges will undoubtedly lead to arrangements in the way we satisfy our needs and wishes that are completely different from the current arrangements and will involve new types of companies and networks.

Tackling the challenge of sustainable development also involves communicating and co-creation with consumers. On a small scale, for instance for an individual hotel or restaurant, sustainability ambitions with respect to sustainable food and drinks and saving energy and water can only be realised if guests are willing to go along with that. Serving more sustainable dishes instead of dishes that come with enormous greenhouse gas emissions and water usage definitely helps to save our environment but will only work if guests are prepared to try them. Installing water-saving showerheads only makes sense if that does not lead to guests showering for 20 instead of 10 minutes. Your customers need to understand what you are trying to do and why you are doing that, and they need to be willing to try out new ways of fulfilling their needs. Obviously, this not only applies at the level of individual companies and their customers, but also at the level of our socio-economic system as a whole. As indicated in the previous sections of this chapter, ultimately, successfully dealing with the challenge of sustainable development requires us to create viable alternatives to our socio-economic system, to the way we have arranged our world to satisfy our needs and wishes. This involves not only finding new ways of satisfying the same needs and wishes but also discussing those needs and wishes themselves. Do we all need an iPhone when there are people who do not yet have access to the Internet and social media? Do we all need to eat meat, even though there are people who currently need to survive on a diet that predominantly consists of rice? Do we really need to travel thousands and thousands kilometres every year to go on multiple holidays, and is it acceptable for all people to do so? These are the types of questions that are directly linked to the concept of sustainable development and the essence of the challenge our society is faced with. Answering these questions and creating appropriate and widely accepted solutions is not something that an individual business or professional, or even an individual industry, can do. It is something that requires the business world and (groups of) citizens, in their roles as consumers and co-creators of the products they consume, to join forces and come up with viable solutions. In other words, just like the challenge of staging successful experiences, the challenge of sustainable development transcends traditional boundaries between individual businesses and professionals, between industries, and between suppliers and consumers. Consequently, tackling this challenge requires new business technologies and business models, which is the topic of the next chapter.

SUMMARY

Based on reading this chapter, we hope you will understand and remember the following:

- The dangers involved with global climate change.
- The interrelatedness of various sustainability problems.
- The two key concepts linked to sustainable development:
  o   needs;
  o   limitations.
- Sustainable development requires changing our political system, our economic system, our social system, our production system, our technological system and more.
- Events, tourism and hospitality have played an important role in the currently unsustainable course of our societies.
- Events, tourism and hospitality could play a crucial role in adjusting this course to a sustainable one.
- The rise of the experience economy and the challenge of realising sustainable development strengthen and reinforce each other.

- Together, these two developments contribute to the blurring of boundaries between industries.
- Experiences could play a crucial role in pursuing sustainable development.

FOOD FOR THOUGHT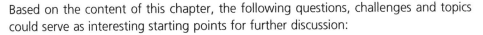

Based on the content of this chapter, the following questions, challenges and topics could serve as interesting starting points for further discussion:

- What needs and wishes, that you currently fulfil through consuming specific products, services or experiences, would you be willing to fulfil differently to contribute to sustainable development?
- This chapter has already provided some examples of how events, tourism and hospitality could contribute to sustainable development. Could you come up with more examples?
- This chapter has already provided some examples of how staging experiences could assist industries outside of events, tourism and hospitality in contributing to sustainable development. Could you come up with more examples?

REFERENCES

Destatte, P. (2010). Foresight: A major tool in tackling sustainable development. *Technological Forecasting & Social Change*, 77, 1575–1587.

Griskevicius, V., Cantú, S. & van Vught, M. (2012). The evolutionary bases for sustainable behaviour: Implications for marketing, policy, and social entrepreneurship. *Journal of Public Policy & Marketing*, 31, 115–128.

Jones, M. (2014). *Sustainable event management: A practical guide* (2nd ed.). New York: Routledge.

Loorbach, D. (2014). *To transition! Governance panarchy in the new transformation.* Rotterdam: Erasmus University Rotterdam.

Maslow, A.H. (1943). A theory of human motivation. *Psychological Review*, 50(4), 370.

Meadows, D., Meadows, D., Randers, J. & Behrens III, W. (Club of Rome) (1972). *The limits to growth: A report for the Club of Rome's project on the predicament of mankind.* New York: Universe Books.

Melissen, F. (2013). Sustainable hospitality: A meaningful notion? *Journal of Sustainable Tourism*, 21(6), 810–824.

Melissen, F. (2016). *4th generation sustainable business models.* Breda: NHTV Breda University of Applied Sciences.

Melissen, F. & Koens, K. (2016). Adding researchers' behaviour to the research agenda: Bridging the science-policy gap in sustainable tourism mobility. *Journal of Sustainable Tourism*, 24(3), 335–349.

Melissen, F. & Moratis, L. (2016). A call for fourth generation sustainable business models. *The Journal of Corporate Citizenship*, 63, 8–16.

Peeters, P. (2017). *Tourism's impact on climate change and its mitigation challenges: How can tourism become 'climate sustainable'?* (dissertation). Delft University of Technology, Delft.

Roorda, N. (2017). *Fundamentals of sustainable development* (2nd ed.). New York: Routledge.

Sennett, R. (2008). *The craftsman.* New Haven, CT: Yale University Press.

United Nations' World Commission on Environment and Development (UNWCED) (Brundtland Commission) (1987). *Our common future (The Brundtland Report).* Oxford: Oxford University Press.

7 Sustainable business models and technologies

The previous chapter has explained that realising sustainable development requires us to develop and implement viable alternatives to our current socio-economic system. This chapter further explores this challenge and discusses the specific contribution required from businesses and professionals in all industries, also in events, tourism and hospitality.

To make this contribution, drastic changes are needed in the business models and business technologies applied by those businesses and professionals. Otherwise, the so-called invisible hand of the free market will most likely delay or even destroy initiatives to create sustainable alternatives to our current socio-economic system. To fully appreciate these self-reinforcing mechanisms incorporated in our current system, we need to understand its foundations and (the behaviour of) the various actors involved in shaping it. This is the topic of the first section of this chapter.

Subsequently, the second section zooms in on the crucial role of businesses and professionals in escaping the lock-in of our current socio-economic system. It describes the ways in which businesses and professionals have so far tried to incorporate sustainability principles in their business models and business technologies. It also explains why these efforts have not yet resulted in significant progress with respect to putting our societies on a truly sustainable course. Finally, it portrays the contours of business models and business technologies that are fully aligned with sustainable development, but also some of the challenges associated with applying them.

The third and final section of this chapter then further elaborates on these challenges and highlights (promising) avenues for tackling them, thereby establishing some specific reference points for businesses and professionals regarding the way in which they could make a significant contribution to realising sustainable development. These reference points relate to the type of leadership required from those making (key) decisions, implications for the way in which businesses and professionals organise themselves and, especially, the way in which they can 'seduce' others – such as (potential) customers – to join them on this journey. Together, these reference points could be translated into specific types of reasoning, learning and actions – a specific type of intelligence: sustainability intelligence. This concept is introduced in this final section and further elaborated in the remaining chapters of this book.

OUR SOCIO-ECONOMIC SYSTEM

The discussion on sustainable development in the previous chapter has repeatedly referred to our socio-economic system and defined it as the way we have arranged our world to satisfy our needs and wishes. Even though this is a helpful working definition, we need a more precise definition to fully understand and appreciate the impact of this system.

The transformation of our society

Socio-economics relates to a specific field within the social sciences that studies how economic activities both are shaped and affected by social processes. This means that it focuses on studying how societies develop over time as a result of and in relation to local and regional economies, as well as the global economy. In turn, the term 'system' refers to a complex whole of (social, economic, political) practices but also to an organised set of doctrines, ideas and principles. Consequently, a socio-economic system can be defined as the organised set of practices, doctrines, ideas and principles that both results from and drives social and economic processes.

As discussed in Chapter 2, over the course of the last few centuries, our society has changed significantly. This process has been called the Industrial Revolution, modernisation or the great transformation. A driving force behind these changes was the development of a number of new technologies, such as (more efficient) steam engines, mechanised cotton spinning, new technologies for iron making, and a number of machine tools like the screw cutting lathe, cylinder boring machine and the milling machine. Combined, these technologies allowed us to exploit natural resources more efficiently. As a result, the productivity of our labour force and our factories increased, which in turn created economic growth, more prosperity, and so on. Over the course of the last two centuries, these technologies were further improved and new ones were developed – with information and communication technology representing an especially important driver of further changes in our society. Simultaneously, we developed new systems for energy supply, mobility, food production, health care, education and science. As indicated in Chapter 2, all of these developments have significantly changed our preferences and cultural habits, causing an on-going process of individualisation and an increased focus on consumption. Simultaneously, the combined effect of factors such as an increased income, higher education levels and access to information for 'the masses' have led to democratisation of decision-making, emancipation of women, human rights and, ultimately, the so-called welfare state (Loorbach, 2014).

It is beyond the scope of this book to provide a detailed description of all relevant developments and interactions between them that have jointly shaped the way we, humans, have decided to arrange our world. However, it is clear that the result of all of these developments is that the social component of our current socio-economic system is drastically different from the situation before this transformation. Many of us now live in cities instead of rural areas. Almost all of us live in countries that are governed by a democratic system. Most of us live in freedom, and the choices we make in our lives are no longer predetermined – by our upbringing or decisions made by a ruling elite – but have become personal choices. A big part of the world's population now has access to education, health care and paid work and, as a result, their living conditions have improved and their material wealth has increased. Not everybody though has these privileges. In the end, we also run the risk of having to pay dearly for the way we have arranged these privileges. However, that side of the coin has already been discussed in the previous chapter and will be addressed again later in this chapter.

This transformation of the social component of our socio-economic system was accompanied and made possible by an economic system based on capitalism. In essence, a capitalist economic system refers to a system in which those who own the capital – the financial resources – needed to manufacture products make the decisions related to that production, and prices and distribution of those products are determined in a market based on competition. The most popular version of capitalism – the most widely diffused around the world – is free market capitalism. This economic system is based on competitive markets where prices for products are determined by supply and demand. The term 'free' refers to the fact that, at least in theory, exchange of money for goods or services on this market is on a voluntary basis. Nobody is forced to sell specific goods or services and neither is anybody forced to buy them. The combination of supply of and demand for specific goods and services determines the price individuals or groups of people, such as organisations, will be willing to pay for them. The same applies to labour; nobody is forced to work for the people who organise production of goods and services, and the salaries these people have to pay their employees for doing the work is once again determined by supply of and demand for those jobs. Ultimately, the free market system is based on competition. If you want to produce specific goods or services, you will be competing for (the best) workers with others who want to produce specific goods and services. If you want to continue to produce those goods and services, you need the financial resources to do so. In other words, you need to sell your goods and services for a price that allows you to buy the (material) resources and pay the employees needed to produce new goods and services. However, you are not the only one offering goods and services to consumers on the market and, therefore, you are competing with those other suppliers for the consumers' money.

Once again, it is beyond the scope of the discussion here to elaborate on all details of our economic system, the principles of capitalism and the rules of the game called the free market. However, it is important to note that the type of social progress described earlier has gone hand in hand with (an increasing popularity and diffusion of) an economic system that is based on free markets that promote competition.

The resulting set of values and worldviews

The previous sub-section has described quite a significant change in the way we have arranged our world and the social and economic systems we have created in doing so. However, this is not all that has changed. As explained by Laszlo (2001), these kinds of drastic changes over the course of humanity's socio-cultural evolution have usually followed a similar pattern, which consists of four stages:

1. In phase 1, (technological) innovations allow for more efficiency in the way we, humans, can exploit natural resources to fulfil our needs.
2. In phase 2, these (technological) innovations change social relations and our relation with the environment, because with higher levels of production comes a faster population growth, which leads to higher societal complexity and a further increase in the impact on the environment.
3. In phase 3, these changed relations lead to new social, political and economic systems.
4. In phase 4, these new systems lead to new sets of values and worldviews.

Over the course of human history, innovations that triggered drastic changes were linked to the control of fire, the domestication of plants and animals, the invention of writing, the lever, the plough, wind and water mills, vessels that allowed navigation of the oceans, weapons, and so on (Laszlo, 2001). Each of these innovations triggered changes in our societies that resemble the four stages described above. If you review the developments described in the previous section, these phases are also recognisable in the process of the last two centuries. With technological innovations such as the steam engine, we were able to even better exploit natural resources to fulfil our needs. In doing so, our social relations changed; we moved to cities, we created factories and a number of other types of organisations aimed at producing goods and services, and, notably, we started to form all kinds of money-based relations with other people. Economic transactions became a part of our everyday lives and the way we fulfil our needs. Even though the way we now fulfil our needs is putting an ever-increasing strain on our natural environment, as discussed in detail in Chapter 6, these changes in our social and economic systems have proved so successful that the world's population has been growing exponentially ever since we introduced them. All these developments have led to our current welfare 'state', which is founded on democracy and (free market) capitalism.

FIGURE 7.1 Pattern of humanity's socio–cultural evolution

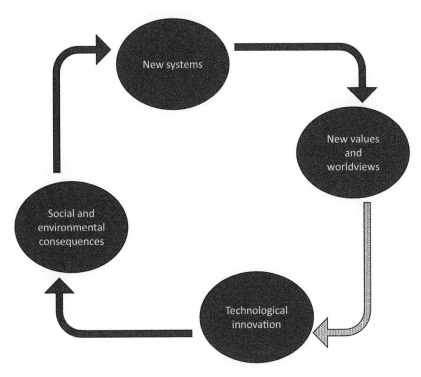

Source: Laszlo, E. (2001). Human evolution in the third millennium. *Futures*, 23(4), 349–372.

What about phase 4, you might ask? Well, we have already gone through that phase as well. As discussed in Chapter 2, most of us now feel that it is up to us, and nobody else, to decide who we are and what we do. We consider it our right as a human being to fulfil our personal needs and to pursue our own dreams. Simultaneously, our current socio–economic system has provided many of us with the material means, technologies – especially information and communication technology, knowledge, desires and imagination to actually pursue our dreams and arrange our lives accordingly (Varul, 2013; Melissen, 2016). In other words, our current socio–economic system comes with a lot of benefits for most of us living in prosperous parts of our world. It has given us freedom, material wealth, health, education, and so on. Our living conditions have drastically improved and many of us can now focus on fulfilling higher-level needs in Maslow's hierarchy of needs, instead of having to worry about whether we will have enough to eat and a place to stay when night falls. Sure, many of these needs and wishes can only be fulfilled through economic transactions with others and, therefore, fulfilling them requires us to earn money. However, most of us seem to accept that as a small price to pay for living in a society full of seemingly endless possibilities. Given that we owe our safety, our freedom, our material wealth and our health to our socio–economic system, we seem perfectly fine with paying off our debts to this system in this way (Varul, 2013).

In fact, by playing our own part in making this system work – by voting for political parties and candidates who promise to make it even more efficient, by working in organisations who produce the goods and services that we crave, by buying the goods and services that are produced – we have actually managed to have it create even more material wealth, more freedom, more possibilities to fulfil our needs and wishes, as time has passed. It is no wonder that we have made the values on which this system is based – free markets based on competition and promoting private property, autonomy and economic growth (Melissen, 2016; Melissen & Moratis, 2016) – more or less our own.

Interestingly, in today's society, these values are almost treated as if they represent fundamental truths or laws, especially since the rise of so-called neoliberalism in the last few decades of the 20th century. Backed up by the successes of socio-economic systems based on these ideas, politicians and economists have been promoting – and have managed to implement (!) – (further) economic liberalisation policies like privatisation, deregulation and free trade. This has resulted in a situation in which the vast majority of (local or regional) economic systems in our world more and more resemble so-called laissez-faire capitalist systems – systems based on the values associated with free markets. The reasoning applied in promoting these values can be traced back to the work of Adam Smith, an 18th-century Scottish economist, philosopher and author of the famous book *The Wealth of Nations* (1776). Smith is commonly acknowledged as laying the foundations for modern economic theory and could be regarded as the spiritual father of many of today's socio-economic systems. The following quotes from *The Wealth of Nations* clearly illustrate the train of thought on which these systems are based:

> It is not from the benevolence of the butcher, the brewer, the baker, that we expect our dinner, but from their regard to their own interest.
> (Smith, 1776, 1976, Book 1, p. 18)

> As every individual, therefore, endeavours as much as he can both to employ his capital in the support of domestic industry, and so to direct that industry that its produce may be of the greatest value; every individual necessarily labors to render the annual revenue of the society as great as he can [. . .] and by directing that industry in such a manner as its produce may be for the greatest value, he intends only his own gain, and he is in this, as in many other cases, led by an invisible hand to promote an end which was no part of his intention.
> (Smith, 1776, 1976, Book 4, p. 477)

In other words, this system is based on the belief that the mechanisms incorporated in free markets – the so-called invisible hand of the free market – ensure that people acting in self-interest – by focusing on private profit, material wealth and private property – automatically contribute to desirable outcomes for all (Bhagwati, 2011). Over time, we, humans, have come to rely on these mechanisms for fulfilling many of our needs and wishes. We have arranged our world based on these values and have actually gone so far as to incorporate rules, regulations and laws in our socio-economic system that enforce them. Companies have to make a profit to survive in this system. In fact, most countries actually have laws stating that organisations only qualify as companies, and are thus allowed to benefit from special rules and regulations within tax systems, if they aim to make a profit. Our politicians, almost without exception, feel it is their duty to take economic growth into account for almost all decisions they make. As indicated earlier, in our roles as consumers and voters, we encourage these companies and politicians to continue focusing on these values by buying those companies' products and by delegating our responsibility for making the right decisions for our city, our region, our country to those politicians. Consequently, most of our socio-economic systems are not only based on the values of the free market but also incorporate a number of self-reinforcing mechanisms to ensure that they will continue to be based on those values. By now, most of us living in (rich) democracies would find it hard to accept or even imagine being part of a socio-economic system that is not based on these values, and many of us – consciously or unconsciously – abide with them in the way we live our lives and many if not most of the decisions we make along the way.

The resulting social dilemma

As indicated earlier, our current socio-economic system and the values on which it is based have benefited many of us in a number of ways. Simultaneously, however, this system and these values are also the main causes for probably the biggest challenge humanity has ever faced: the necessity to adjust the course of our societies to one that matches the principles of sustainable development. To fully appreciate how the values ingrained in our socio-economic system – and thus in the way we have arranged our world to fulfil our needs and wishes – have not only brought us material wealth but may also result in our downfall, it is helpful to refer to the well-known article by Garrett Hardin entitled 'The Tragedy of the Commons' (1968).

In this article, Hardin explains that our socio-economic system and the way it promotes and stimulates all parties in it to engage in self-interested behaviours, has increased humanity's ability and tendency to overpopulate our world and to overuse its resources. He illustrates the resulting problem by using the example of herdsmen using a common pasture – a piece of grassland:

> As a rational being, each herdsman seeks to maximize his gain. Explicitly or implicitly, more or less consciously he asks, 'What is the utility to *me* of adding one more animal to my herd?' This utility has one negative and one positive component.
>
> 1. The positive component is a function of the increment of one animal. Since the herdsman receives all the proceeds from the sale of the additional animal, the positive utility is nearly +1.

2. The negative component is a function of the additional overgrazing created by one more animal. Since, however, the effects of overgrazing are shared by all herdsmen, the utility for any particular decision-making herdsman is only a fraction of –1.

Adding together the component partial utilities, the rational herdsman concludes that the only sensible course for him to pursue is to add another animal to his herd. And another, and another. But this is the conclusion reached by every rational herdsman sharing the commons. Therein is the tragedy. Each man is locked into a system that compels him to increase his herd without limit – in a world that is limited. Ruin is the destination toward all men rush, each pursuing his own best interest in a society that believes in the freedom of the commons.

(Hardin, 1968, p. 1244)

Ultimately, the ever-increasing number of animals will lead to overgrazing and the grassland will degrade. Animals will die and herdsmen will be left with no income and . . . tragedy. In other words, by acting in their own individual (short-term) best interests, these herdsmen are ruining their common grassland and, ultimately, all suffer the tragic consequences. The tragedy of the commons is a specific type of what we have come to understand as a social dilemma (Dawes, 1980). Social dilemmas represent situations in which it (seemingly) pays off for each individual to act in his or her own (short-term) best interest but all people would be better off (in the long run) if all people would act for the common good.

Obviously, with this example, Hardin is referring to what is happening to humanity and our planet. As explained in more detail in Chapter 6, by consistently basing our decisions on (short-term) self-interest, (the effects of) our behaviours are exceeding the carrying capacity of our planet, and all people will (eventually) suffer the consequences. Interestingly, though, it is exactly this type of decision-making that forms the foundation of our socio-economic system. We have followed Adam Smith's advice, so to speak, and have arranged our world based on values such as competition and promoting private property, autonomy and economic growth. What is more, in this system we have incorporated self-reinforcing mechanisms to ensure that we continue to make decisions based on the (short-term) self-interest of our country, our company, our family, and on our own individual (short-term) needs and wishes. This has not only resulted in a situation in which we are ruining our planet but also in severe inequalities in the current distribution of wealth and (thus) power. Most of us in so-called developed countries live privileged lives, but many others still live in poverty, do not have access to proper health care and education, have to fear for their lives as a result or armed conflicts, and so on. The challenge of sustainable development is to resolve these issues. Doing so involves adjusting our socio-economic system to one that is based on equality, inclusiveness and a responsible and sustainable way of interacting with our natural environment (Loorbach, 2014; Melissen, 2016; Melissen & Moratis, 2016). As this section has shown, this is not an easy challenge. Maybe it is best described as arm-wrestling a mightily strong and tenacious invisible hand.

SUSTAINABLE DEVELOPMENT AND THE BUSINESS WORLD

By now, you – the reader – might think that we – the authors of this book – are activists, probably socialists and, most likely, just plain crazy. Apparently, we want to completely overhaul the way we have arranged our world and simply start again from scratch. Just forget about economic principles and let us create a world without money, where everybody is nice to each other and to our planet. We are obviously taking this 'experience thing' quite literally, and seem to think that we could completely do without tangible products, and want to fight invisible hands. In other words, we have lost touch with reality and have obviously gone mad.

Ultimately, we will leave it up to you to decide whether the latter is true – although we would appreciate that you postpone your final judgement to after reading this book! Regardless of the mental state of the authors of this book, the fact remains that some drastic changes to the way we exploit our world's resources are urgently called for. The same applies to the way we distribute wealth across our world's population. This is not some vague dream of a bunch of diplomats at the United Nations. This is something that simply needs to be done for us, humans, to guarantee our survival on this planet in the long run. This is a conclusion reached and now widely communicated by a vast majority of all scientists, more and more worried civilians and grassroots movements, an increasing number of businesses and professionals, and (even) more and more politicians. Opinions on the exact route to follow might differ, but all agree on one thing: we ought to make some changes to the way we have arranged our world to fulfil our needs and wishes, and we ought to do so quickly.

The key question that needs answering then obviously is: who is going to make those changes? The previous chapter has highlighted that businesses and professionals in events, tourism and hospitality could function as catalysts for these changes. This section puts this potential in a wider context by exploring the responsibilities and possibilities of any business or professional to contribute to sustainable development, not just those pertaining to events, tourism and hospitality.

The responsibility of businesses and professionals

Obviously, the way we have currently arranged our world to fulfil our needs and wishes has been shaped by all of us over the course of time. We could try to blame Adam Smith for the negative effects of the socio-economic system we ended up with, but that would be both silly and pointless. Over the years, all of us, in our roles as consumers, voters, employees and employers, owners of both material and financial resources, politicians and members of civil movements, students and scientists, and so on, have jointly shaped the current arrangements. That also implies that, in theory, all of us could try to change these arrangements.

Unfortunately, governments and intergovernmental organisations have so far been rather reluctant to make or promote any (drastic changes) to our socio-economic system. Strict sustainability regulations are few and far between, and tax systems that are truly based on 'the polluter pays' principles have been discussed at great length by a number of individual politicians, political parties, governments and governmental agencies but actual (systematic) implementation is rare if not absent altogether. As discussed earlier, you could debate whether politicians and policy-makers are to blame for that. In most democratic systems around our world, we, voters, have not provided them with a mandate (yet) to make these changes. In fact, most politicians are all too aware that, within the context of four or five year election cycles, such drastic changes – that would probably negatively influence the financial resources of most voters and companies in the short term – would likely guarantee their time in office being restricted to one administration or less. No wonder they are reluctant.

As discussed earlier, we, the general public, in our roles as voters and consumers, are also not exactly showing an overwhelming enthusiasm to change the way we fulfil our needs and wishes. In most countries, the majority of us still vote for those that promise to pursue economic growth, increase our personal incomes and take away barriers that stand in the way of pursuing our (short-term) self-interests. Meanwhile, most of us also still actively contribute to our own tragedy of the commons (Hardin, 1968) on the scale of our planet by enjoying holidays on tropical islands that we travel to by plane or buying that fancy sports car that is sure to not only impress our friends but also make us feel young, confident and desirable (Melissen & Moratis, 2016). Even though many of us are aware of the (long-term) consequences of these types of behaviours for all of us, we persist to a large extent in making choices that favour our personal (short-term) self-interests in the various social dilemmas (Dawes, 1980) ingrained in our everyday lives. Not surprisingly, civil movements, non-governmental agencies, grassroots movements and so on do not (yet) receive the support, nor have the financial means and political power, needed to trigger any drastic changes to our socio-economic system.

So, this basically leaves the business world. Businesses and professionals have a crucial role to play in realising sustainable development. However, it is important to realise that this is not just the result of other stakeholders intentionally looking away from or at least proving to be reluctant to actively address this challenge. First, and maybe even foremost, one could argue that the business world has a moral obligation to contribute to sustainable development. The business world is a key beneficiary of the way we have currently arranged our world to satisfy our needs and wishes. Businesses and professionals make (significant) profits based on the current arrangements. As those arrangements are the cause of problems that affect us all, it would be quite natural for these parties to feel prompted to resolve them; especially since the ways many of them produce goods and services to make those profits are based on consuming significant amounts of natural resources and those production processes often come with pollution and disturbances to (local, regional and global) ecosystems. In other words, the ecological footprint associated with those production processes – as well as the processes involved with delivering the final products to customers and seducing potential customers to buy them – contributes quite significantly to the past and current overexploitation of Earth's resources. Further, the way a significant part of the business world has operated over the course of the last two centuries has clearly contributed to an unequal distribution of wealth across the globe and across social groups in our societies. To put it bluntly: many of our business leaders have willingly participated in the 'winner takes all' game called the free market. Obviously, one could argue that they had no choice because this is the only way to survive in our current socio-economic system. However, one could just as easily argue that those that have benefited from the rules of the game automatically bear a huge responsibility in assuring that others do not suffer the (disproportionate) negative consequences. In other words, the business world has a specific moral obligation to address the negative environmental and social consequences of our current system.

Second, the way businesses and professionals fulfil their role in our socio-economic system significantly impacts the behaviour of all other stakeholders in this system. In essence, they finance the current system. Our welfare state would not exist without the profits made by businesses and professionals. In most countries, national, regional and local governments rely on the taxes paid by companies – profit tax, employees – income tax, and consumers – value-added tax (VAT) or goods and services tax (GST) – to finance (national, regional and local) infrastructure, health care, education, safety, and so on. In some countries, politicians even need to rely on the direct financial support of companies for election campaigns. Most of us, in our role as consumers, rely on those companies to provide the products, services and experiences we crave. Most of us generate the money we need to pay for those products, services and experiences by working for those companies. Chapter 6 has already highlighted the way businesses and professionals in events, tourism and hospitality are intertwined with all levels of our societies. The same could be said for most other companies because they produce what we need to satisfy our needs and wishes. They pay our salaries and we live next to them, and so on. For most of us, businesses and professionals in a range of industries serve as co-creators of our lives (Melissen & Moratis, 2016).

Therefore, if we are to make drastic changes to the way we have arranged our world to fulfil our needs and wishes, the business world simply needs to be involved. Based on the arguments presented in this section, businesses and professionals – in events, tourism and hospitality, and in almost any other industry – are 'inextricably both part of the problem as well as the solution' (Warhurst, 2005, p. 155).

The business world's contribution so far

The best way to review the way businesses and professionals (can and do) contribute to sustainable development is to review the so-called business models they apply. A business model describes the rationale of how a company creates value, delivers value, and captures value (Osterwalder & Pigneur, 2010). In other words, the business models of companies relate to three key elements of the way in which they operate (Bocken et al., 2014; Melissen & Moratis, 2016):

1. The products, services and/or experiences they offer or provide to customers, including the way they are produced and the natural resources used for that.
2. The way in which they deliver these products, services or experiences to their customers.
3. The way in which they deal with costs and revenues.

Over the years, numerous businesses and professionals have already tried to incorporate sustainability principles in their business models. Most of these initiatives have focused on the first element mentioned above – the products, services and/or experiences that they offer and especially the way in which they are produced, including the natural resources needed for doing so. Many companies have adjusted the design of their tangible products and the processes needed to produce them to accommodate applying so-called recycling, cradle-to-cradle and circular economy principles and techniques. Companies around the world have also managed to (sometimes significantly) reduce pollution and the (non–renewable) energy needed for producing and using their products. A company widely recognised as one of the frontrunners in this area is Interface, a global carpet manufacturer. Through a range of initiatives and innovations they have managed to significantly reduce their dependence on oil as a raw material needed to produce carpet tiles. Almost all carpets that they now produce contain a significant portion of recycled materials, not only through setting up a network of carpet reclamation companies and leasing their carpets to their customers instead of selling them but, for instance, also through using reclaimed fishing nets in the nylon incorporated in these carpets. Based on these actions, it now looks like Interface might come very close to realising their ambition of reducing the ecological footprint of their production processes to zero. In fact, recently they have launched a new mission called Climate Take Back, which states that they do not want to stop there and actually aim to further improve their production processes and, consequently, create a negative ecological footprint, for instance by absorbing more greenhouse gases than they emit.

A range of other companies has made similar changes to their products and production processes. Many of these initiatives have contributed to reducing the raw materials and energy needed to produce and consume specific products, services and experiences. Others stimulate and engage in the use and production of renewable energy through switching to energy suppliers that apply solar and wind energy to generate electricity instead of oil, gas and coal, or even installing solar panels or wind turbines themselves. Overall, quite a few companies across our globe have addressed the environmental component of sustainable development in the (first two out of the three elements listed earlier of the) business models they apply.

Others have not stopped at addressing the environmental component and also engage in initiatives to address their social impact. In fact, these days the mission statements of quite a few companies, especially bigger companies and companies that are listed on the stock exchange, include ambitions with respect to making a positive contribution to the social component of sustainable development. Some choose to do so through investing in the working conditions and overall wellbeing of their own employees, while others actively contribute to improving the living conditions in local communities in which they operate or contribute materials/man hours/money to – or even set up their own – charity projects across the globe. Usually, these initiatives are part of so-called Corporate Social Responsibility (CSR) or Corporate Citizenship programmes. By engaging in initiatives that are, strictly speaking, not linked to their primary processes, you could argue that these companies also address the third key element of business models mentioned earlier. These days, many companies actually consider it their responsibility to (publicly) report on all consequences of their functioning from a people, planet and profit perspective – the well-known three Ps of the so-called triple bottom line introduced by John Elkington (1997). Companies like Coca-Cola have even introduced the position of Chief Sustainability Officer to coordinate and report on all the various initiatives they engage in – both within their own company and in wider society – and have set up their own foundation to cooperate in a range of projects across the globe with partners such as local and regional governments, aid organisations, foundations of other companies, and so on. It is quite interesting to visit the Coca-Cola website and review the various topics they focus on. Clearly, for companies such as Coca-Cola, sustainable development has become a multifaceted concept that they address in a number of ways.

Some businesses and professionals have taken matters one step further yet and explicitly focus on creating economic value through creating social value (Porter & Kramer, 2011). The business models applied by these businesses and professionals are often referred to as social or societal business models (Melissen & Moratis, 2016; Stubbs & Cocklin, 2008). The idea behind these business models is that, instead of having to rely on donations for survival, the best way to create significant environmental and social value across the globe is to organise those actions based on self-sustaining or even profit-focused business models. One of the best known examples of the latter is the Grameen Group: a network of businesses designed to alleviate poverty in Bangladesh. One of these businesses focuses on lending money to people who do not qualify for a loan from a regular bank, whereas another one has teamed up with the French company Danone in providing cheap but healthy nutrition to poor families. In 2006, the founder of the original company – the Grameen Bank – Muhammed Yunus was awarded the Nobel Peace Prize for these initiatives.

CASE STUDY 7.1   **PATAGONIA'S ACTIVIST BUSINESS MODEL: A COMPANY TURNED NGO?**

Lars Moratis

Readers of *The New York Times* might have been caught by surprise when seeing the full-page advertisement of a company urging people not to buy their stuff. Yes, you read that correctly: *not* to buy the stuff this company sells. That must at least sound somewhat counterintuitive if not outright crazy to a lot of people.

The advertisement was placed on 25 November 2011, the day before Black Friday. Black Friday is the day when the largest shopping-spree in the United States takes place. It got its name by being the proverbial first day in the year that retailers covered their operational costs and started to make a profit from selling their products. Business figures then turn from 'red' into 'black'.

So, was this advertisement a joke? No, it was not. Actually, it was a very serious initiative of a company called Patagonia to attract the attention of readers to an idea that is central to this company. Patagonia, a US-based outdoor clothing and equipment company, has become a true sustainability leader over the past years. Still, the company is not your typical sustainability leader who tries to contribute to environmental quality and social wellbeing by conducting business activities in slightly more sustainable fashion every day, but one which challenges the very socio-economic system that they – like all companies and consumers – are part of and that dictates our ideas about value creation. In fact, what Patagonia aimed for with this thought-through advertisement, is to challenge our modern culture of consumption. As the advertisement reads, this culture of consumption 'puts the economy of natural systems that support all life firmly in the red. We're now using the resources of one-and-a-half planets on our one and only planet. Because Patagonia wants to be in business for a good long time – and leave a world inhabitable for our kids – we want to do the opposite of every other business today. We ask you to buy less and to reflect before you spend a dime on this jacket or anything else.'

You may find it strange for a business to act in such a way. But just think of it: all of our consumption comes with a negative footprint, usually both in an environmental and a social sense. And that is exactly what Patagonia realised, despite all their efforts to become as sustainable as possible as a company. One of the most remarkable things is that they are fully open about this in the advertisement: 'The environmental cost of everything we make is astonishing. Consider the R2® Jacket shown, one of our best sellers. To make it required 135 liters of water, enough to meet the daily needs (three glasses a day) of 45 people. Its journey from its origin as 60% recycled polyester to our Reno warehouse generated nearly 20 pounds of carbon dioxide, 24 times the weight of the finished product. This jacket left behind, on its way to Reno, two-thirds its weight in waste. And this is a 60% recycled polyester jacket, knit and sewn to a high standard; it is exceptionally durable, so you won't have to replace it as often.'

While the advertisement has become a (sustainability) marketing classic, it has spurred Patagonia to further reconsider the ways they create value and reinvent their business model. Next to providing full product and supply chain transparency through its 'Footprint Chronicles', one of the initiatives the company took was to forge a partnership with eBay, developing a Patagonia-branded eBay channel where owners of Patagonia clothing who wanted to get rid of their jackets, vests, trousers and the like could simply offer their second-hand stuff to others. Patagonia also offered to repair and refurbish customers' goods in order to bring the quality of their offerings up to par again and receive more money for selling them. Quite smart – not only to keep people from buying new clothes and keep existing goods from being turned into waste, but also because Patagonia signals the enduring quality of its products, develops a new revenue stream from repair and refurbishment and taps into an entire new market segment and customer base through selling used Patagonia clothing. This campaign has evolved in the past couple of years into the 'Worn wear: Better than new' program, which celebrates the stories of people wearing Patagonia clothing, emphasises the value of repair and refurbishment, and offers an easy way to recycle the company's products. Currently, Patagonia operates the largest repair and refurbishing plant in the United States, employing over 40 people dedicated to extend the life of their products.

And as a final interesting feature of this company, in 2016 they published the book *Tools for Grassroots Activists – Best Practices for Success in the Environmental Movement*, containing lessons and ingredients for, among other things, taking on businesses by environmental activists. So, what are we dealing with here? A company in disguise as an NGO? A marketing-savvy sustainable business? Or just next-generation smart, responsible and successful entrepreneurship? You decide. You may find your answer in (not) buying that cool Patagonia jacket.

It would be fair to say that, over the years, many different types of companies have addressed a number of sustainability problems in a number of ways. Specific products are now produced in ways that require significant lower quantities of (various) natural resources and cause significantly less pollution and disturbances to ecosystems. Initiatives such as the Grameen Bank have provided opportunities to many people in poorer regions of our world – especially women – to create ways of generating an (increased) income. Those are clearly steps in the right direction within the context of adjusting the course of our societies to a sustainable one. Therefore, you might wonder why the problem of unsustainability has not yet been solved. Why are scientists and activists apparently still very worried and talking about a crisis? Why do specific politicians – and especially former politicians who no longer have to worry about re-election – continue to state that it is time for drastic actions? Why are more and more media channels reporting with quite serious tones of voice about the problems that apparently are still there and even becoming more serious as time passes? Why do authors of books on designing, staging and managing experiences feel the need to address this topic so extensively? The answer is both simple and sobering: those steps are still (way) too small, and the resulting changes to the way we have arranged our world to fulfil our needs and wishes are taking place at a rate that is still (way) too slow, to have the desired and needed effect.

One of the most important explanations for this links to the self-reinforcing mechanisms in our current socio-economic system discussed earlier (Melissen & Moratis, 2016). For companies to survive in our current system, which is based on the principles of the free market, they need to make a profit. Making profits requires a sizable market share, because you need the revenues generated by selling your products to pay for the materials and other resources to produce new products, and you need to do so in a way that benefits from the so-called principle of economies of scale – simply put: the more products you produce, the lower the costs per product because you can spread out investments for production facilities over a higher number of products. In the free market, for many companies, the only option to survive in the long run is to increase their profits based on increasing their market share. Otherwise, competitors will grab that market share, be able to lower their prices as a result and, consequently, put you out of business. Otherwise, shareholders will be disappointed about the return on their investment, prices for stocks in your company will drop and your possibilities to acquire the financial means for investing in new production facilities or maintaining the old ones will disappear. The reality thus is that most companies need to assess their sustainability initiatives within the context of these mechanisms. Consequently, most companies, also those who are genuinely motivated to contribute to sustainable development, are forced to look for ways of addressing sustainability that also contribute to making (more) profits. This implies that sustainability initiatives are usually treated as a business case – whether a company engages in them also depends on their contribution to cost reduction, profit margin, risk reduction, reputation and brand value (Schaltegger et al., 2011). Given that, as discussed earlier, both governments and consumers mostly further reinforce a focus on generating more revenues and reducing costs, through the regulations and tax systems they implement and the products they buy, it is no surprise that sustainability principles have not yet been fully incorporated in the business models applied by most businesses and professionals. As Marques and Mintzberg (2015) indicate, sustainability initiatives are mostly treated as add-ons, as icing on the cake. Whether they like it or not, most businesses and professionals are 'competing in the same baking contest: a baking contest in which the judges surely value a great icing, but in the end prizes are only awarded to those that have used the recipe of the free market in baking their cake' (Melissen & Moratis, 2016, p. 11). Wayne Visser (2011) has described this as the curse of CSR: the business models of companies in our socio-economic system have not really changed (yet) as a result of the self-reinforcing mechanisms incorporated in this system and, as a result, the overall picture is that the business world still mostly focuses on creating economic value, which is done 'at the expense of, and even through destroying, environmental and social value' (Melissen & Moratis, 2016, p.12).

Unfortunately, the same pretty much applies to companies claiming to use social business models. Take the example of the Grameen Bank. This bank offers loans to poor people. Usually, these loans are for much smaller amounts of money – so-called microcredits – than loans offered to (rich) people by regular banks. This implies that the costs involved per loan are higher per money unit because for

FIGURE 7.2 The baking contest called the free market

Artist: Anabella Meijer (www.kanai.nl)

instance administration costs are more or less the same for a loan of US$100 and a loan of US$10,000 dollars. Given that the Grameen Bank is operating as a for-profit company on the free market, this pretty much forces the bank to charge higher interest rates. This, in turn, increases the chances of borrowers not being able to repay the loan plus interest (in time), thus increasing the risks for the bank in offering those loans, which once again forces them to increase interest rates. Meanwhile, borrowers run an increased risk of ending up in a so-called debt trap – having to borrow even more money to be able to pay back earlier loans. Similar mechanisms have caused many more companies that started out with an explicit social or environmental mission to make significant concessions to their original mission to survive in the marketplace shaped by our current socio-economic system. Even though these companies set out to do things differently, the choice to operate as a company in the free market oftentimes forces them to play by the rules of that game. The idea of creating economic value through creating societal value has certainly gained popularity over the years, especially as a result of the introduction of the Creating Shared Value concept by management gurus Michael Porter and Mark Kramer in their famous article 'Creating Shared Value: Redefining Capitalism and the Role of the Corporation in Society' (2011). Such ambitions can now be found in the CSR programmes and missions of quite a few companies, including some influential and globally operating multinationals. However, and unfortunately, this concept has not fundamentally changed the role of the business world in our socio-economic system. Most companies that express such ambitions still (have to) abide with the existing rules of the game. Consequently, the actual contribution of the business world to realising sustainable development does not (yet) live up to the promises incorporated in the Creating Shared Value concept (Crane et al., 2014).

Sustainable business models and technologies

Some of the questions that thus need answering are: what would business models of companies have to look like to contribute to sustainable development at the rate that is required? How can businesses and professionals escape the lock-in of our current socio-economic system? The honest answer to these types of questions is: we are not quite sure yet. If answering these questions was that simple, we would have probably not ended up in the mess we find ourselves in. However, researchers and professionals have already developed a number of ideas, and have implemented and reviewed a number of variations of what could be considered to represent various prototypes of (truly) sustainable business models and technologies. These variations have been labelled social enterprises, B-corps, circular economy business models, sharing economy business models, and so on. In the end, obviously, the name given to a business model does not really matter; what matters is its contribution to realising sustainable development.

Lüdeke-Freund (2009, pp. 66–67) has tried to capture the essence of a sustainable business model by stating that it represents 'the activity system of a firm which allocates resources and coordinates activities in a value creation process which overcomes the public/private benefit discrepancy.' He continues by explaining that this should be done by

> extending value propositions to integrate public and private benefits [. . .], making customers involved and responsible partners in value creation processes [. . .], taking advantage of partnerships which enhance resources and activities [. . .], [. . .] and dedicating resources and activities to secure free, legitimate and legal behaviour and to explore currently neglected opportunities in non-market spheres.

Obviously, this would imply changes to all three key elements of a business model highlighted in the previous sub-section:

1. The products, services and/or experiences that these companies offer or provide to customers need to be based on value creation processes that integrate public and private benefits.
2. The delivery of these products, services and/or experiences to customers is based on involvement of and responsible partnerships with those customers.
3. Capturing value is not necessarily expressed (just) in terms of profits, and the context in which value is created is not necessarily limited to (just) the (logic of the) so-called free market.

In other words, sustainable business models are business models that (aim to) bridge the gap between self-interest and the common good. These business models cannot rely on an invisible hand to ensure that self-interest leads to results in the interest of wider society – we have tried Adam Smith's recipe and the resulting cakes have left a rather unpleasant aftertaste.

Therefore, sustainable business models actually need to be based on the opposite reference point: they need to purposely align the interests of the company with the interests of wider society. If we are to prevent new problems and repair the damages already done by our current socio-economic system, this involves much more than minimising the environmental impact of value creation processes through advanced physical technologies. There is no doubt that we will need those technologies but we will also need new so-called social technologies (Laukkanen & Patala, 2014). Social technologies refer to the way we organise our societies, and ourselves, including the businesses and professionals who co-create our societies and our lives. Earlier in this chapter and the previous one, these social technologies have been described as the arrangements for fulfilling our needs and wishes. Adjustments to these arrangements, and possibly designing and implementing new arrangements, will have to be based on the requirements linked to putting our societies on a sustainable course. As discussed earlier, these requirements relate to equality, inclusiveness and a responsible and sustainable way of interacting with our natural environment. Quite possibly, this will have to involve 'redefining what we consider to represent our needs in relation to what the Earth can provide and the search for an alternative to [free market] capitalism as the system assisting us in meeting those needs' (Melissen and Moratis, 2016, p. 13). It will definitely involve incorporating mechanisms to avoid or resolve some of the social dilemmas that lie at the core of unsustainable behaviour of people and organisations in our societies. This is not a simple task, to say the least. Doing so will probably require experimenting and taking risks, breaking some of the 'rules' laid down by (various actors within the) current arrangements, and developing and adjusting new rules along the way. This is not something an individual professional nor an individual business can do in isolation. The required changes and associated innovations in physical and social technologies are simply too complex, as is the context – our current socio-economic system with all its self-reinforcing mechanisms – in which they need to be developed and implemented (Bocken et al., 2014; Warhurst, 2005). Businesses and professionals who apply a sustainable business model thus have to collaborate with all stakeholders (directly or indirectly) involved with defining, producing and consuming the products, services and/or experiences that these models deliver. This includes other businesses and professionals, policy-makers and public authorities, civil and grassroots movements (Murphy & Bendell, 1997, 1999), *and* consumers! Even though the details of the arrangements that need to be developed may still be rather vague, one thing is crystal clear: to avoid a tragedy of the commons, the commons need to come together in shaping those arrangements to ensure that they serve the common good, also in the long run.

REFERENCE POINTS FOR SUSTAINABLE BUSINESSES AND PROFESSIONALS

So far, we have established that businesses models that are aligned with the principles of sustainable development are applied by businesses and professionals who collaborate with all stakeholders affected by their actions. Consequently, these businesses and professionals at the very least partly base these actions and the decisions they make on the interests, the views and the preferences of those stakeholders. Together with these stakeholders, these businesses and professionals need to decide on the value creation processes that will form the core of their business models and how they can ensure that these processes serve the interests of all stakeholders and thus the common good.

Ethical leadership, distribution of control and powers of persuasion

There is a marked contrast between serving the common good and (only) focusing on reducing costs, increasing profit margins and overcoming competitors based on the rules of the free market game. Basing your decisions, at least partly, on how your company can best serve the common good is something that not everybody will understand. One could even argue that doing so goes against some of the values that have become ingrained in the way most of us live our lives. As indicated earlier in this chapter, most people, especially those living in (rich) democracies, will not automatically accept and will probably find it hard to imagine living their lives and making decisions based on other values than the ones that form the core of our current socio-economic system. We have grown so accustomed to living our lives and making our decisions based on those 'old' values that switching to 'new' ones almost feels unnatural. Consequently, if and when a business or professional decides to start doing things differently, to base decisions on the principles of sustainable development, this might very well lead to some raised eyebrows, mistrust, even confusion. This requires courage and vision of those making those decisions (Melissen & Moratis, 2016). It requires conviction and commitment to not stop at answering the question whether you are doing things in the right way but to also address – and invite others to join you in answering – the question whether you are doing the right things for the right reasons. Steadfastly basing your actions on finding answers to both questions, even when others – including your own colleagues, employees and customers – might sometimes react in ways that clearly show they suspect you have completely lost the plot, requires something that is probably best described as ethical leadership (Ciulla, 2005).

However, leadership means nothing if nobody is willing to follow you and join you in your quest to base your company's business model on the principles of sustainable development. In fact, as discussed earlier, doing so is not something that one business or one professional can accomplish without the help of others. Developing and implementing value creation processes that truly integrate public and private benefits requires developing and implementing advanced, oftentimes new, physical and social technologies. These cannot be developed and implemented without the support and involvement of others. You will need to join forces with parties such as other companies, policy-makers and researchers, maybe even activists, to get access to enough resources, imagination and knowledge to create them. Even if your company is lucky enough to have all those resources, enough imagination and the required knowledge in house, you still need those other parties to support you in experimenting with alternatives to the arrangements incorporated in our current socio-economic system. You still need their support to provide you with a so-called (social) licence to operate (Warhurst, 2005), otherwise you will be all alone in fighting the mighty invisible hand of the free market and the outcome of that fight is pretty predictable based on the discussion presented in the previous sections of this chapter. However, if you want those other parties to share their expertise, their imagination and their knowledge, and to support you in setting up the value creation processes that form the core of your business model, you will have to accept that they will probably like to have a say in what value will be created and how. You will have to accept the concept of distributed control (Loorbach, 2014): giving up some autonomy and share power with respect to decisions about your company and the business model you apply with people outside of your company. Given that you are now collaborating with others in creating value based on integrating public and private benefits means that your needs and wishes as a business or professional are no longer the only ones to consider in making decisions about the value creation processes that you bring to the table (Stubbs & Cocklin, 2008).

Finally, you will probably also need considerable powers of persuasion to make all this work. For instance, you might have to lobby and team up with influential other parties 'to persuade policy-makers and public authorities to adjust regulatory systems or to at least allow you to not follow current regulations to the letter' (Melissen & Moratis, 2016, p. 14). You will definitely have to convince those assisting you and supporting you in developing and implementing new physical and social technologies that you are 'for real'. Within the context of our current socio-economic system, it might not be a sinecure to make others believe that you really want to 'be part of a community or network that is based on long-term commitment and true reciprocity rather than short-term gains and opportunism' (Melissen & Moratis, 2016, p. 15). As discussed earlier, most of us have grown so accustomed to living our lives within a context based on pursuing self-interest that it might take some time and effort to convince people that you really want to do things differently and to have them join you in your quest or allow you to join theirs. And then, finally, there is the customer. There is really no point in implementing a sustainable business model if it fulfils non-existing needs and wishes. A business model without customers is not a business model but a hobby! A sustainable business model can only contribute to sustainable development if consumers are willing to accept it as an appropriate way of satisfying their needs and wishes. So far, businesses and professionals who have incorporated sustainability principles into the products, services and/or experiences they offer, and the way in which they produce and deliver them, have not always found it easy to seduce enough consumers to actually consume them. Most of us, the general public, are pretty aware of the unsustainable course of our societies. We know driving a car or flying an aeroplane is contributing to climate change. We are perfectly aware of the fact that we should really wear an extra sweater instead of turning up the thermostat in our house. More and more of us understand that eating meat comes with consumption of enormous amounts of water and greenhouse gas emissions. Nobody can say that he or she is not aware of the fact that people in specific regions of our world have to live their lives in circumstances that can only be described as inhuman. And still, we continue to consume large quantities of products and services that contribute to these problems. Therefore, changing our consumption patterns and convincing consumers to satisfy their needs and wishes through products, services and/or experiences produced by sustainable business models might very well be the biggest challenge for businesses and professionals applying them. This will require them to develop some impressive powers of persuasion.

Naïve, native and narrative intelligence

Obviously, the specific physical and social technologies that have to be developed within the context of applying a specific sustainable business model depend on the specific products, services and/or experiences involved. A sustainable business model for an event will look quite different from a sustainable business model for a hotel. The physical technologies involved with sustainable transport of visitors to festival grounds are different from the physical technologies involved with sustainable heating of hotel rooms, although some of the basic principles – such as using renewable energy sources instead of oil, gas and coal – might be similar. The social technologies involved with accounting for the interests of local residents living near the grounds of a hard-rock music festival will differ from the social technologies needed to account for the interests of local residents living in the neighbourhood of a five-star hotel, although some of the basic principles – such as open communication and possibly creating opportunities to benefit from your presence – might again be similar. Given that visitors to a hard-rock music festival and guests in a five-star hotel might not always be the same type of people, with the same preferences, needs and wishes, persuading them to display sustainable behaviour and consume sustainable products, services and/or experiences might require different strategies. Then again, in essence, people are not that different. We might dress differently, we might talk differently, but we all want to be happy, safe, loved, and so on. We all move on to higher-level needs in Maslow's hierarchy once our basic needs are satisfied. Therefore, strategies to influence different customer segments can probably apply common principles. Principles that are based on a full understanding of what makes people behave the way they behave – what makes them tick. The same applies to convincing other stakeholders to join you and support you in your efforts to develop and implement a sustainable business model. A seasoned politician and an environmental activist will talk differently, probably dress differently, but they are both still people.

FIGURE 7.3 Sustainability intelligence

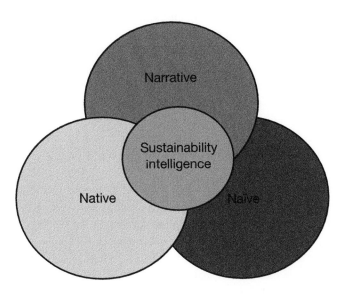

In other words, even though the details of sustainable business models might differ depending on the context in which they are applied, the basic reference points on which they are based will be the same. Regardless of the specific products, services and/or experiences that you offer, the trains of thought that you will have to apply in doing so will be quite similar if you want to do so in a sustainable manner. The specific (physical and social) technologies to be incorporated in your business model might differ but the way of reasoning on which they are based is the same. If we refer to this way of reasoning as sustainability intelligence, three specific types of sustainability intelligence can be distinguished that constitute important reference points for developing and implementing sustainable business models (Melissen & Moratis, 2016, 2017):

1. naïve intelligence;
2. native intelligence;
3. narrative intelligence.

Naïve intelligence relates to the types of reasoning, learning and actions needed to escape the lock-in of our current socio-economic system. Given that the types of arrangements needed to do so will be quite different from what is generally considered 'normal' or 'logical' within the context of our current socio-economic system, you need to be able to look at things differently and do things differently. Developing these arrangements cannot only rely on existing knowledge and technologies and thus requires a certain freshness, openness and intuitiveness to come up with new solutions, a new way of doing things. Given that some of these solutions and actions will probably raise some eyebrows at first and be considered by some as rather naïve, trivial or primitive (Melissen & Moratis, 2016), this might take some perseverance. You might be taking some (mental) punches before you will be able to convince others of the fact that your solutions and actions are not naïve, trivial or primitive but rather 'intelligent' from a sustainable development perspective and thus from the perspective of your *and* their interests. You might call this thinking and acting consciously naïve because this is the only way to escape the lock-in. As such, naïve intelligence is not the same as ignorance but rather relates to applying 'a certain level of healthy and deliberate unprejudiced appreciation of old and new ideas, and the assumptions behind existing and new business models, through a truly reflexive process' (Melissen & Moratis, 2017, p. 70).

Native intelligence relates to the types of reasoning, learning and actions needed to convince others – policy-makers, civil movements, employees, consumers, and so on – to participate in and support (shaping) your value creation processes and using the products, services and/or experiences they produce. Convincing these 'others' will need to be based on a full understanding of what makes them tick. Synonyms for native are terms like inborn, natural, innate and normal. Native relates to: what makes people do the things they do? What makes them behave the way they do? What makes them make the decisions they make? Native intelligence thus relates to using these mechanisms to convince or even seduce others to join you in making your sustainable business model a success. Simultaneously, the term 'native' is also often used in relation to indigenous people. A specific characteristic of these people is 'age-old knowledge and capacity [. . .] to solve problems based on ancient wisdom and without relying on modern technologies in doing so' (Melissen & Moratis, 2017, p. 71). Applying this type of intelligence links to understanding the importance of local value creation processes and local networks, a reciprocal relationship with nature, and taking matters into your own hands instead of relying on an invisible hand. Together, these two interpretations of the word native explain what is meant by native intelligence: types of reasoning, learning and actions that are based on a full understanding of people, their behaviours, how these behaviours have evolved over time, and how to tap into the evolutionary processes that shaped us as humans in adjusting the course of our societies (Griskevicius et al., 2012). How to do the latter is addressed in more detail in the next chapter.

Narrative intelligence relates to the types of reasoning, learning and actions needed to successfully make use of the fact that people are 'narrative animals' (Mateas & Sengers, 1999). In order for others to join and support you in your efforts to base your actions and decisions as a business or professional on the principles of sustainable development, this needs to make sense and appeal to them. If consumers are going to consider your products, services and/or experiences as appropriate means of satisfying their needs, they need to understand the benefits involved with consuming them. Regardless of the specific party you are reaching out to, it will involve creating a picture of what the value is that your business model is going to create and ensuring that the picture is appealing. You need to be able to explain what it is that you are aiming for. This requires communication and storytelling techniques.

It probably involves co-creating a description with others of what it is that your sustainable business model is going to bring to them. Ultimately, your sustainable business model cannot but be based on a specific narrative: a description of the arrangements involved with it and the benefits these bring to all involved.

Interestingly, these three types of sustainability intelligence are actually quite closely linked to some of the topics discussed in the first five chapters of this book. The healthy and deliberate unprejudiced appreciation of old and new ideas that forms the basis of naïve intelligence is very similar to the types of reasoning involved in any design process, also those aimed at designing experiences. Understanding what make people tick has been discussed in Chapter 2 and is crucial not only to sustainable business models but also to designing, staging and managing experiences successfully. The relevance of a proper and appealing storyline as well as co-creation with customers has been highlighted repeatedly in the first part of this book. If any business or professional should be able to co-create appealing narratives, it should be those that stage experiences.

Not surprisingly, Chapter 6 has already concluded that the rise of the experience economy and the pursuit of sustainable development represent two developments that not only fit with each other but also strengthen and reinforce each other. Based on the reference points that have been established in this chapter, the remaining chapters of this book further explore how experiences can be designed, staged and managed successfully in a sustainable manner.

SUMMARY

Based on reading this chapter, we hope you will understand and remember the following:

- The way our socio-economic system has changed over the course of the last two centuries.
- These changes are linked and form a key explanation for the unsustainable course of our societies.
- The invisible hand of free markets.
- The tragedy of the commons.
- The roles of values, worldviews and social dilemmas in explaining the challenges involved with pursuing sustainable development.
- The responsibility of businesses and professionals in realising sustainable development.
- The way the business world so far has tried to contribute to sustainable development.
- The reference points for truly sustainable business models and technologies.

- The roles of ethical leadership, distribution of control and powers of persuasion in pursuing sustainable development as a business or professional.
- The three types of intelligence that play a crucial role in developing and implementing sustainable business models and technologies:
  - o   naïve intelligence;
  - o   native intelligence;
  - o   narrative intelligence.
- The apparent link between sustainability intelligence and designing, staging and managing experiences.

FOOD FOR THOUGHT

Based on the content of this chapter, the following questions, challenges and topics could serve as interesting starting points for further discussion:

- Which company would you consider to be the most sustainable company in the world? Why?

- How does this company apply sustainability intelligence? How could they apply it even more?

- How many of the activities you engage in, in your daily life, are (ultimately) based on economic transactions? Is this a problem, from a sustainable development perspective? Why?

- To what extent do you possess sustainability intelligence? Do you already apply it in your daily life? Why?

- How would you describe your worldview?

REFERENCES

Bhagwati, J. (2011). Markets and morality. *American Economic Review: Papers and Proceedings 2011*, 101(3), 162–165.

Bocken, N., Short, S., Rana, P. & Evans, S. (2014). A literature and practice review to develop sustainable business model archetypes. *Journal of Cleaner Production*, 65, 42–56.

Ciulla, J. (2005). The state of leadership ethics and the work that lies before us. *Business Ethics: A European Review*, 14, 323–335.

Crane, A., Palazzo, G., Spence, L. & Matten, D. (2014). Contesting the value of 'creating shared value'. *California Management Review*, 56, 130–153.

Dawes, R.M. (1980). Social dilemmas. *Annual Review of Psychology*, 31(1), 169–193.

Elkington, J. (1997). *Cannibals with forks: The triple bottom line of 21st century business*. Oxford: Capstone.

Griskevicius, V., Cantú, S. & van Vught, M. (2012). The evolutionary bases for sustainable behaviour: Implications for marketing, policy, and social entrepreneurship. *Journal of Public Policy & Marketing*, 31, 115–128.

Hardin, G.R. (1968). The tragedy of the commons. *Science*, 162, 1243–1248.

Laszlo, E. (2001). Human evolution in the third millennium. *Futures*, 23(4), 349–372.

Loorbach, D. (2014). *To transition! Governance panarchy in the new transformation*. Rotterdam: Erasmus University Rotterdam.

Laukkanen, M. & Patala, S. (2014). Analysing barriers to sustainable business model innovation: Innovation systems approach. *International Journal of Innovation Management*, 18, 1440010.

Lüdeke-Freund, F. (2009). *Business model concepts in corporate sustainability contexts: From rhetoric to a generic template for 'business models for sustainability'*. Working paper. Lüneberg: Center for Sustainability Management, Leuphana Universität Lüneburg.

Marques, J. & Mintzberg, H. (2015). Why corporate social responsibility isn't a piece of cake. *MIT Sloan Management Review*, 56, 7–11.

Mateas, M. & Sengers, P. (1999). Narrative intelligence. (1999): *Proceedings of the AAAI fall symposium on narrative intelligence* (pp. 1–10). Palo Alto, CA: AAAI Press.

Melissen, F. (2016). *Fourth generation sustainable business models*. Breda: NHTV Breda University of Applied Sciences.

Melissen, F. & Moratis, L. (2016). A call for fourth generation sustainable business models. *The Journal of Corporate Citizenship*, 63, 8–16.

Melissen, F. & Moratis, L. (2017). Developing fourth generation sustainability-oriented business models: Towards naïve, native, and narrative intelligence. In S.O. Idowu, S. Vertigans, & A. Schiopoiu Burlea (Eds.), *Corporate social responsibility in times of crisis: Practices and cases from Europe, Africa and the world* (pp. 59–76). Berlin: Springer.

Murphy, D. & Bendell, J. (1997). *In the company of partners: Business, environmental groups and sustainable development post-Rio*. Bristol: The Policy Press.

Murphy, D.F. & Bendell, J. (1999). *Partners in time? Business, NGOs and sustainable development. UNRISD Discussion Paper, 109*. Geneva: United Nations Research Institute for Social Development.

Osterwalder, A. & Pigneur, Y. (2010). *Business model generation: A handbook for visionaries, game changers, and challengers*. Hoboken, NJ: John Wiley & Sons.

Porter, M. & Kramer, M. (2011). Creating shared value. *Harvard Business Review*, 89, 62–77.

Schaltegger, S., Lüdeke-Freund, F. & Hansen, E. (2011). *Business cases for sustainability and the role of business models innovation: Developing a conceptual framework*. Lüneberg: Centre for Sustainability Management.

Smith, A. (1776, 1976). *The wealth of nations*. Chicago, IL: Chicago University Press.

Stubbs, W. & Cocklin, C. (2008). Conceptualizing a 'sustainable business model'. *Organization & Environment*, 21, 103–127.

Varul, M. (2013). Towards a consumerist critique of capitalism: A socialist defence of consumer culture. *Ephemera – theory and politics in organization*, 13, 293–315.

Visser, W. (2011). *The age of responsibility: CSR 2.0 and the new DNA of business*. London: Wiley.

Warhurst, A. (2005). Future roles of business in society: The expanding boundaries of corporate social responsibility and a compelling case for partnership. *Futures*, 37, 151–168.

PART III

CO-CREATING
SUSTAINABLE
EXPERIENCES

Sustainability and experiences: a match made in heaven?

INTRODUCTION

The previous two chapters have addressed the topic of sustainable development. They have also established that the challenge of sustainable development and the rise of the experience economy represent two developments that not only seem to fit with each other but also strengthen and reinforce each other. If you would have to pick one type of business and professional who would or, at the very least, could be adept at applying sustainability intelligence, you would pick those that focus on designing, staging and managing experiences. What is more, the industries that are naturally linked to staging experiences – events, tourism and hospitality – represent industries that could be argued to be perfectly poised to act as catalysts in adjusting the course of our societies to a more sustainable one.

This chapter further explores what is needed to turn this apparent link between sustainability and experiences into a healthy, possibly even blossoming relationship. The first section discusses the various levels of intimacy in this relationship that

FIGURE 8.1 Experiences and sustainability: a blossoming relationship?

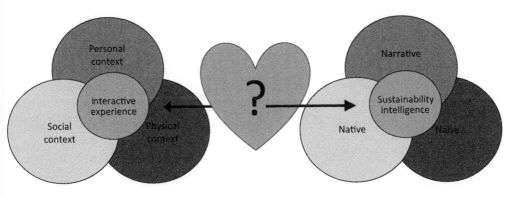

businesses and professionals offering those experiences could and maybe even should aim for. It also addresses some of the reference points for and challenges involved in doing so. Promising avenues for tackling one specific challenge – i.e. convincing or even 'seducing' consumers to accept or even 'learn to prefer' sustainable ways of fulfilling their needs and wishes – is discussed in more detail in the second section of this chapter. The third and final section then puts these reference points and challenges into context by linking them to what has been discussed in the first five chapters of this book. In doing so, it also explains why staging experiences in a sustainable manner requires addressing this topic as early as in the design of those experiences.

SUSTAINABLE EXPERIENCES: FROM THE BASICS TO GOING ALL OUT

As indicated in the previous chapter, the specific physical and social technologies involved in applying sustainable business models depend on the specific products, services and/or experiences created by those business models. The same applies to businesses and professionals offering experiences; this still represents a range of companies with a wide variety of experiences that incorporate very different tangible and intangible components. Even if we limit ourselves to businesses and professionals within events, tourism and hospitality, it is clear that the physical and social technologies applied by a mega-sports event are completely different from the ones applied by a small bed and breakfast. However, the underlying logic for incorporating sustainable development principles into the experience offered, the way it is staged, and the way the business or professional doing so interacts with 'relevant others' is pretty much the same. Basically, you could distinguish four levels of ambition in addressing sustainability by companies offering experiences – four levels or generations of strategic orientation with respect to integration of sustainable development principles into the business models they apply (Melissen & Moratis, 2016).

Level 1: addressing your environmental impact

Trying to reduce the negative environmental impact associated with the ultimate product offered to and consumed by customers is something that a number of companies already do. You could even argue that this is the least any company could or actually should do – not just from an ethical perspective, but also from a business-economic perspective. Even though changes to our socio-economic system might not be happening at the rate required for long-term sustainable development yet, at least clearly showing that you put effort into addressing your own negative environmental impact as a company is slowly but surely becoming the norm in today's market place. These days, most companies and governmental organisations will not book hotel rooms (for their employees) in hotels that do not at least meet the standards of specific environmental certification schemes. Even though most consumers are not willing to pay more for sustainable products and services (yet), more and more of us now prefer the sustainable alternative if it is offered for the same price. This is a clear trend in the market place and one that not a lot of companies can afford to neglect. Especially in the long run, given the magnitude of the problems our societies are faced with and ever-increasing attention paid to these problems by the media, policy-makers, civil movements and your competitors alike, not doing so would seriously damage your company's so-called (social) licence to operate. This also applies to businesses and professionals operating in events, tourism and hospitality, and for any other type of company offering experiences.

Many if not most experiences consist of intangible *and* tangible components. A restaurant offering a fine-dining experience serves food and drinks, and usually this is done in a specific building. A theme park offering thrills and excitement uses rollercoasters but also parades and shows with various tangible attributes to let you escape reality for a day, within the context of a physical world specifically created to support these touch points and your overall customer journey, also through offering food, drinks, gifts, souvenirs, and so on. A hotel offers hospitality and this concept is based on the behaviour of staff in combination with offering you food and/or drinks and accommodation. Beyond the context of events, tourism and hospitality, almost all companies that apply experiences as part of their value proposition also incorporate tangible elements in the ultimate product they offer to their customers. Consider the example in Chapter 6 regarding the fashion boutique: a clothing shop offering not only clothes but also food and drinks to customers within the context of staging an experience based on creating an environment in which you can pleasantly interact with likeminded people and decide on what scarf would best compliment your facial features while discussing the state of our world. Some of these shops are actually the physical components of a much broader concept based on combining physical outlets with a website offering all clothing available in the physical outlets and much more for online sales. For some brands, physical boutiques have now been turned into showrooms and meeting places to promote the brand, while the vast majority of the actual economic transactions between the company and customers take place online.

All of these tangible components of the various types of touch points used to create customer journeys that appeal to consumers require natural resources to create them and to deliver them to customers. That means all of the principles and techniques for reducing pollution and the use of (non-renewable) energy and material resources discussed in the previous two chapters could, in theory, be applied by any business or professional offering experiences. Any company offering food and drinks can address the environmental consequences linked to doing so, regardless of whether this represents their core business – such as for a restaurant – or something they have added to their original business model as a smart way of responding to the rise of the experience economy – such as clothing shops offering food and drinks. Opportunities to serve local, seasonal and organic produce, as well as vegetarian and vegan options, are 'growing' by the day, as is the willingness of consumers to at least try them. Rollercoasters require a lot of energy to operate them but the ride is just as exciting if it is powered by electricity generated by solar panels instead of gas or coal. The latest LED light bulbs can create the same pleasant, warm atmosphere in your restaurant or hotel room as any other type of light bulbs. The actual clothing offered by a physical outlet and online can be produced using recycled materials, in a factory that does not emit enormous amounts of greenhouse gases and pollute air, water and soil. Speaking of clothing, why could staff involved in the intangible component of experiences – the ones offering food and drinks, playing roles in shows, communicating with customers, and so on – not wear uniforms produced by those sustainable clothing companies instead of the unsustainable ones. Staff operating backstage, such as cleaning staff, do not have to use petrol-powered vehicles to get from one end of the theme park to the other; there are plenty of electricity-powered alternatives. Finally, just the actual decision to adapt your business model and base it more on selling experiences and less on selling (tangible) products opens up a world of possibilities to reduce the amounts of natural resources required and pollution and disturbances caused by your company, regardless of the sector in which you operate.

It is beyond the scope of this book and actually impossible to review or even simply list all options available to almost any business or professional to minimise the negative environmental impact associated with staging experiences. Smart solutions, sustainable alternatives and technological innovations for almost any tangible product, production process and delivery process are already known, available and promoted by a growing number of companies, policy-makers, civil movements and researchers alike. What is more, the rise of the experience economy only reinforces the possibilities for almost all companies to address the environmental component of sustainable development through staging experiences. Therefore, for any business or professional, trying to reduce their negative environmental impact through or linked to staging experiences is pretty much the least they can do.

Level 2: also address your social (and economic) impact

Businesses and professionals staging experiences need not limit themselves to addressing their environmental impact; they can also address the social component of sustainable development. As discussed in Chapter 6, this social component relates to fulfilling people's needs and wishes and ensuring a decent quality of life for all.

One of the most obvious ways for companies staging experiences to address this component is to address the working conditions and overall wellbeing of their own employees. This involves paying them a decent salary, letting them work reasonable working hours, providing them with safe and healthy working environments, treating them fairly and with respect, and so on. However, this also involves a number of the issues discussed in Chapter 5, such as job rotation, empowerment and creating opportunities to fulfil social needs. As has been highlighted in that chapter, some companies in events, tourism and hospitality could be argued to suffer from 'warm body syndrome', quite the opposite of caring for the wellbeing of your employees. Obviously, from a sustainable development perspective, this is simply unacceptable. Companies claiming to operate sustainably should at the very least address the needs and wishes of their own employees. Similar to addressing environmental issues, this is not only a requirement from an ethical perspective, but also from a business–economic perspective. Time and time again, research has shown that companies that invest in their employees – through higher wages, training and development opportunities, empowerment, and so on – are directly rewarded for those efforts through better performance and higher productivity. This is especially true for companies that stage experiences because an important element of those experiences is the interaction quality – which is based on the expertise, attitude and behaviour of employees that interact with customers. Better-trained, knowledgeable, satisfied and committed staff are far more likely to interact with customers in ways that meet or even exceed those customers' expectations. The same applies to those working backstage; if they know what they are doing, why they are doing that and – probably most importantly – want to be doing that, this significantly improves overall performance of the organisation. In other words, investing in employees' wellbeing not only benefits those employees but also the company employing them. It is a no-brainer, really.

Interestingly, one could argue that if any type of company would be capable of addressing the needs and wishes of employees, it would be those staging experiences. The first five chapters of this book have reviewed what you would need to know, understand and do to meet or even exceed the expectations of customers. Obviously, the very same principles and techniques could be applied to employees. Their values, their higher order Maslow needs, their responses to cues and stimuli, and their ways of learning are not fundamentally different from those of customers. Therefore, many of the approaches that could be used to address the needs and wishes of customers could also be applied to address the needs and wishes of employees.

What is more, addressing particular sustainability aspects can prove to be a complex challenge. As highlighted in Chapter 7, successfully dealing with some of these challenges requires adjusting and developing new physical and social technologies, which can require specific expertise, perseverance and imagination. You will need all the help you can get to make this work, also from your own employees. Some of those employees might very well have interesting ideas about how to do things differently, more efficiently, using fewer resources – in a more sustainable way. Simultaneously, by informing employees about and involving them in decision-making with respect to sustainability initiatives, not only will their understanding and knowledge of these initiatives increase, their support for these initiatives and their overall engagement with the company will increase as well, especially given the fact that working on sustainability can provide purpose and make work activities more meaningful. Just as consumption has increasingly become a way to express who you are or want to be for today's consumers, 'making a difference through their [. . .] job' (Glavas, 2012, p. 5) has more and more become a priority for today's employees. Consequently, engaging in sustainability initiatives, such as reducing the negative environmental impact of staging specific experiences, in turn can lead to 'a positive influence on the engagement, productivity and wellbeing of employees' (Glavas, 2012, p. 14). In other words, investing in employees is crucial both from a sustainable development and from a business–economic perspective, while investing in sustainability initiatives and involving employees in those initiatives is a very promising way of doing so. Maybe, just maybe, this is the type of self-reinforcing mechanisms that could counterbalance those incorporated in the game called the free market. At the very least, the mechanisms at work here deserve our attention and, therefore, are discussed in more detail in the next section of this chapter.

Within the context of the discussion presented in this section, it is important to note that caring for the wellbeing of your employees is obviously not the only way to address the social component of sustainable development. A business or professional staging experiences could also address the impact of staging them in local communities. A number of the issues involved have already been discussed in Chapter 6, especially with respect to businesses and professionals operating in events, tourism and hospitality. Once again, given that not only the physical environment but also the social environment in which you stage experiences can significantly influence the overall experience of your customers, it not only makes sense from a sustainable development perspective to address these issues but also from a business–economic perspective. If a hotel, restaurant or event causes local businesses to go bankrupt, you cannot expect local inhabitants to welcome your guests or visitors with open arms. If your festival, conference or theme park disturbs the local community through causing traffic jams or noise pollution, it is hard to imagine local people directing your customers to your entrance with a smile. Even though you are probably not legally responsible for rubbish left by your customers on the streets outside of your festival grounds or hotel, it is not unreasonable to say that you are at least partially and morally responsible for cleaning up. Obviously, the specific aspects that you could address depend on the location and specifics of the experience you stage. These are also not limited to businesses and professionals operating in events, tourism and hospitality. Fashion boutiques serving drinks need to be careful not to send their customers on their way home in their car after having selected exceptionally bright coloured trousers, if that choice was clearly influenced by a high amount of alcohol consumption. In fact, those same boutiques ought to account for the impact of serving alcohol on the café next door – it might not appreciate the competition.

Obviously, addressing the social component of sustainable development is not limited to your own employees and local communities. Some of the tangible products you use to stage your experiences might very well have been produced in different parts of the world. If you take the social impact of your business model seriously, you also account for working conditions of those employees and the impact of production of your tangibles on those local communities in decisions you make regarding the tangibles to be used in staging your experiences. Maybe you could use your influence as an important client of a factory on the other side of the world to improve working conditions of its workers. Perhaps you could join forces with non-governmental agencies to improve the lives of people living there. Once again, the options available to almost any business or professional to address the social impact associated with staging the experiences they offer are almost endless.

What is more, there is no reason why you would have to stop reducing the negative impact of your experiences. Both with respect to environmental and social issues, businesses and professionals can engage in a number of initiatives to contribute to improving the state of our natural world or the quality of life of people. In fact, numerous companies do so, also those offering experiences as their core product. This ranges from Disney giving more than US$400 million to non-profit organisations around the world helping kids, families and communities in need to a local restaurant handing out free meals to homeless people. These types of initiatives are often referred to as CSR, Corporate Citizenship, philanthropy, accounting for the Triple Bottom Line, or simply 'giving back to the world'. Many of them make a difference – a positive difference. What distinguishes this second level of ambition with respect to incorporating sustainable development principles in the business model applied from the third level is that the core product offered to consumers – the experience staged for customers – is still mostly based on serving the (financial) interests of the company involved. If those interests allow for it – or sometimes even are served by investing in sustainability, for instance through creating a positive brand image for potential customers – companies applying these business models can and often do make sizable contributions to sustainable development.

Level 3: creating economic value through creating societal value

Chapter 7 has already indicated how – at least in theory – businesses and professionals could take matters a step further. They could apply so-called social or societal business models and purposely set out to create societal value through operating as a business. Even though the discussion in the previous chapter has highlighted that the road to doing so is full of nasty traps and it might be difficult to fully escape the impact of the invisible hand of the free market, one could argue that if any type of company could give it a good try it would be those staging experiences.

A very interesting example in this respect is the Eden Project – a visitor attraction in Cornwall, UK. The park is located in a reclaimed kaolinite pit. The core of this visitor attraction is formed by two huge biomes – domes that house plants. Each of them replicates a specific type of environment: (1) a rainforest, and (2) a Mediterranean environment. The park also hosts pop concerts, and includes gardens, classrooms, art exhibitions and sculptures, such as a giant bee and the so-called WEEE Man: a towering figure made from discarded electronics that shows the average amount of electrical waste generated by one person over a lifetime. This project is set up as a company in the sense that it needs to generate enough financial resources through funding, loans and sales (of entry tickets) to survive. However,

FIGURE 8.2 The Eden Project

Courtesy of: the Eden Project

the purpose of this project – as conceived by its initiator Tim Smit – is not to make as much profit as possible but to educate people on the relationship between people and plants. As such, this project helps to raise awareness about environmental problems *and* possible solutions. To support the latter, the Eden Project is currently trying to raise enough money to build a geothermal power plant to create enough renewable energy for the Eden Project and the surrounding community – some 5,000 houses of people living near the attraction park. Furthermore, this initiative has given rise to a number of (international) spin-off projects with respect to educating people on environmentally responsible practices. At the heart of all of this lie the experiences staged in the attraction park: experiences based on being immersed in a rainforest without having to step onto an aeroplane to travel to Brazil; experiences based on actually interacting with plants; experiences based on the crucial role of water for our ecosystems as well as experiences that apply the principles of biophilia – a concept discussed in Chapter 6 – to stimulate greater appreciation among visitors for the natural environment and thus encourage them to engage in sustainable behaviour during their visit and also after leaving the park; and, finally, experiences that people apparently want to consume, given that the park now attracts over a million visitors a year. Obviously, it is impossible to measure the exact (lasting) impact this project has on the behaviour of its visitors once they have returned home. The answer to the question whether it has truly managed to create a transformative experience is probably different for different types of visitors. However, the concept of biophilia suggests that it would not be unreasonable to expect at least some of them to become more environmentally aware and change at least some of their behaviours accordingly.

This specific example highlights the potential of businesses and professionals to create societal value through staging experiences. There is no better environment which lets people try out sustainable alternatives to satisfying some of their everyday needs and wishes than pleasant, exciting experiences staged by those who know how to stage them successfully. Chapter 6 has already highlighted some practical examples of not only minimising the negative environmental consequences of the experience itself but also of how that same experience could create a positive impact by encouraging people and showing them how to apply sustainable solutions and alternatives in their own homes and daily lives. A water-saving showerhead within the context of a hotel room that guarantees guests have a pleasant stay is much more likely to appeal to them than one shown in a television commercial that only refers to the amount of water saved. Clearly, the best place to discover that a vegan meal using local, seasonal and organic ingredients can be just as tasty as a steak flown in from the other side of the world is a restaurant with a chef who knows exactly what he or she is doing. If that chef is also willing to share some tips and tricks with guests during a pleasant conversation about the amount of greenhouse gas emissions saved by choosing this dish on the menu, those guests might be very well inclined to eat meat less regularly. In the events industry, we can see an increase in events that are explicitly based on promoting sustainable alternatives and behaviours and, interestingly, many of them are quite successful in attracting enough visitors to cover the costs involved and even make a profit. Several dining in the dark restaurants – such as the one we designed in Chapter 4 – that were initiated with the specific purpose of offering visually handicapped people an opportunity to work in hospitality and/or raise awareness among the general public about both the impact of a visual handicap on someone's life and the positive contribution those people can make to society have proven very successful, also in economic terms. In other words, effectively escaping the lock-in of our current socio-economic system might be difficult, but businesses and professionals staging experiences as the product they have to offer to consumers on the free market can still get very close to realising the ambition of creating societal value through creating economic value.

Level 4: kicking our current socio-economic system in the . . .

As discussed in Chapter 7, the highest level of ambition would be to not stop at making a positive contribution to (reducing or resolving) specific environmental and social problems but to contribute to actually taking away the cause of these problems. This would imply staging experiences that contribute to realising the kind of drastic changes to our socio-economic system needed to put our societies on a truly sustainable course. Businesses and professionals with this level of ambition would likely collaborate with other stakeholders in experimenting with viable alternatives to this system – alternatives based on inclusiveness, equality and sustainable ways of interacting with our natural environment. Doing so would require them to apply business models that include concepts like distributed control and exploring new ways of operating as a company – ways that are not based on the reference points of the free market. Obviously, the specific physical and social technologies involved in staging such experiences depend not only on the preferences and expertise of the businesses and professionals staging them but also on the specific context in which they are staged and the specific needs and wishes of the parties with whom these businesses and professionals would collaborate. How to apply naïve, native and narrative intelligence in co-creating a blossoming relationship between specific experiences and sustainable development is not something for which standard procedures can be established. Simultaneously, one could argue that the Eden Project described earlier in this section already highlights some interesting avenues for doing so. To further illustrate what applying these reference points could look like in practice, consider the example of a hotel located in a neighbourhood of a big city that suffers some of the negative consequences of urban tourism within the context of our current socio-economic system.

Some cities in the world have become so popular as destinations for tourists that more and more inhabitants of those cities no longer see tourism as a positive thing but rather as something that is worsening their quality of life. For these contexts, tourism is not only linked to negative environmental consequences – for instance through the greenhouse gas emissions involved with transporting those tourists from around the world to the city – but also to negative social consequences. A typical example of the free market mechanisms at work regarding the latter relates to the rise of AirBnB in many neighbourhoods in these cities and the fact that its popularity has led to more and more professional investors buying and renting out complete houses and apartments. The potential negative impacts on a neighbourhood are obvious. The ratio between inhabitants and tourists changes completely because of a decrease in the number of inhabitants and a further increase in the number of tourists. Those tourists no longer stay in a room in a house of a local inhabitant, with whom they interact and who shows them the way, but in an apartment owned by someone who lives somewhere thousands of kilometres away from the city. The inhabitants who still live there often feel their neighbourhood has been taken over by investors and tourists and no longer feels like their neighbourhood – obviously not exactly positively influencing their attitude towards tourists, which in turn does not exactly help to create a positive interaction between tourists and remaining inhabitants. If you add to that the further possible disturbances through noise, litter left on the streets, and so on, the downward spiral that can result from these mechanisms becomes obvious.

Now imagine a hotel in this neighbourhood that actively wants to contribute to resolving (some of) these issues. Together with residents, maybe this hotel could persuade city policy-makers to set up an experiment in the neighbourhood. Part of this experiment could be to no longer allow people renting out (parts of) houses

FIGURE 8.3 The concept of sustainable hospitality

Artist: Anabella Meijer (www.kanai.nl)

or apartments if they do not actually live there themselves – something some cities have already implemented. The hotel could offer to work together with those inhabitants who want to (continue to) rent out (parts of) their house or apartment to tourists through AirBnB and together shape a hospitality concept for the neighbourhood based on a positive relationship between residents and tourists. A concept based on sustainability principles and that benefits all parties: residents, tourists, local entrepreneurs *and* the environment. As an expert on hospitality concepts and principles, the hotel could play a crucial role in making this work. For example, as an expert in designing and staging experiences, it could take the lead in collectively creating surroundings that unleash the positive effects of biophilia. By planting trees along the streets in the neighbourhood and ensuring that the hotel and other accommodation offered, including the AirBnB houses and apartments, have plants and pictures of nature as key ingredients in the decoration of guestrooms and breakfast areas, more sustainable behaviour of both tourists and inhabitants could be encouraged. The hotel could open up its network of sustainable suppliers and distributors to other (micro-)businesses in the neighbourhood to ensure that more and more of them apply sustainable practices and use sustainable products. It could join forces with local (micro-)businesses in setting up sustainable food and energy production and consumption systems, for instance through collectively working with local and regional farmers in serving local/regional produce and investing in renewable energy projects. The hotel could not only serve as inspirational employer for local residents but also as the place where all parties meet to discuss new sustainability initiatives. It could also be a key meeting place for local residents and tourists, where they get to know and understand each other. Obviously, the hotel would ensure that it worked with influential individuals and organisations in the neighbourhood to ensure that these developments and resulting benefits reach all inhabitants of the local community and not just those eager and confident enough to step in at the early stages.

This example has highlighted just a small selection of the numerous actions experience-staging businesses and professionals, such as hotels, could take based on truly incorporating the principles of sustainable development in their business models. Obviously, for this particular hotel, realising its ambitions would only work if it were able and willing to truly collaborate with all other (local) stakeholders involved. In this specific example, the hotel might very well become an important player in this network but at the centre of the network of collaborating parties we would not find the business–economic interests of the hotel. Rather, at the centre we would find sustainable and inclusive hospitality as the central concept and building block for redeveloping the local community *and* for the experience that those collaborating parties collectively stage for tourists *and* inhabitants.

ATTRACT, LURE, ENTICE, CONVINCE OR SEDUCE CONSUMERS

Obviously, not all businesses and professionals staging experiences are ready (yet) to implement the kind of drastic changes to their business models that are linked to the level 4 ambitions described in the previous section. Doing so not only requires courage, conviction and a thick skin; it is also risky. Ultimately, any experiment to create viable (local, regional or global) alternatives to our current socio–economic system is still an experiment – and experiments can fail. What is more, introducing the kind of changes linked to the first three ambition levels can already prove quite a challenge because of the physical technologies required for successfully reducing the negative consequences associated with staging specific experiences. Those technologies might be expensive, difficult to combine with other physical technologies or the social technologies used to stage those experiences, or simply not available yet. However, more often than not, physical technologies are not the main problem. As Parrish (2007, p. 846) states, 'it is not human technology so much as patterns of human activity that are challenging the sustainability of human development'. As discussed in detail in the previous chapters, realising sustainable development is actually mostly about finding ways to resolve the social dilemmas that lie at the core of unsustainability. Resolving these dilemmas revolves around finding ways to change people's behaviour. A crucial group of people in this respect are consumers. Many of the products we choose to buy and consume contribute significantly to overexploiting our natural resources and – directly and indirectly – to an unequal distribution of wealth across all people in our societies.

Regardless of the specific ambition level regarding sustainability of businesses and professionals staging experiences, those experiences can only contribute to solving these problems if people actually consume them. Staging sustainable experiences without customers is like a wedding with only one of the happy couple showing up; the invitation card can look great and the wedding chapel ever so charming but with only the bride present the actual ceremony will never happen. Experiences that cause less environmental damage can only make a difference if and when consumers choose these experiences over ones that cause more environmental damage. Businesses and professionals who aim to make a positive contribution to the social component of sustainable development through staging experiences can only make a significant contribution if and when enough people consume them. Unfortunately, the previous chapters have shown that consumers are not always inclined or easily persuaded to go for the (more) sustainable alternative. Therefore, a key question that needs answering is: how could you convince (more) consumers to (buy and) consume (more) sustainable experiences as a means to fulfil (more of) their needs and wishes?

Accounting for the gap, different types of goals and the relevance of context

Oftentimes, promoting sustainable behaviour is assumed to involve changing people's values and attitudes. This assumption can be traced back to the dominant role of Ajzen's (1991) theory of planned behaviour – and modified versions of this theory – in psychology and especially in research dedicated to promoting sustainable (consumer) behaviour. The key reference point underlying these kinds of theories is that people's behaviour can be explained and predicted based on the combination of their attitudes and/or values and/or beliefs, social norms, and their perceived behavioural control. As an individual, there are many ways in which you could make a (small) contribution to sustainable development, for instance through buying and consuming different products. Simultaneously, more and more people actually want to preserve our natural environment, would like climate change to be dealt with successfully, and feel the unequal distribution of wealth across societies is a problem that should be solved. Consequently, one could argue that the social norm is slowly but surely shifting towards more sustainable behaviour. Therefore, if those theories are correct, this means that unsustainable behaviours by individuals must be the result of anti-sustainable values and attitudes of those individuals.

Interestingly though, many of those individuals engaging in unsustainable behaviour actually feel a bit guilty if and when they display unsustainable behaviour. We all know the feeling: 'I know I should really turn down the thermostat and wear an extra sweater but it feels so nice if the house is all warm and cosy' or 'I should really not buy a plastic bag to put my groceries in but I forgot to bring my canvas bag – again!' The fact is that research shows that while many consumers are reluctant to buy and consume/use sustainable products, services and experiences, these same consumers often do value the environment and fully support the idea of sustainable development (see e.g. Vringer et al., 2015). Obviously, the conclusion reached in Chapter 2 is correct: we, people, are rather complicated. Our real-life behaviour can often not be explained and predicted based on our values and attitudes. This contrast between our values and attitudes on the one hand and our actual behaviour on the other is usually referred to as the attitude-behaviour gap or intention-behaviour gap. Not surprisingly, therefore, trying to find (all) the factors that explain (all) these gaps has received and still receives quite a bit of attention in (scientific and non-scientific) literature and by all kinds of professionals, especially in relation to promoting sustainable behaviour. Even though we might not have found all answers (yet), some things are pretty clear by now.

First and foremost, it has become clear that a lot of the decisions we make, especially with respect to our buying and consumption behaviour, are not based on consciously weighing all options and choosing the one with the highest objective utility every time we buy or consume a product, service or experience. Many of these decisions are actually made unconsciously or automatically and are based on habits and routines, as well as being influenced by the same type of lock-in effects discussed in the previous chapters in relation to our current socio-economic system. These lock-in effects relate to dominant social and cultural practices in the communities and societies we are part of. This explains why it is usually quite a big step for people to install solar panels on their roofs if they were to be the first to do so in their neighbourhood but as soon as some more people have installed them this significantly increases the likelihood of other people installing them. The impact of habits and routines is also one of the explanations of the fact that most media campaigns by governments aimed at promoting sustainable behaviours do not have the desired effect. Many of us probably agree with the underlying message of those campaigns when we see the advertisements. However, this does not automatically make us change our habits and routines, especially not with respect to products, services and experiences we buy and consume regularly. The message sent through those campaigns is not what we think about when we make the decision to buy or consume them; most of the times when we buy or consume them we think about a number of other things such as 'I should really remember to give my mother a call' or 'Wow, look at that guy, what was he thinking when he put on those shoes?' because the decision to buy or consume them is actually made unconsciously. We usually just buy and consume what we always buy and consume. What further complicates matters is that on those occasions when we are inclined and ready to make a conscious decision with respect to a specific type of product, service or experience we want to buy, accounting for sustainability aspects in that decision is not always easy. These days, most producers claim their products, services or experiences are sustainable, green or environmentally responsible. It can be quite a challenge to determine whether the product you are considering buying actually lives up to those claims. It is often even more difficult to determine which alternative is the most sustainable one. What is more, you might think it is more important that a product does not harm the environment, whereas someone else feels it is more important that a product contributes to helping the world's poor.

What can businesses and professionals staging sustainable experiences deduce from all this? First and foremost, if you communicate about the sustainability aspects of your experience to and with consumers, you need to be honest and open about what you are doing and why you are doing it. Consumers have heard it all before and are bombarded with beautiful promises all the time. By now, they do not necessarily trust the business world to be environmentally and socially responsible; they have been confronted with too much so-called greenwashing and have seen too many reports on sustainability scandals to just take your word for it. Therefore, you need to back up any claims you make with details about the actual impact of your experiences, including all the tangible and intangible components incorporated in staging them (Cho, 2015). You also need to grab their attention – entice or seduce them to make a conscious decision instead of just doing what they have been doing so far – and do so in a way that resonates with what they value, what they find important. This might very well involve accounting for the fact that different customer segments will have different priorities and different values when it comes to what is the most important sustainability aspect to address. Sometimes, this might even require accounting for differences between members of one and the same household or family (Collins, 2015) for which you stage those experiences. A father, mother, 12-year-old son and 16-year-old daughter visiting your theme park together might very well have very different thoughts about whether it is acceptable or not to eat meat, to include wild animals in your shows, or to offer handsome 16-year-old boys a summer job operating your roller-coaster.

Within this context, you also need to account for the fact that sustainability often links to conflicts between the various goals people pursue in their lives. Steg et al. (2014) explain that, when it comes to deciding between unsustainable and sustainable behaviour, most people are confronted with a conflict between their hedonic and gain goals on the one hand and normative goals on the other. Hedonic goals relate to focusing on improving short-term feelings through avoiding effort or seeking pleasure and excitement. Gain goals relate to costs and benefits involved with specific behaviour in relation to one's personal resources, such as the time and money required to engage in specific behaviour. Normative goals are directly linked to what people consider appropriate behaviour, to their values and beliefs. Oftentimes, unsustainable behaviour is considered to be easier, cheaper and more fun than sustainable behaviour. We all know that a Porsche 911 requires a lot more natural resources to take you from A to B than a fully electric Volvo station car. However, you can buy them second hand for a lot less than that Volvo. You are not bound to petrol stations that have electricity charging facilities and . . . when you open the roof top while driving 140 kilometres per hour, well, you feel alive!

If your challenge is to entice or seduce people to buy and consume your sustainable experiences, you need to make allowance for these types of conflicts at work in most people's brains. One approach to doing so is to make sustainable experiences just as fun, exciting and cheap as unsustainable ones or, even better, to make them more fun, more exciting and even cheaper. Sometimes, this is actually not necessarily a mission impossible. Organic, local and seasonal food can be just as tasty as a steak flown in from across the globe, and does not have to be more expensive. Another approach would be to strengthen normative goals. One way to do so is to change the context for sustainable behaviour and to make sure that this context incorporates cues and stimuli that support this type of behaviour. Earlier, the positive impact of biophilia on sustainable behaviour has already been highlighted. Smart choices with respect to (creating) the physical context for staging an experience could very well promote sustainable behaviour. Given that experiences usually involve interaction with staff members, staff could also play a vital role through creating a social context in which sustainability is promoted by not only displaying sustainable behaviour themselves but also referring to the sustainable behaviour of other customers/visitors/guests. The latter could also be incorporated in storylines communicated in other ways at various touch points of the customer journey, for instance in the welcome message for guests in the 'what to do' guide in their hotel room. The key is to balance these two approaches well because solely promoting sustainable experiences through linking to hedonic and gain goals 'make these goals more influential in [future] decision-making, thereby weakening [the potential positive impact of] normative goals' (Steg et al., 2014, p. 106).

Ultimately, convincing consumers to buy and consume sustainable experiences probably needs to be based on combining three approaches (Hall, 2013):

1. A utilitarian approach aimed at providing people with (honest and detailed) information, possibly even educating them on some specific sustainability issues linked to the experience you stage for them.
2. A social/psychological approach that acknowledges the fact that better or more information not always leads to 'better' behaviour or choices because of the impact of factors such as dominant social and cultural practices, habits and routines, and context.
3. A system of provision approach aimed at changing the context for people's choices and behaviour.

The second and third approach both try to change the context for people's choices and behaviour but whereas the second one focuses on trying to nudge (Thaler & Sunstein, 2008) people to make more sustainable choices by changing the environment without actually restricting their choices, the third one takes a more structural or fundamental approach by trying to change (parts of) the (socio-economic) system in which these choices are made and these behaviours are displayed.

Two typical examples of nudging or social marketing that fit the second approach would be to

> *not* arrange for the in-room television [in a hotel] to switch on automatically and display a welcome message and hotel information as soon as the key card is inserted in the wall slot. Obviously a nice welcome message and practical information for guests make perfect sense [from an experience perspective].

However, using the television to do so usually results in guests leaving the television switched on, even though many of them would not switch on the television themselves the moment they (first) entered the room. Many would simply (first) take time to unpack, put their toiletries in the bathroom, read some of the brochures available in the room [such as that 'what to do' guide mentioned earlier], admire the view from the hotel room, possibly have a nap, and so on. This simple change of context immediately reduces the amount of energy used [without necessarily negatively influencing the overall guest experience if welcoming guests is done differently, for instance at the moment of arrival in the hotel by staff at the reception desk, who take the opportunity to also immediately bring some sustainability aspects of the hotel to the attention of the guest]. Another example would be to place coffee makers in hallways close to some comfortable seats and a nice table on which information on the hotel's sustainability initiatives is displayed, instead of having small coffee makers in every guest room – a potentially elegant but simple way to use less equipment, and thus less resources to create them, while stimulating guests and staff to interact and discuss these initiatives.

(Melissen, 2017, p. 160)

A typical example of applying the first approach would be the Eden Project, whereas an example of the third approach would be the hotel trying to resolve the negative effects of urban tourism in a specific neighbourhood, both discussed in the previous section. All of these examples show that businesses and professionals staging experiences could very well apply all three approaches suggested above. Obviously, the specific details of actions to be taken by individual businesses or professionals depend on the specific (types of) sustainable experiences they want to stage and the specific (characteristics of the) consumers they want to target buying and consuming them. However, the attitude-behaviour gap, the differences between different people's values and even between the multiple goals of one and the same person, and the relevance of the context in which they need to decide on and engage in specific sustainable experiences, represent crucial aspects that any business or professional staging them needs to account for.

Unleash the beast within?

A very interesting perspective with respect to tackling the challenge of convincing consumers to go for (more) sustainable ways of fulfilling their needs and wishes is provided by Griskevicius et al. (2012). In their paper, they look beyond the Industrial Revolution and the rise of free market capitalism and review the evolutionary bases for the behaviour of people. They use the following example for explaining what it means to apply an evolutionary approach to reviewing people's behaviour:

When asking *why* children prefer doughnuts over spinach, for example, one answer is that doughnuts taste better and elicit more pleasure than spinach. An evolutionary approach, however, would also ask why sweetened, fatty foods taste good and elicit more pleasure in the first place. In this case, the reason is that humans have inherited a tendency to crave fatty and sweet foods, such as meat and ripe fruit [. . .]. These types of foods provided our ancestors with much-needed calories in a food-scarce environment and did so more effectively than foods low in fat and sugar [. . .]. In our modern world of supermarkets and convenience stores, although people know that they should resist Ben & Jerry's latest combination of ice cream, cookies, and brownies, their evolved mechanisms continue to signal the adaptive benefits of fatty and sweet foods. This evolutionary explanation for food preferences is known as an ultimate explanation or cause.

(Griskevicius et al., 2012, p. 116)

Based on the same train of thought, these authors suggest that we could distinguish five evolutionary tendencies that might very well contribute to explaining some of the environmental and social problems we face today:

1. our propensity for self-interest;
2. our motivation for relative rather than absolute status;
3. our proclivity to unconsciously copy others;
4. our predisposition to be short-sighted;
5. our proneness to disregard impalpable concerns.

Griskevicius et al. (2012) suggest that it might be wise to not try to fight these tendencies but rather accept that they (still) play an important role in explaining the choices we make and the behaviours we display today, even though the circumstances in which we live our lives have changed considerably. Instead of fighting these tendencies within the context of pursuing sustainable development, it might be smart, and sometimes more effective, to promote sustainability through making use of them. Once again, the simple example they use to illustrate this logic is linked to our preference for fat and sugar. In promoting more healthy lifestyles, maybe we should not try to convince people to not crave sweet and fatty foods but try to change (the taste of) healthy food into food that gives us the same cues of sweetness and fattiness. Salad dressing is a perfect example of how to make vegetables taste fattier and tangier. Medication that is flavoured with the taste of sweets is another example.

How could we use the same logic in promoting sustainable choices and behaviour by relating to the five tendencies mentioned earlier? With respect to our propensity for self-interest, for example, it is important to realise that self-interest is not necessarily limited to the interests of one person. The principle of natural selection – to which this tendency is linked – relates to our motivation to pursue survival of our own genes, not to survival of our species. The deeply ingrained motivation in people to have their genes survive encourages them to make selfish choices but could also be used to promote sustainable choices. People share their genes with family and kin. The herdsmen in Hardin's explanation of the tragedy of the commons, as discussed in Chapter 7, probably not just looked at the utility of an extra animal for themselves but also for their family. Social dilemmas linked to sustainability often involve us making choices that serve the interests of our own family, our own children right here and right now instead of the interests of all people belonging to future generations in the long term. What would happen if we did not promote sustainability by referring to what is best for our species, for our entire world, but rather to what is best for our family, our kin? Griskevicius et al. (2012) indicate that recent research shows that sustainability messages that emphasise the impact of specific decisions or behaviours on one's own family or kin are more effective than messages that stress the impact on our world as a whole. Given that businesses and professionals staging experiences often do so for whole families or groups of people who are otherwise related or (close) friends – sometimes even for you and someone you could very well imagine being your future husband/wife and father/mother of your children, this is a reference point that they could certainly take on board in promoting sustainable experiences.

Griskevicius et al. (2012) continue their discussion by pointing to a number of other mechanisms linked to this first and the other four tendencies that could potentially be used to promote sustainability. For instance, by linking people's desire for relative status to costly signalling theory – which basically states that natural selection makes us favour people who engage in activities that involve high costs, a lot of energy, high risk or a lot of time because the fact that they can afford to do so tells us something about their ambitions, skills, perseverance, and so on – one could argue that making huge efforts as a business or professional in pursuing sustainability, even taking some risks in doing so, actually makes you more attractive for consumers as a potential co-creator of their lives. This can be even more so, if you can offer them clear (physical or virtual) signs or tags that they could use to promote their involvement with this sustainability leader to others (Melissen & Moratis, 2016). These mechanisms are especially interesting for businesses and professionals staging experiences because these experiences involve them (and their staff) directly interacting with those consumers in co-creating the ultimate experience. What is more, as discussed in Chapter 1, an important aspect of staging successful experiences can relate to providing so-called (physical) evidence to customers of a specific service or process having been completed. Providing this evidence could very well be done in the form of the tags and signs customers could use to show off their involvement with you – the experience provider – thus simultaneously offering a good chance of further promoting your brand's or independent company's (sustainable) personality (and the experiences you offer) to other consumers. Another example of the mechanisms discussed in this paper relates to the inclination of people surviving in hunter-gatherer groups in days long gone to help others if they returned the favour, especially if those others go first. Helping each other was a key to survival in a dangerous, unpredictable world. Businesses and professionals staging experiences could use these so-called reciprocal altruism and social obligation mechanisms in promoting sustainable experiences by trying to create a community or family feeling linked to the experiences they stage as a means to entice consumers to support them in their sustainability efforts by displaying the types of behaviours that would help make them a success (Melissen & Moratis, 2016). Obviously, creating this community or family feeling would also allow for making use of the tendency of people to make decisions that favour people close to them, as discussed earlier. Simultaneously, it would also tap into the need of people to feel connected to others, to belong to specific social groups, and the fact that in today's individualised society people increasingly fulfil this need through consuming experiences, as discussed in Chapter 2.

It is beyond the scope of this section to review all five tendencies established by Griskevicius et al. (2012), and the mechanisms linked to them that could be used to promote sustainability, in full detail. If you are triggered to know more, make sure that you read this interesting and thought-provoking paper. Here, the relevance of an evolutionary perspective on promoting sustainability could be concluded to offer an interesting and promising avenue for businesses and professionals aiming to stage (more) sustainable experiences. However, it is also important to note that basing your strategy for convincing consumers to buy and consume your (more) sustainable experiences only on these types of mechanisms might not be the smartest move from a wider sustainable development perspective. As indicated earlier, with respect to the various goals that often conflict within the context of individual people's decision-making, solely promoting sustainable experiences through linking to hedonic and gain goals might actually weaken the potential positive impact of normative goals. One could argue that the same applies to focusing exclusively on mechanisms based on self-interest, short-sightedness and (personal) benefits that can be witnessed and experienced right here, right now. Doing so might actually hinder efforts of the highest ambition level discussed in the previous section – efforts aimed at creating viable (local) alternatives to our current socio-economic system based on principles such as inclusiveness, equality and sustainable ways of interacting with our natural environment. Therefore, the best advice probably is to balance all approaches described in this section carefully.

SUSTAINABILITY AND EXPERIENCES: LIKE TWO PEAS IN A POD

By now, it is pretty clear that there is no reason why staging experiences and pursuing sustainable development could not go hand in hand, and actually reinforce each other. Both experiences and sustainability challenges have become an increasingly important part of all of our lives and represent a crucial topic to address for almost all businesses and professionals.

The first five chapters of this book have shown that one can distinguish different types of experiences that could be staged by businesses and professionals as the product they offer to their customers. Some of these experiences, such as specific peak experiences or memorable encounters, represent one-off events that might make a lasting impression on you – because they were very enjoyable or exciting – but usually do not represent immersing yourself in a different 'world' or life-changing events. In contrast, transformative experiences are much more immersive in nature and provoke learning and sustained changes in the people consuming them. The fact that companies stage these experiences implies that they have become part of the way we interact with other people within the context of our current socio-economic system and they are usually based on an economic transaction between those offering them and those consuming them. Consequently, aspects such as branding and communicating about what the company offering those experiences stands for, believes in, have gained importance. We, consumers, do not want to consume experiences offered by just anyone; our consumption patterns have too much (symbolic) meaning for us, in relation to who we are and who we want to be, to co-create our lives through consuming experiences staged by businesses and professionals who do not have the same values and beliefs. The word 'co-create' forms a key element in all this because consuming experiences requires us, consumers, to interact with those staging them. Through specific touch points and customer journeys based on specific cues and stimuli we are triggered to immerse ourselves in the storyline and dramatic structure of the experience and to display behaviours that enhance the ultimate experience. To ensure that the ultimate experience lives up to our expectations, the businesses and professionals staging them need to design them carefully, stage them in accordance with that design, and manage a range of processes and people in doing so. All this involves focusing on both tangible and intangible components of the overall experience, as well as on-stage and backstage processes. A specific complication for these businesses and professionals is that we, consumers, all have very different reasons for wanting to consume specific experiences, based on different (types of) needs and wishes, values and personalities. Our particular needs and wishes, values and personalities also make us react differently to the same cues and stimuli. The first part of this book has highlighted a number of theories, methods, tools and techniques that could prove helpful in dealing with this complication and designing, staging and managing experiences successfully.

Interestingly, a number of these reference points for and complications involved with successfully designing, staging and managing experiences bear great resemblance to the reference points for and complications involved with tackling sustainability, as discussed in this chapter and the preceding two chapters. As a business or professional, you could tackle this issue in different ways, ranging from straight-forward reduction of your negative environmental impact to efforts that truly change the lives of all stakeholders linked to your business activities and the (local) social and environmental system in which you operate. One of the ways you could try to make a contribution to sustainable development is to have a lasting effect on the behaviour of your customers – also after the experience you stage for them has ended. To do so, you need to understand how to motivate them to change their behaviour. The ultimate challenge is to stage your experiences in a way that contributes to creating a viable alternative to our current socio-economic system. However, doing so will have to smartly negotiate or avoid the lock-in effects of our current system dominated by interactions between people based on economic transactions and conflicting interests. The only way you could expect to do so is to involve your customers and other stakeholders in doing so. Regardless of your ambition level with respect to pursuing sustainable development, you need to co-create the solutions with those parties. This requires accounting for their interests, their values, their needs and wishes, and so on. This also implies that communicating to and with them about your ambitions as well as your actions need to be based on a thorough understanding of their behaviour and what makes them tick. A complication involved with this is that different people might very well have different preferences, different priorities, and react differently to the same cues and stimuli. However, including the right cues and stimuli in your communication and the context in which you stage experiences for them is actually a critical success factor for realising your sustainability ambitions.

All this means that the theories, models, tools and techniques discussed in the first five chapters of this book could not only prove useful for successfully designing, staging and managing experiences within the context of our current socio-economic system but also for trying to adjust it to a more sustainable system. Accounting for people's values, personalities and possible peculiarities forms the key to both. The people with whom you will be co-creating the ultimate experience are the same people. Your staff members play a crucial role in realising both ambitions, as does treating them well and involving them in what you do, how you do that *and* why you do that. The tangible products and artefacts that you use in staging experiences are the same tangible products and artefacts that require natural resources to produce and use them. Collaborating with the suppliers of those products, as well as the suppliers of specific services, is key to both ambitions. And finally, the experiences you stage to be successful in our current socio-economic system and contribute to adjusting it to a more sustainable system are the same experiences. This means that staging and managing them carefully is extremely important but, ultimately, whether this will lead to success is very much dependent on how they were designed. Staging experiences based on a design that does not account for the specific preferences and peculiarities of the different types of people who you would like to consume them is a mission impossible – this also applies for sustainable experiences. Managing the processes and people involved with staging them will more than likely result in headaches and frustration rather than the desired results if the design process did not address how to manage them effectively and efficiently – the same is true for trying to focus on the sustainability aspect in managing these processes and people. In other words, successfully staging and managing sustainable experiences cannot be done without addressing all reference points and complications involved in doing so in the design of these experiences. Therefore, how to integrate sustainability principles into this design is the topic of the next chapter.

SUMMARY

Based on reading this chapter, we hope you will understand and remember the following:

- The four levels of ambition with respect to pursuing sustainable development through designing, staging and managing experiences.
- The relevance of accounting for the attitude-behaviour gap, different types of goals and the context in stimulating sustainable behaviour.
- The three approaches to convincing consumers to buy and consume sustainable experiences:
    o   a utilitarian approach;
    o   a social/psychological approach or nudging;
    o   a system of provision approach.
- The five evolutionary tendencies that could explain unsustainable behaviour *and* be used to promote sustainable behaviour:
    o   our propensity for self-interest;
    o   our motivation for relative rather than absolute status;
    o   our proclivity to unconsciously copy others;
    o   our predisposition to be short-sighted;
    o   our proneness to disregard impalpable concerns.
- Successfully staging and managing sustainable experiences is anything but a mission impossible *but* doing so requires addressing all reference points and complications involved with doing so in the design of these experiences.

FOOD FOR THOUGHT

Based on the content of this chapter, the following questions, challenges and topics could serve as interesting starting points for further discussion:

- In your opinion, is 'a match made in heaven' the right description for the relationship between experiences and sustainability? In answering this question, address the following aspects:
    o   Is the answer to this question the same for all four ambition levels?
    o   How could you combine hedonic, gain and normative goals in one and the same (overall) experience?
    o   How can experiences unleash a sustainable beast within?

REFERENCES

Ajzen, I. (1991). The theory of planned behaviour. *Organizational Behavior and Human Decision Processes*, 50, 179–211.

Cho, Y.-N. (2015). Different shades of green consciousness: The interplay of sustainability labeling and environmental impact on product evaluations. *Journal of Business Ethics*, 128(1), 73–82.

Collins, R. (2015). Keeping it in the family? Re-focusing household sustainability. *Geoforum*, 60, 22–32.

Glavas, A. (2012). Employee engagement and sustainability: A model for implementing meaningfulness at and in work. *Journal of Corporate Citizenship*, 46, 13–29.

Griskevicius, V., Cantú, S. & van Vugt, M. (2012). The evolutionary bases for sustainable behaviour: Implications for marketing, policy, and social entrepreneurship. *Journal of Public Policy & Marketing*, 31, 115–128.

Hall, M.C. (2013). Framing behavioural approaches to understanding and governing sustainable tourism consumption: beyond neoliberalism, 'nudging' and green growth? *Journal of Sustainable Tourism*, 21(7), 1091–1109.

Melissen, F. (2017). Hotels and sustainability. In R.C. Wood (Ed.): *Hotel accommodation management* (pp. 152–163). New York: Routledge.

Melissen, F. & Moratis, L. (2016). A call for fourth generation sustainable business models. *The Journal of Corporate Citizenship*, 63, 8–16.

Parrish, B.D. (2007). Designing the sustainable enterprise. *Futures*, 39(7), 846–860.

Steg, L., Bolderdijk, J.W., Keizer, K. & Perlaviciute, G. (2014). An integrated framework for encouraging pro-environmental behaviour: The role of values, situational factors and goals. *Journal of Environmental Psychology*, 38, 104–115.

Thaler, R.H. & Sunstein, C.R. (2008). *Nudge: Improving decisions about health, wealth and happiness*. London: Yale University Press.

Vringer, K., Vollebergh, H.R., van Soest, D., van der Heijden, E. & Dietz, F. (2015). *Sustainable consumption dilemmas. OECD Environmental Working Papers, 84*. Paris: OECD Publishing.

9 Designing sustainable experiences and businesses

INTRODUCTION

The previous chapter has concluded that successfully staging and managing experiences and pursuing sustainable development can (and should) go hand in hand but requires addressing both challenges in the design of those experiences. This chapter discusses and illustrates how the reference points for and complications involved with various ambition levels with respect to staging sustainable experiences can be accounted for within the context of applying the comprehensive approach to experience design presented in Chapter 4. It illustrates how this approach can offer a promising avenue for merging solutions for both challenges, thus leading to opportunities to design, stage and manage sustainable experiences successfully.

The first four sections are linked to the four ambition levels described in the previous chapter, ranging from merely addressing your (negative) environmental impact to experimenting with viable alternatives to our current socio-economic system. For each ambition level, obvious routes and opportunities to integrate sustainability principles into the design of the experience that will be staged are discussed and illustrated. The fifth and final section of this chapter then discusses the implications of doing so at a more abstract level: how would that change the role of experiences in our lives and our society? It concludes with explaining how the answer to this question illustrates that staging sustainable experiences instead of unsustainable ones need not be an inconvenience or burden for the businesses and professionals involved but rather presents a promising avenue for their long-term success based on making a crucial contribution to our future societies.

AMBITION LEVEL 1

This ambition level relates to reducing the negative environmental impact associated with staging experiences for your customers. A straightforward way of integrating this ambition into the design of these experiences is to include this ambition as an objective in the first step of the design process. You could do so for an experience that is designed from scratch but also for redesigning an existing experience with the objective to reduce its negative environmental impact. Obviously, once you have set this as an objective, you will need to specify this objective in more detail in the setting requirements step. Would you like to use fewer materials, more recycled materials, cause less pollution, emit less greenhouse gas emissions, a combination of these aspects, all of them, or something else? As with any requirement, it really helps to be as specific as possible and quantify your ambitions. If you have included these ambitions in your requirements, applying the design approach presented in Chapter 4 automatically ensures that they will be accounted for in generating design alternatives and evaluating them, for instance within the context of a multi-criteria analysis. Obviously, the higher the weight assigned to the criteria linked to your objective to reduce your environmental impact and the requirements that have specified this objective, the more influence this aspect will have on the ultimate choice for a specific alternative.

Tangible and intangible components

The actual environmental impact of the experience you stage can be related to both the tangible and intangible components of the various touch points of the customer journey(s) offered to customers. For example, for a hotel a significant portion of the greenhouse gas emissions linked to the hospitality experience are directly associated with the building in which you stage it. Choices you make with respect to the materials used in constructing this building, furnishing and decorating rooms and public spaces such as the lobby and restaurant, and so on, all relate to specific amounts of greenhouse gas emissions associated with producing them and transporting them to the site of the hotel. The same applies to the way you heat or cool this building but also to other types of environmental impacts. Ultimately, the list of choices that influences the environmental impact of staging this experience is almost endless. In some way or another, all of these choices are directly linked to choices you make in the design process. What type of decoration is used to shape the physical context for a specific touch point? Some types of decoration come with significantly less environmental impact, for instance because they have been created using recycled materials or the specific supplier of that decoration uses electric vehicles to deliver the components to your hotel. What type of interaction with staff is going to take place to shape the social context for a specific touch point? If you opt for serving à la carte breakfast instead of a breakfast buffet, significantly less food will be wasted.

One could argue that just the decision to incorporate the environmental impact in the objectives for the design process and the requirements the ultimate design will have to meet, will probably trigger the design team to come up with or think of more sustainable alternatives for the touch-point alternatives they generate in step 5 of this process. By accounting for the environmental impact of touch-point alternatives in the evaluation stage and thus of the touch points to be included in the ultimate design of the customer journey(s), you can make sure that these choices are also based on this impact. More importantly, by integrating sustainability aspects into the design of experiences, you will probably find that contrary to popular belief – or maybe, by now, we should actually say: views of the uninformed? – (sub-)solutions that make the ultimate experience pleasant or attractive to customers and (sub-)solutions that make it less unsustainable do not have to conflict. In fact, quite often they can reinforce and strengthen each other. The same applies for business-economic and sustainability interests supposedly being mutually exclusive. In many if not most real-life contexts, this is simply not true.

The example of an à la carte breakfast versus a breakfast buffet illustrates this perfectly. Hospitality managers often write off the à la carte option because it is assumed to be too costly. And yes, staff costs involved with this option are probably higher than for a buffet. However, food waste is a lot lower for the à la carte version. A number of ingredients can be bought in so-called bulk packaging instead of small packages or even individually packaged items – which not only reduces packaging materials but also the volume that needs to be transported and stored. Put together, all this not only saves natural resources but also costs. What is more, by serving breakfast à la carte, staff get more chances to talk to guests, respond quickly to their needs and wishes, establish a relationship, talk about other touch points in the overall guest journey you have created for them, and increase their anticipation while collecting valuable information about their preferences to allow you to customise breakfast and other touch points accordingly. By making it explicit that your motivation to go for the à la carte option is also based on sustainability ambitions, you get a chance to involve your guests in these ambitions, which increases the chances of those same guests helping you to save water and energy by adjusting their behaviour once they return to their hotel room – a topic returned to later in this chapter. Obviously, if your guests use less water and energy, this not only saves natural resources but also money. And so on, and so on. Hospitality and sustainability are not mutually exclusive – they could even be argued to represent two sides of the same coin because sustainability *is all about* caring for the needs of people and our planet, and treating them accordingly. The same applies to most other types of experiences. Experiences that are more sustainable are not necessarily more expensive or less effective from the perspective of satisfying the needs and wishes of customers. In fact, with a little bit of effort and imagination, oftentimes merging these three perspectives is possible and can even lead to some interesting synergies. However, the chances for creating these synergies increase significantly if you purposely explore them early in the design of the experiences you would like to stage.

From products to services to experiences

This specific example of a hotel serving breakfast à la carte instead of through a breakfast buffet is also a nice illustration of the positive sustainability effects of transforming products and services into experiences. In generic terms, a move from simply handing over tangible products to customers – either by selling them or within the context of providing a specific service – to staging experiences for them usually represents a move into a more sustainable direction. Earlier in this book, the underlying logic for this reference point has already been illustrated through using the example of copiers and printers. By no longer selling these machines but leasing them, producers of copiers and printers can create more opportunities for reusing (parts of) them. They also create better opportunities for maintenance, including software updates and replacing old parts with improved versions, thus creating better opportunities to control energy, paper and ink usage of those machines. Obviously, this reference point not only applies to producers of copiers and printers; in theory, it could apply to businesses and professionals offering just about any type of product or service to consumers. For all of these businesses and professionals, the design approach presented in Chapter 4, as well as the theories, methods, tools and techniques discussed in all other chapters of this book, could prove very helpful in successfully designing, staging and managing these experiences.

However, businesses and professionals who already focus on staging an experience as the overall product they offer to consumers can often still improve the design of this experience – and consequently also staging it and managing the processes involved – by revisiting its design based on this reference point. A hotel serving breakfast within the context of staging a hospitality experience is certainly not the only example of how this could reduce the environmental impact while maintaining

FIGURE 9.1 Customisation and sustainability: a symbiotic relationship

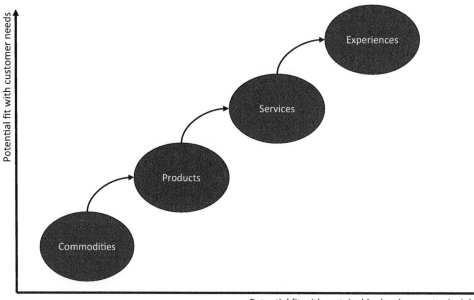

or even improving the ultimate experience provided to customers without necessarily increasing overall costs involved. Obviously, the train of thought applied to the hotel example could also apply to any other business or professional offering food and drink within the context of the overall experience they stage. Take, for example, a zoo that sells food and drinks to customers through various outlets in the park. Some of these outlets might sell sandwiches wrapped in plastic and canned drinks, so that visitors can have lunch while continuing their stroll through the park. Changing these outlets into areas where you can sit at a table and where staff members come over to you to take your order and serve your meal – not wrapped in plastic and canned but on a nice plate and in cheerful cups that can be used again, and again, and again – could very well result in the same synergies described in the hotel example. In fact, by consciously designing this area as an area in which staff and visitors can interact in a way that reinforces all of your ambitions – based on providing staff with smart scripts and instructions, and themed outfits – within the context of a physical environment that further strengthens the overall storyline of your park, you might very well change a dime in a dozen food outlets into a touch point that plays a crucial role both in reducing your environmental impact *and* in meeting and exceeding your visitors' expectations. Obviously, this logic could also be applied to other tangibles – not just food and drinks. Maybe a theatre could use a QR code to give visitors access to an interactive platform displayed on their mobile phone instead of a paper version of the programme. Why would a gift shop in a theme park have to sell plastic versions of the main characters in its shows? If you really put your mind to it, surely it must be possible to come up with a sustainable alternative that also makes families remember the great time they had in your park and rave about that to others. The design approach presented in this book – as well as all the supporting theories, methods, tools and techniques discussed within the context of successfully designing, staging and managing experiences – will probably prove very useful in doing so.

Involve others in your design process and join theirs

For some elements incorporated in the experience you stage, you might rely on others to actually produce and deliver them. A specialised company usually produces the souvenirs a theme park sells to its visitors. Most restaurants do not grow vegetables and do not catch fish themselves. Reducing the environmental impact of the experiences you stage therefore often requires collaborating with suppliers. Sometimes, you might even have to switch supplier to reduce your environmental impact, if your current supplier is unwilling to adjust their offer. At other times, more sustainable alternatives might not be available yet. In those circumstances, it might be wise to have representatives of your suppliers actively contribute to your design process or for you to contribute to their design processes. Quite possibly, those representatives could point out changes you could make to the design of your experiences that would allow them to create more sustainable alternatives for the products or services you need in staging those experiences. Similarly, maybe your expertise in designing, staging and managing experiences could assist your suppliers

CASE STUDY 9.1 **USER-CENTRED DESIGN IN SUSTAINABLE PRODUCT DEVELOPMENT**

Xavier Font

Companies that aim to be more sustainable have designed their products based on making an improved impact on the local economies and societies, and reducing their negative impacts on the environment. These have usually followed lists of criteria, such as those from the Global Sustainable Tourism Council, that codify industry best practice. While these are conceptually appropriate, they lack something rather important: customer relevance.

Taking a user-centred design approach to the design of sustainable tourism products is rather different. It requires a company to consider what are the consumer needs and desires from a holiday, and the development of an empathetic understanding through observation and engagement, in order to identify the design problem and suggest 'how might we' statements that fit the consumer needs, while also offering products that nudge the consumer to enjoy their holiday in a more sustainable way. The difference may seem subtle, but it is not. Consumers do not set out to be unsustainable in their behaviour. This is a by-product; hence, the design of experiences needs to both satisfy essential enjoyment aspects while also using more resilient resources or using them in ways that they will deteriorate less.

This can be exemplified with the design of activities in a campsite outside Barcelona (Spain), where the management commissioned researchers to devise a strategy to engage consumers in reducing their negative environmental impacts. Instead of designing a consumer education campaign on water, energy and waste management, the team first worked to understand what it was that made the customers of the campsite behave the way they did. And this generated surprising results.

The findings suggested that customers were aware of and felt uneasy about their own impacts, but their lack of knowledge about their options made them behave unsustainably, because they simply followed the most convenient options offered to them. For example, most families were not used to cooking on a camping gas stove, so they bought ready-made food that was quick to heat up, but that was heavily packaged. Although families wanted to relax and enjoy the destination informally, excursions offered to them suggested the need to travel considerable distances in organised groups to have an experience. The impacts resulted from poor product design.

The research team therefore went about the design of meaningful memorable experiences that brought the family together, which was understood to be the aim of their camping holidays. A sunrise beach breakfast picnic, a sensory garden walk, a camping stove recipe book, a pick your own fruit farm visit, were some of the more than 25 experiences that were mocked up and prototyped with the campsite users, and helped improve the design of the products. All these experiences used local produce and low-carbon transport (or no transport at all), but this was never mentioned; the emphasis was placed on personalised and unique family fun, in an informal setting. Customer satisfaction improved and customer willingness to engage in requests from management increased, thanks to having built a rapport. The negative impacts were reduced, and the positive impact on the economy increased, but this was a result of customers being given positive and enjoyable options, rather than being denied the chance to enjoy themselves on holiday, which is how many sustainability messages often come across.

Based on: Font, X., English, R. & Gkritzali, A. (resubmitted). Sustainable tourism product development with user-centred design. *Tourism Management*.

in developing sustainable – experience-based – alternatives for the products and services they deliver to you. The same applies to experiences that are staged by multiple businesses and professionals, such as the fly-drive holiday mentioned in the introduction section of Chapter 5. Obviously, one could argue that the car rental company, the wildlife reserves, the theme parks and the theatres that contribute specific elements to this holiday booked at a travel agency all stage a separate experience. However, for the holidaymakers they also represent touch points within one overall extended experience. If the travel agency wants to address the environmental impact of the holidays it offers to its customers, it will have to collaborate with all of these parties in doing so. Once again, the travel agency has two basic options at its disposal: (1) switch supplier, or (2) work with existing suppliers to reduce the environmental impact of specific components of the overall holiday. And also, once again, using some of the reference points and the design approach presented in this book could probably turn out to be very helpful in jointly exploring more sustainable alternatives *and* avoiding the lock-in of popular beliefs such as 'pleasure and sustainability cannot go together' and 'reducing the environmental impact would be too expensive'.

AMBITION LEVEL 2

This ambition level relates to not only addressing the environmental impact of experiences staged but also their social and economic consequences. Businesses and professionals who aim for a contribution to sustainable development at this ambition level account for their overall impact with respect to the well-known triple bottom line: people, planet and profit. They do so without necessarily changing their core product or business model but they do usually aim at moving beyond simply reducing their negative impacts and also aim to make positive contributions.

The social component

As indicated in the previous chapter, one of the most obvious ways to account for the social component is to address the working conditions and wellbeing of your own employees. Given that staff members with the right expertise, attitude and behaviour are crucial to staging successful experiences, this not only contributes to the people component of the triple bottom line but also to the profit component. More qualified and motivated employees increase the chances of staging experiences the way they have been designed and also allows for staging experiences that demand more from staff to make them successful. What is more, involving employees in sustainability initiatives, such as those linked to the planet element or external projects supporting people in need, will significantly increase the chances of those efforts being successful.

Chapter 8 has already indicated that if any type of business or professional should be able to accommodate for the needs and wishes of employees, it should be those staging experiences. All of the theories, models, tools and techniques discussed in the first five chapters could also be applied to ensure proper working conditions for employees and improve their wellbeing. What is more, the comprehensive approach to designing experiences presented in Chapter 4 could serve as a key reference point for doing so. Even though the primary purpose of this approach is to design experiences to be staged for customers, it could also be used to design the experiences of employees. A working day of an employee represents a customer journey full of touch points that together shape the experience of that employee just like the customer journey of a customer spending a day/evening at your hotel, theme park, restaurant or theatre. Similarly, an extended period of working for your company represents an extended or even transformative experience for your employees just like spending a year backpacking through Australia would for a young person taking a year off after secondary school.

You, the employer, also have some clear advantages in designing the working day or career path of your employees compared to designing the customer journeys of customers. Creating appropriate personas as the starting point for the design process should be absolutely no problem because the people they represent, your employees, are not only known to you – you know them personally – but you can also get together with them and even involve them in designing their own working day/career path. Their values, their preferences, their priorities and their dreams should hold no secrets for you. The ways they react to specific cues and stimuli are either already known to you or you could explore all options that could be incorporated in their customer journeys face-to-face. You could apply many of the methods, tools and techniques discussed in Chapters 3 and 4 to make absolutely sure that choices made have the optimal effect on the ultimate experiences of your employees. You could organise a session based on the Stated Preference method to evaluate design alternatives together with the ones that will be 'consuming' the ultimate design. Rapid prototyping is something that is often difficult to apply in designing experiences for customers but in designing the working day of an employee, there are ample opportunities to make use of this approach in the design process. You could have employees 'test' new working methods, new tools, new ways of collaborating, switching roles, and so on. Finally, you can involve your employees directly in the improving details step of the design process. Interestingly, the very same blueprints you create or have created for staging experiences for customers establish a direct link between the design of the customer journey of customers and the customer journey of your employees. These blueprints contain all the relevant moments of interaction between those customers and your employees as well as the backstage processes your employees need to execute to successfully stage the experience for customers. This is a perfect opportunity to create a two-layered version of those blueprints: one layer that displays all processes involved with ensuring an optimal experience for customers and one layer that displays all processes involved with ensuring an optimal experience for your employees, including the 'backstage' processes that you, as an employer, will have to execute to successfully stage the latter.

However, this is not the only direct link that could be established between the design process for customer experiences and the design process for employee experiences. For one, obviously, the physical context in which customers are immersed is oftentimes the very same physical context in which your employees are immersed. Therefore, it would be wise to also account for the impact of this context on employees in choices made with respect to physical environments for

FIGURE 9.2 Concurrent design of guests' and employees' customer journeys

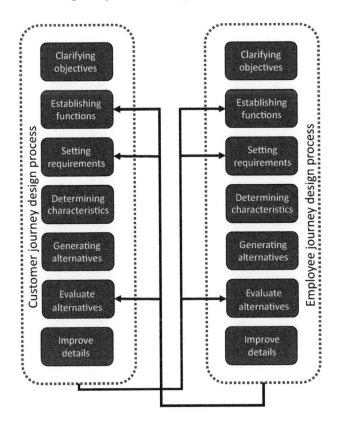

touch points included in the customer journeys of customers. Similar to the first ambition level, a straightforward way of doing so is incorporating this impact in the design objectives, requirements and evaluation procedures applied in the design of these customer journeys. In other words, businesses and professionals who aim at accounting for all three components of the triple bottom line in the experiences they stage for their customers not only need to address the environmental impact of those experiences in designing them but also the social and economic impact. An example of the latter would be to account for the economic impact of an event in designing it. Why not make it an objective and requirement to design this event in such a way that it would (financially) benefit local entrepreneurs by using them as suppliers for some of the products and services you require to execute the event successfully? Why not design it to accommodate for your visitors to also visit local shops, restaurants, stay over in local bed and breakfasts and hotels, and so on? Interestingly, doing so would probably enhance your opportunities to reduce your environmental impact as well because you would be using more local produce, require fewer natural resources than if you were to supply some of these services yourself, reduce transport distances for visitors travelling between your event location and the places they eat and sleep, and so on.

From reducing your negative impact to having a positive one

Ensuring that local entrepreneurs benefit from your presence represents a clear example of how you would not have to stop at reducing your negative environmental, social and economic impact but could also purposely set out to create a positive contribution. An interesting approach to making a positive contribution to the social component of sustainable development would be to not only optimise the experience of current employees but to offer opportunities for people who have a hard time in today's job market to work for your company. For instance, why not try to create jobs in your company for people with specific disabilities or from disadvantaged social backgrounds? The dining in the dark restaurant example discussed in Chapter 4 has already shown that doing so and staging experiences that appeal to customers can go together. Obviously, this specific restaurant was actually purposely designed with this objective in mind. However, even if creating such jobs is not your primary objective, doing so could very well be accounted for in the design of the experiences you stage.

Take the hotel example from the previous section. This hotel could aim to create jobs for local youth who are finding it especially difficult to land a first job after dropping out from secondary/high school. Once again, it could be very helpful to purposely design these jobs using the same design approach used for designing the experiences this hotel stages for its customers. The same logic, methods, tools and techniques that can be used for designing the working days and career paths of 'regular' staff can also be used to create jobs for local youth. Given that this group of (potential) employees might for instance have different backgrounds, and less experience and formal training than your current staff, implies that the personas that form the starting point for this design process will be different and thus also the ultimate design. However, the underlying logic and the design steps that need to be applied in coming up with an experience that would appeal to them, fit with their values, their ways of responding to cues and stimuli, and so on, would be exactly the same. In fact, similar to the way multiple (different) personas can be incorporated in one and the same design process for creating an overall (customisable) experience for multiple customer segments, designing the overall working experience that your company offers to its (current and future) employees can also be based on multiple (different) personas. In Chapter 4, a dining in the dark experience was designed for Pipa the journalist and Richard the businessman, using the design approach presented in that chapter. The very same approach could be used to design a working experience staged by your hotel for Karl – an experienced chef and hospitality person by nature – and Shaniqua – an 18-year-old high school drop-out from a broken home. Obviously, once again, it is important for your hotel to incorporate some of the characteristics of the design of the working experience for your employees in the design of the hospitality experience for your guests. You have already chosen to go for an à la carte version of providing breakfast for your guests. One could argue that this is a perfect match with creating jobs for people like Shaniqua. By serving breakfast à la carte, Shaniqua gets a chance to talk to guests and get to know them. This allows her to work on her interpersonal skills, and to learn about the needs and wishes of guests first hand. You could ensure – through including this as a requirement in the design of your working methods and schedules – that she is part of a team that also includes experienced staff members, so that they can coach Shaniqua and help her develop herself as a hospitality professional. By making your ambitions with respect to creating jobs for local youth explicit – through incorporating that in the design process of your hospitality experience – Shaniqua and her colleagues get a chance to involve your guests in these ambitions and share their stories with them. Most likely, this will not only further enhance Shaniqua's experience but also that of your guests. In other words, by letting the specifics and outcomes of one design process feed into the other, and vice versa, there is every chance that both ultimate designs will be all the better for it.

Looking beyond the borders of your organisation

Earlier, it has already been established that the same logic could apply to merging the environmental and business-economic perspectives, as well as to merging the ambitions to reduce your environmental impact and to contribute to the local economy. Smartly applying the design approach presented in Chapter 4 not only to create an optimal experience for (all of) your customers but also in accounting for the triple bottom line therefore clearly provides a promising avenue for staging experiences that are truly based on balancing the interests of people, planet and profit. Simultaneously, it could also provide an important reference point for decisions with respect to making a contribution to resolving environmental and social problems that are not directly linked to the customer experience you stage.

A number of companies with 'ambition level 2' also engage in so-called corporate philanthropy or corporate citizenship projects to contribute to improving the state of our natural world or the quality of life of people, even if those aspects are not directly influenced by products, services or experiences they offer to consumers.

The hotel example referred to earlier in this chapter could illustrate how engaging in these types of initiatives could also benefit from linking decisions with respect to these efforts to a comprehensive approach to designing experiences. The hotel – or maybe, by now, we should simply refer to it as 'our hotel', given that we, authors and readers of this chapter, are basically jointly 'designing' it in our minds along the way – already serves breakfast à la carte and employs people like Shaniqua. Obviously, however, by now our hotel goes further than just minimising food waste and creating jobs for local youth. We also save water and energy because we have installed water-saving showerheads and LED light bulbs. Companies that use a lot of recycled materials supply our furnishings and decoration and together we have even managed to design carpet and bathroom tiles that are easy to clean, fit in with the atmosphere we are trying to create, incorporate our logo, and are produced in a way that absorbs carbon dioxide instead of emitting it. The food we serve in our à la carte breakfast room and in our restaurant contains a number of locally and regionally grown, seasonal and organic ingredients and our menu includes a number of vegetarian and vegan dishes, thereby reducing greenhouse gas emissions, water usage and supporting local and regional urban and rural farmers, as well as improving the health of our guests. However, we did not want to stop there. We wanted to 'give back to the world' that has allowed us to stage our hospitality experience in a way that is clearly appreciated by our guests and makes a healthy profit. Simultaneously, we felt it was important to do something that fits in with who we are, what we are all about. Therefore, we decided to base our decisions on the preferences and priorities of the people most important to us: our guests and our employees. We did not just want to pick a topic or an organisation to work with from the many topics you could address as a company and the range of organisations out there that you could work with. We decided to design our own project!

For designing this project, we used the same method we have used for designing our guest experience and our working environment. In fact, it turned out that this was a perfect opportunity and occasion to review both these designs and update them. Therefore, we set up a design team consisting of Shaniqua, Karl, our hotel manager, our facility manager and James, one of our most loyal guests, to concurrently (re)design all three. The corporate citizenship project they came up with aims at working with local youth in cleaning up and improving the streets in our neighbourhood. Shaniqua leads this project, not only because she knows exactly how to get through to young people in our neighbourhood but also, as it turns out, she actually felt a little bit guilty about the fact that she was offered a job in our hotel, while some of her friends and acquaintances are still without a job and are finding it hard to feel that they have a purpose in life. This is a perfect opportunity for her to help out some of them and by doing so she no longer feels the need to hold back in really making the most of the opportunities given to her in our hotel. In fact, it would be fair to say that allowing her to spend some of her working hours on this project has resulted in her really coming into her own and flourishing in her regular work as a hospitality professional as well. However, it was actually James who originally came up with the idea for this project. He has always felt that our hotel is lovely and a great place to spend a few days away from home but he also thought that our neighbourhood could need a little makeover. He also remembered some very pleasant talks he had with Shaniqua during breakfast and her stories about her friends and the problems they face. During the design process, the design team established that James was definitely not the only guest feeling that the neighbourhood in which our hotel is located is not always up to par with the experience offered within our building. They also discovered that a number of our employees have really enjoyed working with people like Shaniqua and would be eager to do more. Finally, while discussing options to make the streets around the hotel look better, the design team also made sure to address one specific aspect of our own building that has bugged them for years: those ugly air conditioning units – whatever they are called – 'pasted' onto the walls of our hotel. As it turns out, both our employees and our guests hated them and felt they ruined the appearance of our otherwise beautiful hotel. What is more, they used a considerable amount of energy. After talking to more of our guests, the design team discovered that they actually would not mind a hotel room without air conditioning. Opening the window is just as effective. What is more, many of them actually felt it was a bit strange that we focused so much on sustainability in the way we have furnished and decorated our hotel, in everything we do, and then forget about that aspect. Needless to say, we no longer have air conditioning in our hotel!

AMBITION LEVEL 3

The previous section has shown the logic and benefits of making sure that the specifics addressed in and outcomes created by one design process feed into other design processes used for coming up with the experiences you will be staging for various stakeholders involved with or affected by your business activities, such as employees and guests but also those benefiting from your corporate citizenship initiatives. Our hotel example has shown – be it in a rather informal way – how these design processes are all linked through incorporating objectives, requirements and evaluation procedures that capture the essence of all other design efforts. Regardless of whether you can actually talk to the people involved and have them join the design team or you need to rely on market research and creating personas for addressing the needs, wishes, values and peculiarities of specific groups of people, the steps involved and the underlying logic are the same. However, so far, the core product you are offering as a business or professional staging experiences has not fundamentally changed. Essentially, you are still staging experiences for your customers to make a profit, even though you might be doing so in a way that fully accounts for all social, environmental and economic impacts associated with doing so.

Experiences as a means to create societal value

If and when businesses or professionals staging experiences would like to go yet a step further in incorporating sustainability principles in the way they operate, this would change. The third ambition level implies changing your business model into a so-called social or societal business model, which specifically aims at creating economic value through creating societal value. The Eden Project described in the previous chapter represents a very interesting example of a company staging experiences that could be argued to come very close to doing so. One could argue that the same applies to the dining in the dark restaurant designed in Chapter 4.

Obviously, the hotel we have been using as an example in this chapter could apply some of the same principles on which the Eden Project and the dining in the dark restaurant are based. Instead of staging experiences for its guests in a socially and environmentally responsible way, accompanied by specific initiatives to create a positive social and/or environmental and/or economic impact, it could also turn things around. For instance, staging a hospitality experience for guests that is able to support itself financially could become the means to have a significant and lasting impact on the behaviour of those guests once they have returned home. If staging the experience can stimulate them to save water and energy in their daily lives, to get involved with community projects, to start influencing the companies they work for to become more sustainable, and so on, the ultimate societal value this experience could create is huge. However, to realise this ambition it is no longer sufficient to incorporate this aim in the design process creating this experience as just one of the objectives to be realised by the ultimate design. Including this ambition as one of the requirements to be met by design alternatives and one of the criteria on which evaluation of these alternatives is based will not do the trick.

Instead, you will probably have to (re)design the overall experience you stage for your guests from scratch. The logical starting point for doing so is the personas you use as the reference point for designing this experience. Obviously, these personas still need to encompass information on the generic values, needs and wishes, preferences and peculiarities of your (potential) guests to allow you to stage experiences that appeal to them. However, they now also need to include specific and more detailed information with respect to their values and priorities when it comes to sustainable development. Some people think climate change is the most pressing problem of our societies and are convinced this problem is caused by us, humans, whereas others feel helping the world's poor is a top priority, while climate change will more than likely be solved through technological advancements anyway. The differences in these views impact the way in which you would try to bring about a sustained change in their life in a sustainable direction. The touch points and incorporated cues and stimuli that you have to create to shape a customer journey that will have the desired effect will clearly be very different. The blueprints that guide the actions and reactions of your staff members will have to account for these differences. In fact, more than likely, the hotel will look different, the atmosphere will be different, the sustainability initiatives you engage in will be different, and so on. If you aim to have both types of guests consume your experience, you will have to find ways to create physical and social contexts for the various touch points incorporated in their guest journeys that could satisfy or even exceed the expectations of both. This may sound extremely complicated – and to be honest, it is not an easy challenge – but, in essence, designing this transformative experience is actually very much the same challenge as trying to create a dining in the dark experience that appeals to both Pipa the journalist and Richard the businessman. Ultimately, it is not that different from designing a two-day gaming event that satisfies the needs of both Steve the hardware engineer and Hannah the game (software) developer, as described in the example of UXtream in Chapter 4. The steps you have to go through in designing this experience are the same. The reference points for successfully completing these steps and thus guaranteeing that you will end up with an optimal design are identical. What has changed is your main objective as the business or professional staging this experience. What has definitely changed is that you will now have to include bringing about a sustained change in guests' behaviour, in a sustainable direction and also after they have left the hotel, in step 2 of the design process as one of the key functions that needs to be fulfilled by the overall experience. Obviously, this also changes what the house(s) of quality and the morphological chart(s) that will be created in steps 4 and 5 will look like. However, the train of thought that you need to apply throughout this design process is *not* fundamentally different from that applied in a design process aimed at creating experiences that contribute to making as much profit as possible. The end result is though!

Getting your customers on board

It goes without saying that in designing this experience a number of the aspects discussed in the previous chapter with respect to how to promote more sustainable behaviour could prove essential to address in this process. Maybe the hotel could make smart use of the positive effects of biophilia by using furnishing and decoration (materials) that create a feeling of being immersed in a natural environment. Perhaps the hotel could counteract our propensity for self-interest by highlighting the financial benefits of using an electric car instead of a petrol one and tap into our need to be excited while doing so – a hotel Tesla roadster free to be used by guests. It could apply the art of nudging by first listing all vegan and vegetarian dishes on the menu and add a sentence along the lines of 'we also have dishes with meat or fish, should you so desire'. Or maybe, the hotel feels that this is still accommodating behaviour that is not in line with what it stands for and what it wants to accomplish, thus removing any ingredients from the menu that are not considered sustainable – creating a system of provision that removes the unsustainable choice. Quite possibly, it would compensate for this – in the eyes of some – drastic choice by using sustainable ingredients that manage to give the same signals to our brains as fatty and sweet foods did, thus further reinforcing the message that sustainable is not necessarily less pleasurable. Obviously, the hotel is very likely to follow up on the suggestion included in the previous chapter to *not* display a welcome message

---

on a television that automatically switches at the moment guests enter their hotel room and to *not* place a small coffee maker in their rooms but rather install some nice coffee lounges in the hallways of the hotel where guests and staff can discuss how to make a real difference. It would be foolish for the hotel to not apply its expertise when it comes to creating a storyline with the right dramatic structure, backed up with an eye for detail in both the physical and social context it creates for each and every touch point in the customer journeys it provides to its guests, to make sure that the message it is trying to get across is understood, accepted and embraced by those guests. In any case, the hotel is open and honest about its ambitions and is willing to share details on all its social, environmental and economic impacts with guests. The only way you can expect to make a sustained and sustainable difference in guests' lives is if you are for real!

Ultimately, it does not really matter whether you are trying to satisfy the hedonic goals of your guests or trying to bring about a sustained change in their behaviour in a sustainable direction; the design approach presented in Chapter 4 and all other theories, methods, tools and techniques presented in this book can guide you in ensuring that the choices you make for the touch points to be included in the ultimate customer journeys of your guests – or other types of consumers in case you are staging another type of experience than a hotel – are the right ones. To be brutally honest though, you would hurt the feelings – and dent the confidence – of the authors if you were to decide to only use it for the first and ignore all options to do the second – if only to some degree – after coming so far in reading this book.

AMBITION LEVEL 4

Obviously, however, where it gets really interesting is ambition level 4. This level relates to staging experiences as part of an (explicit) effort to put our societies on a (more) sustainable course by creating (local, regional or global) alternatives to our current socio-economic system. Chapter 8 has illustrated the types of actions a business or professional could take to do so through the example of a hotel located in a neighbourhood in a big city that suffers some of the negative consequences of urban tourism. The hotel in this example collaborates with a number of (local) stakeholders to collectively stage an experience for local residents, local and regional (micro-)businesses and tourists based on the concept of sustainable and inclusive hospitality. Some of the actions involved relate to collaborating with local AirBnB owners, improving the local surroundings, setting up a sustainable food and energy production and consumption system, employing local residents, and serving as the meeting place for discussing current and new initiatives.

Our hotel is your hotel

As ambitious – or maybe extreme, in the eyes of the non-naïve – the example described in Chapter 8 might seem (at first sight), one could argue that our hotel

– the one we have co-created in this chapter – already bears some resemblance to it. We already employ local youth and are involved in a project to clean up and improve the streets in our neighbourhood. The hospitality experience we stage for our guests is already very much explicitly based on promoting sustainability. Our business model is already based on trying to create economic value through creating societal value. Therefore, you could say that turning our hotel into an ambition level 4-hotel would not have to be too big a jump and maybe even represents the logical next step.

The design approach presented in Chapter 4 could, once again, prove very helpful in realising this ambition. One of the crucial concepts involved with truly incorporating the principles of sustainable development in your business model is distributed control. If and when you decide to purposely create a blossoming relationship between the experiences you stage and sustainable development, you need to account for all stakeholders directly and indirectly impacted by these experiences in designing them. In fact, within the context of ambition level 4, the specific experiences to be staged would probably not be just your decision. You are now staging experiences within the context of a network of players who jointly want to create an (local) alternative to our current socio-economic system. Therefore, these players will want to have a say in which needs and wishes of this network you will be satisfying and the way in which you will be doing so. Simultaneously, you can bring your expertise with respect to staging experiences to the table, including a comprehensive design approach. This approach could very well prove extremely useful in structuring discussions with and between all stakeholders on these needs and wishes and the experiences to be staged.

Our personas are your personas; our functions are your functions

Our hotel will be contributing to redeveloping the neighbourhood in which it is located based on the concept of sustainable and inclusive hospitality. As an expert on hospitality experiences, it could offer to take the lead – not in a hierarchical sense but through inspiring and assisting all players in the network – in refining and fleshing out this concept and what it could mean for the actions to be taken by all involved. In essence, this could be done in the same way we designed the experience to be staged at ambition level 3. However, we, the hotel, are no longer the only ones staging this experience; staging it is a joint effort of all players in the network. What is more, this experience is staged not just to satisfy the needs and wishes of our guests and our employees but also those of all other inhabitants of the neighbourhood, guests who do not stay at our hotel but in one of the local AirBnBs, local and regional farmers and other (micro-)businesses involved in setting up a sustainable food and energy production and consumption system, *and* our natural world. Like level 3, the logical starting point for designing this overall experience is to translate the needs and wishes of all of these stakeholders into personas. The fact that you are designing this experience together with (representatives of) the people who are represented by these personas, helps in encompassing all relevant information with respect to their values, needs and wishes, preferences, priorities and peculiarities. To make absolutely sure that the (local) alternatives (to our current socio–economic system) that are generated in this design process are not only based on principles such as equality and inclusiveness but also on a sustainable way of interacting with our natural world, it is probably wise to move beyond addressing the latter as a requirement and to incorporate the natural world as one of the personas whose needs and wishes need to be satisfied. If that feels a bit too odd for you, maybe you could at least introduce a persona that represents people living in this neighbourhood 40 or 50 years from now. A smart way of ensuring that the needs of this persona are addressed sufficiently in the design process could be to purposely focus on the children of members of the design team as inspiration for creating them, thus following the advice of Griskevicius et al. (2012) with respect to focusing on the impact of decisions on one's own family and kin in mitigating our propensity for self-interest and proneness to disregard impalpable concerns.

Obviously, the specific experiences that we, our hotel, will be staging represent just parts of this whole puzzle. However, these parts are crucial to solving this puzzle and need to fit with the other parts. For instance, maybe one function that the overall experience to be staged by all players in the network is going to fulfil

FIGURE 9.3 A multi-layered design process

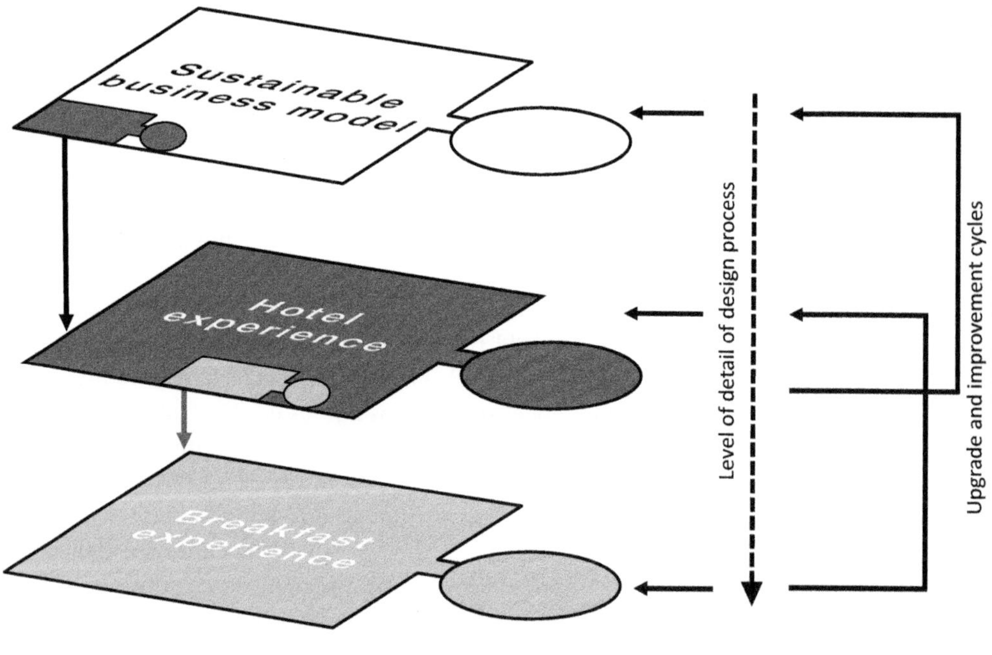

is to store electricity. This electricity is generated by wind turbines and solar panels installed by the urban and rural farmers with whom a food and energy production and consumption system is going to be set up. This could change the role of our hotel's Tesla roadster from just a nice experience and way to promote the use of electric vehicles to also being an integral part of the local infrastructure for storing electricity; maybe the batteries in all electric vehicles in our neighbourhood could be used to store electricity. This idea might sound crazy to some of you but it has already been experimented with in some real-life neighbourhoods! However, to make sure that our hotel can play its role in this system, the design of the Tesla roadster experience we offer to our guests needs to account for that role in the bigger whole. Obviously, the same applies to the food and drinks we serve, and the way we do so, in our breakfast room and restaurant; these touch points in the customer journeys of our guests are inextricably linked to that same food and energy production and consumption system set up in and by our neighbourhood. Hiring people like Shaniqua is very much linked to the neighbourhood's ambition to ensure that the overall sustainable hospitality experience to be staged benefits all inhabitants of the neighbourhood and not just those eager and confident enough to step in at the early stages, and so on. In other words, the specific experiences that we stage as a hotel basically represent touch points within the overall experience staged by the network we are a part of. Decisions made at the level of this network need to be accounted for in the design of the specific experiences our hotel stages and vice versa. For specific aspects, this will involve feeding the specifics and outcomes of one design process into the other as personas whose needs and wishes need to be satisfied or functions that need to be performed by the ultimate design. For other aspects, it may be enough to account for them through incorporating specific requirements or criteria to be used in evaluating design alternatives.

Earlier in this chapter, it has been established that such a multi-layered design process – very likely also resulting in multi-layered blueprints for the people involved – sounds extremely complicated. However, it has also been established that, in essence, it is not that much different from the dining in the dark and UXtream examples discussed in Chapter 4. The number of personas, functions and requirements might be bigger – and thus the resulting houses of quality and morphological charts might be more complicated – but the reference points for successfully completing all basic design steps and thus guaranteeing that you will end up with an optimal design are identical. For all of these design efforts, you will be dealing with an overall experience at a more abstract level and specific experiences or touch points at a more detailed level. Therefore, the overall design process for all of these efforts actually involves multiple (levels of) design processes that are linked. With respect to creating sustainable experiences that live up to level 4 sustainability ambitions, in theory, this still holds true. The overall design process consists of multiple (levels of) design processes that differ with respect to the level of abstraction/detail, and are linked and interdependent. However, it would be strange to say that these processes are not more complicated than those involved with designing a dining in the dark restaurant or even UXtream. The design processes described in this section involve experimenting with alternatives to our current socio-economic system and business models and technologies that would fit in with these alternatives. That *is* a big step. For one, the number of stakeholders (directly) involved with these processes can be huge. These stakeholders could have very different interests, and you will have to treat our natural world as an actual stakeholder represented by an actual persona in the design process. Furthermore, the number of and variety in (touch points and) experiences involved with shaping the overall experience to be staged by a specific network can be quite significant. Of course, this complicates matters. Playing simultaneous chess on 20 boards is more complicated than doing the same on 10 boards, even though the rules of the games you are playing on all boards are identical. The same applies to designing the overall experience and all more detailed experiences and touch points involved within a context such as that provided by a hotel aiming to contribute to redeveloping a neighbourhood based on the concept of sustainable and inclusive hospitality. The design principles and rules that you could apply to do so are the same as those involved with designing an experience staged by a single provider simply aiming to please hedonic goals of specific homogeneous customer segments to make a healthy profit. The challenge to successfully complete this design process is not the same. However, neither are the rewards!

FROM CANVAS-DRIVEN TO COMMUNITY-ORIENTED NETWORKS

The introduction to this book has claimed that businesses and professionals who aim to remain successful in today's and tomorrow's marketplace need to be able to tackle two key developments: (1) the rise of the experience economy, and (2) the challenges posed by realising sustainable development of our societies. This and the previous eight chapters have explored and illustrated both developments in detail, as well as reference points for dealing with them intelligently. Before translating these reference points into key competencies for current and future professionals within the context of successfully designing, staging and managing experiences, this section reflects on the combined impact of these reference points on the business models and technologies likely to be applied by businesses and professionals who actually *will be* successful tomorrow and the day after tomorrow.

One could argue that the rise of the experience economy is just one stage or step within a continuous and continuing change in the preferences of consumers. Within the context of a society in which the symbolic value of consumption is ever-increasing, the spiritual fathers of the experience economy (Pine and Gilmore, 1999) have already suggested that maybe by now businesses and professionals should start focusing on staging experiences that assist consumers in transforming themselves instead of just stimulating or exciting them. Others have suggested yet another stage in our economies and refer to a so-called meaningful economy as a way of tapping into the trend of more and more people seeking to live meaningful lives and an increased willingness to express that in their (consumption and work related) decision-making (Drewell & Larsson, 2017).

Within the context of a society in which the problems associated with our current socio-economic system and the ways in which we exploit our natural resources and distribute wealth across (people in) our world are increasingly noticeable and acknowledged, the social license to operate for businesses and professionals is likely to depend more and more on their contribution to resolving these issues. Some have suggested that we are on the verge of a shift in our socio-cultural evolution as a species, as we (have to) adapt our ends and means from being based on conquest, colonisation and consumption to being based on connection, communication and consciousness (Laszlo, 2001). Obviously, this would change the way in which businesses and professionals (would have to) contribute to our societies. Others simply point out that if businesses and professionals are to contribute to sustainable development at the rate required and, increasingly, expected from them by other stakeholders, they need to start applying different business models and technologies. Various concepts, definitions and reference points have already been suggested as forming the basis for these business models and technologies of tomorrow, such as the Creating Shared Value concept proposed by Porter and Kramer (2011), the definition of a sustainable business model put forward by Lüdeke-Freund (2009) and the three types of sustainability intelligence distinguished by Melissen and Moratis (2016).

By now, it should be pretty clear to you, as reader, that it is our firm belief, as authors of this book, that businesses and professionals could very well concurrently address the challenges posed by the rise of the experience economy and the currently unsustainable course of our societies through designing, staging and managing experiences. This book has presented a number of reference points – including a comprehensive approach to designing experiences that allows for accounting for all of these reference points – that could guide businesses and professionals in staging experiences that not only appeal to consumers but also contribute to sustainable development. Specific ambition levels with respect to merging these two perspectives have been presented and illustrated.

By now, it should also be pretty clear to you that the business models and technologies applied by businesses and professionals who will be able to successfully design, stage and manage these sustainable experiences tomorrow and the day after tomorrow will likely look different from the ones applied by most of the (key) companies that shaped today's socio-economic system. The train of thought applied by the latter could probably best be summarised as being based on the so-called Business Model Canvas, displayed in Figure 9.4.

The Business Model Canvas (Osterwalder and Pigneur, 2010) is a representation of the nine business model building blocks that are 'normally' considered by companies in developing or describing the way they operate. These nine building blocks are based on the rationale that the essence of a company is linked to creating value for customers, delivering this value to those customers *and* capturing this value within the context of the rules of the free market. However, the train of

FIGURE 9.4 The Business Model Canvas

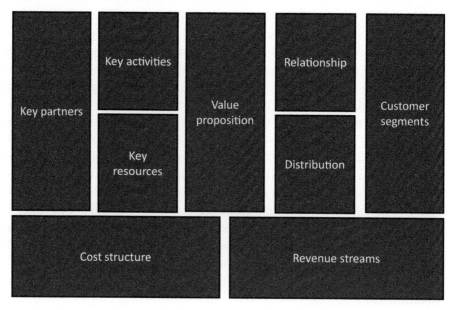

Adapted from: Osterwalder, A. & Pigneur, Y. (2010). *Business model generation: A handbook for visionaries, game changers, and challengers.* Hoboken: John Wiley & Sons.

thought presented in this book suggests that the reference points on which this rationale is based are slowly but surely losing their relevance, especially for businesses and professionals aiming to design, stage and manage sustainable experiences.

Designing, staging and managing sustainable experiences at ambition level 4 is based on creating value that is not necessarily expressed in terms of money and not just for customers. The partners involved in doing so are not just the suppliers of the materials and technologies you need to stage the specific experiences you bring to the table but everyone involved with and impacted by the overall experiences staged by the network of stakeholders you are a part of. You no longer treat natural resources as just an asset to your company but as a key stakeholder of this network. Your value proposition is not just based on aspects such as price, efficiency and the customer experience you offer but also on your contribution to that overall experience, and so on. The specifics of the business model and technologies you apply depend on the characteristics and preferences of this network and the overall experience to be staged by this network. Some of these experiences might be experimenting with (local) alternatives to our current socio–economic system and therefore they might involve very different ways of dealing with value from that suggested by the Business Model Canvas and the rules of the free market.

However, even if your ambition level with respect to staging sustainable experiences is a little bit more modest, you will probably find out that this 'old' way of looking

FIGURE 9.5 The EFQM model

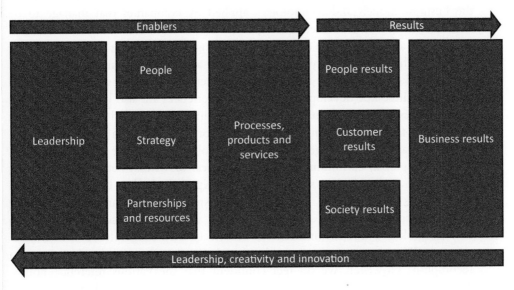

Source: www.efqm.org

at the way a company operates is not helping you to realise these ambitions. Maybe the well-known EFQM model (Figure 9.5) could offer a better perspective on the role and position of a company in today's and tomorrow's society. This model suggests that you reflect on the values and ethics that form the basis for your organisation and thus the type of leadership required for your company to be successful. It reinforces the relevance of creating a culture that allows your employees to not only pursue the company's goals but also their personal goals. Instead of merely addressing ways to capture value (from the market) as the ultimate goal, this model suggests that you also review your results in terms of your impact on your customers, other people and wider society – including our natural world. Finally, it stresses the need to promote fairness and equality but also to focus on the needs and expectations of stakeholders and not just the needs and expectations of shareholders. Doing so requires (collective) learning and innovation (with respect to both physical *and* social technologies), not just repeating what we have been doing for so long.

It is beyond the scope of this book to discuss the EFQM model in full detail. The same applies to some of the other alternative methods, tools and techniques for reviewing a company's activities and success that have been developed over the years. There is a wide range of books, papers and websites out there that could assist you in exploring them. Some of them might prove helpful in creating the business models and technologies needed for successfully designing, staging and managing the experiences you are/will be staging, some may not.

The two developments addressed in this book – the rise of the experience economy and the need for sustainable development – will surely have a significant impact on the business models and technologies applied by companies that manage to be successful in our future societies. Regardless of whether these future societies will be based on a transformation economy, a meaningful economy or a socio-economic system of which we do not yet know the name and details, sustainable experiences look very likely to play a key role in shaping them because they are directly linked to both of these key developments. These experiences are also likely to be staged by businesses and professionals who apply business models and technologies that allow them to play a meaningful role in collaboration (based on co-creation) with other companies and a range of (other) stakeholders within the context of (local, regional or global) community-oriented (physical or virtual) networks. Providing a generally applicable but still detailed description of what these models and technologies will look like for the specific experiences you are/will be staging within the specific context of your network is a mission impossible. The authors of this book are not fortune-tellers, nor necessarily stakeholders within your network. We are not the ones to decide what you and yours should set out to accomplish. However, we do feel confident that the various reference points, theories, methods, tools and techniques this book has presented might prove helpful in creating both those networks and the appropriate business models and technologies.

SUMMARY

Based on reading this chapter, we hope you will understand and remember the following:

- How the comprehensive approach to experience design presented in Chapter 4 could be used to create (more) sustainable experiences at all four ambition levels with respect to pursuing sustainable development through staging experiences.

- The relevance of accounting for both tangible and intangible elements in the design of sustainable experiences.

- The crucial role of involving others in your design process for (more) sustainable experiences.

- How experiences could be used to create societal value.

- Designing, staging and managing sustainable experiences implies a move from applying Business Model Canvas-driven business models and technologies to applying community-oriented, networked business models and technologies.

- How the various reference points, theories, models, tools and techniques presented in this book could assist you in successfully designing, staging and managing sustainable experiences, and developing the appropriate business models and technologies to do so.

FOOD FOR THOUGHT

Based on the content of this chapter, the following questions, challenges and topics could serve as interesting starting points for further discussion:

- Apply the comprehensive approach to experience design presented in Chapter 4 to design your own example of an experience that truly incorporates the principles of sustainable development.

- Compare your design with the design of others. Assist each other in improving details, and discuss key reference points for actually staging this experience in 'real' life.

REFERENCES

Drewell, M. & Larsson, B. (2017). *The rise of the meaningful economy: A megatrend where meaning is a new currency* (Kindle ed.). Stockholm: the Foresight Group.

Griskevicius, V., Cantú, S. & van Vugt, M. (2012). The evolutionary bases for sustainable behaviour: Implications for marketing, policy, and social entrepreneurship. *Journal of Public Policy & Marketing*, 31, 115–128.

Laszlo, E. (2001). Human evolution in the third millennium. *Futures*, 23(4), 349–372.

Lüdeke-Freund, F. (2009). *Business model concepts in corporate sustainability contexts: From rhetoric to a generic template for 'business models for sustainability'*. *Working paper*. Lüneberg: Center for Sustainability Management, Leuphana Universität Lüneburg.

Melissen, F. & Moratis, L. (2016). A call for fourth generation sustainable business models. *The Journal of Corporate Citizenship*, 63, 8–16.

Osterwalder, A. & Pigneur, Y. (2010). *Business model generation: A handbook for visionaries, game changers, and challengers*. Hoboken, NJ: John Wiley & Sons.

Pine, B.J. & Gilmore, J.H. (1999). *The experience economy: Work is theatre and every business a stage*. Boston, MA: Harvard Business Press.

Porter, M. & Kramer, M. (2011). Creating shared value. *Harvard Business Review*, 89, 62–77.

10 ... or rather, the epilogue

INTRODUCTION

Way back when the first rough sketches for this book were created, we – the authors – came up with some first ideas for this final chapter. These ideas basically amounted to having this chapter revolve around listing and explaining all competencies you – the reader – will have to master to be able to successfully design, stage and manage experiences in events, tourism and hospitality, or any other industry for that matter. Why? First, we have been involved in writing textbooks before and most of those also end with a chapter on competencies. It has always felt like the logical way to conclude the train of thought presented in a textbook. To be honest, a second reason is that we probably also felt, at that time, that this would be a way to please your professor – if you, the one reading this book, are a student, you probably know best that professors tend to *love* competencies. However, it also felt like the obvious way to satisfy one of your needs as a reader, regardless of whether you are a student or a professional. Most readers like a straightforward, no-nonsense (management) summary, right?

By now, at this moment in time, we have come to realise that we would be wrong to *bore* you with a lengthy discussion on the backgrounds to the concept of competencies, a long list of competencies of particular relevance to designing, staging and managing experiences, and detailed explanations for each of them. After coming this far in trying to explain what designing, staging and managing experiences is all about, it would be silly to ignore the (negative) impact of such a final chapter on the overall experience we have staged for you – our reader. Obviously, reading this book is also an experience. If we want to make sure this experience turns into an extended (Yes, we know, some of the previous chapters are a bit long; sorry!) or transformative experience that you will remember for the right reasons, we ought to apply our own reference points and design approach in creating an appropriate dramatic structure. We should incorporate a fitting arc for the last touch point in the journey of our hero – you, our reader. You have borne with us for nine chapters. If you are still with us in this final chapter, you have definitely earned that typical final moment in a hero's story – the moment when the hero takes a deep breath and relaxes after the final climax of the plot. In literature, this moment is called the denouement, which is when all strands of a story come together; any final loose ends are tied up; and all remaining secrets are revealed. Regardless of whether you are a fan of fantasy novels, or into thrillers or more of a Shakespeare person, this should sound familiar to you. Therefore, instead of getting bogged down in the details of extensive lists of competencies, let us take a moment to relax and casually reflect on your journey thus far.

YOUR JOURNEY

It started with us introducing you to the rise of the Experience Economy and the insights of various academics regarding where this came from and where it is going. The first chapter also highlighted consumers' ever-increasing need for experiences and the resulting challenge for businesses and professionals to design, stage and manage them in ways that are tailored to the wishes of (individual or groups of) consumers. All of this provided a first inciting incident: the moment you (might have) realised that you did not yet have the knowledge, skills and/or tools to do so. Some would call this the stage in competency development in which you move from unconscious incompetence – not being aware of what you do not know or cannot do – to conscious incompetence. Obviously, we would not do this, because we promised you that we would not get bogged down in the details of the concept of competencies.

Subsequently, the next few chapters exposed you to the tip of the iceberg with respect to theories, methods, tools and techniques from the worlds of the social sciences and design science. They showed how the social sciences could help us understand why people want experiences and how experiences can turn into memories or instigate transformations. They also highlighted some of the methods, tools and techniques that could be used to design machines, processes, products and services, as well as the steps that need to be completed in doing so. As authors with a background in both fields, we hope that these chapters have made you curious to learn more about both. If so, you might want to have a closer look at some of the articles and books we have referred to in these chapters or some of the other work of the people who wrote them.

These chapters also created a tension; a tension between social science insights, which are mostly related to intrapersonal aspects such as personality and self-actualisation, and design science, which usually focuses on creating tangible and virtual artefacts. This tension was purposely created by us to create a build-up to the climax in Chapter 4, in which these two worlds finally came together in shaping a comprehensive approach to designing experiences. We will leave it to you whether this chapter actually represented a high in the overall experience of reading this book but do hope that we have managed to have this approach come to life for you in the examples of the dining in the dark restaurant and the UXtream event. Most importantly, we hope that it will prove helpful to you in designing the experiences your (future) customers really want. However, it is important to realise that the secret to becoming a competent experience designer is not just reading a chapter on designing experiences. You need more than knowledge; you also need specific skills, attitudes and behaviours that come with it to become a proficient experience designer. Luckily, steadfastly sticking to the steps of this approach and making full use of the various methods, tools and techniques discussed in this chapter is very likely to assist you in developing that kind of craftmanship and ultimately reaching the stage of being consciously competent. Sure, it could take some time to truly master the experience design process, being able to play with it. During this journey, it is important to always remember one thing: do not be afraid to make mistakes along the way. Just ensure you reflect on them and never make the same mistake twice. Make full use of the guidance that could be provided by experienced designers. Enjoy the journey and (!) then reap the rewards of completing it.

Maybe it also helps to know that we have gone through pretty much the same process. Chapter 4 has required quite a few iterations to become what it is now. When writing some of the other chapters, especially Chapters 5, 8 and 9, we developed some new insights that we felt we needed to incorporate in a truly comprehensive approach to designing experiences. In ensuring a coherent storyline and optimal dramatic structure for the whole book, we had to return to some other touch points in the overall customer journeys of our personas as well. Chapters and examples that we thought we got right straightaway turned out to require some improvements and sometimes even a full redesign. Then again, a design process without iterations is not a design process!

Obviously, after a period of tension and a peak, you need a period of relaxation. In this book, this part of the journey came in the shape of Chapter 5. This chapter should have helped you to develop an understanding of the link between designing experiences, in the way described in Chapter 4, and actually staging those experiences. Chapter 5 introduced you to some of the basics of managing the staging of experiences at an operational and tactical level. This chapter could have easily turned into a book on its own, especially if we had elaborated on (all details involved with) aspects such as project management, leadership and quality assurance. Some of the content of this chapter was developed based on our own careers as (experience) managers but most of it was conveyed to us by some of the professionals we have had the privilege to visit, talk to, learn from and work with over the years. Ultimately, this chapter touched upon some of the key aspects you need to consider within the specific context of managing the staging of experiences without trying to provide you with a full discussion on the generic topic of management. Many others have already written insightful papers, chapters and books on this topic – better than we ever could. Therefore, we suggest and urge you make full use of their work in filling in the details of the overall train of thought presented in this chapter.

Chapter 6 was the so-called McGuffin of this book; an unexpected turn in what seemed to be a straightforward plot of a story in which we all live happily ever after, cheerfully moving from one experience to the next. This chapter confronted you with the harsh reality of the true story of our planet and our species, which will not have a happy ending if we continue on the road we are on. As indicated in this chapter, we cannot simply point a condemnatory finger at big multinationals, oil companies or our governments for overexploiting our planet's resources and not caring about the lives of the less privileged in our world; all of us are to blame for this, also those already working or planning to start a career in the events, tourism and hospitality industries.

We are writing this on the day that the BBC reported that most of the Great Barrier Reef should probably be considered lost. Our local newspaper, also today, reported that the wind turbines planned close to the home of one of us will probably not be built after all because too many people have complained about the negative impact on the aesthetics of the local landscape – they say they understand the need for renewable energy but do not want these monstrous towers ruining their view from their living rooms.

Chapter 7 further explained the situation: the planet is in peril and our hero is caught in a system that is extremely hard to escape from. If this book were a James Bond movie, you would now be held captive by SPECTRE or some other evil organisation, with your loved ones in danger and a lethal weapon pointed at your face. Is this the end? Is it all over?

Some (would) say we desperately need a so-called *deus ex machina* for this story to have a happy ending with someone or something, appearing out of nowhere, helping us stop global warming and teaching us how to live our lives in ways that do not harm other people or nature. However, instead of putting all of our eggs in a basket that might very well never be sent to us, we should probably realise that resolving this dilemma is something that requires a contribution from all of us. This is not something we can leave to the United Nations or our governments. This is something that all of us – in our roles as voters, consumers, suppliers, employees, employers, neighbours, friends, and so on – should tackle together. What is more, Chapter 7 pointed you to a glimmer of hope of particular interest to you, namely the paperclip your captor left behind on the table which you could use to get your handcuffs off: experiences!

Experiences could be both a red herring and the solution. They will turn out to be a red herring if and when we continue to only focus on partying and having fun in designing, staging and managing them. They could also prove to be our saviour or narrow escape if and when we start to incorporate the principles of sharing, caring and transformation in the way we design, stage and manage them. Experiences could very well help us escape the lock-in of our current socio-economic system and fight the invisible hand of the free market. You could say Chapter 7 has handed you, our hero, with some secret weapons to fight your captors: naïve, native and narrative intelligence. At first sight, they seem a perfect fit with experiences. They could be the key to resolving our dilemma. But, the clock is ticking.

This means tension is building again. However, before we finally find out whether our hero will manage to break free in the end, there is one final twist in the story. Chapter 8 provided this final twist by putting you to the test. It introduced you to four ambition levels with respect to merging the perspectives of the experience economy and sustainable development, four ways of using your secret weapons to escape. Will you save yourself and get away? Will you save yourself and your loved ones without facing the enemy? Will you save yourself and your loved ones *and* report back to headquarters that there is a powerful enemy out there? Or will you gather all of your friends and colleagues – your avengers, if that is your thing – to collectively create a safe haven that protects you from the powers of your common enemy and then invite others to join you in that safe haven?

Obviously, heroes make up their own minds. We cannot tell you what to do. This choice is yours to make. Will you add a sheep to your herd grazing the commons, or will you account for the natural boundaries of the commons and make a different choice? Maybe you want to make sure that your children will also be able to rely on what the commons can give them. You might join forces with others to make the commons future-proof. If so, what will you bring to this group? What will be your role and status in this group? Obviously, you are not the only one faced with these types of decisions. Your decisions are not the only ones that will determine what happens to the commons. However, your decisions do matter, especially if your decision is to try to influence the decisions of others as well. Your decisions do play a role, and possibly a crucial role, in how the story of our commons, our planet, will end.

Chapter 9 presented one possible end to this story. It is an end that involves you designing, staging and managing experiences that positively impact our planet, the people you work with, the communities you operate and live in, and the people for which you stage them. This is our preferred journey for our hero. This is what we would like to happen to you.

We are fully aware of the fact that you might (still) think we are mad for writing this down. We know that there is every chance that, to you, we are merely the writers of a book that seemed interesting (at first) or even that someone else made you read. Who are we to tell you what to do or think? If you had to create a persona representing us, what values, beliefs, traits and personality would you give us? Would you assign us with naïve intelligence or just naivety? Would we be the jester or the sage?

Whatever choice you make, we do hope that you will continue on your journey to becoming a true craftsman in designing, staging and managing experiences. We do hope that you will ultimately master all competencies involved.

Regardless of your own personal ambitions in relation to sustainable development, you will need to master competencies linked to design to be successful in today's and tomorrow's experience economy. You need to understand the design process, be skilled in applying design methods, tools and techniques, and smart in choosing the right ones for the right steps. Obviously, you may come across methods, tools and techniques that were not discussed in this book. Make sure to try them, test them, see how they work for you, and fill your toolbox with them and share them with others. Analyse best practices in the world around you and step forward to ask other designers about their work and their insights.

You will also certainly need competencies linked to understanding and steering human behaviour. You will repeatedly need to read up on (the latest) consumer trends and talk to your customers, staff and stakeholders. You will need to ask the right questions, and listen and observe, to establish the right objectives, functions and requirements for the experiences you design, stage and manage. You need the confidence to apply iterations and redesign your experiences if and when needed. You need to be aware of your own values, personality and cultural background in doing all this because what is normal to you might not be normal to others. Be aware of your own ethics and behaviours and how they affect others during your interactions with them.

Finally, you do need to understand the system you are a part of and the various roles and responsibilities you have in relation to it. This system could be the supply chain of commodities that is slowly but surely being transformed into a system based on experiences. It could be the organisation you work in or for. It could also be the community you work or live in, or the market system in which you operate. Every one of these systems has its own boundaries and limitations, its own ways to relax those and escape routes. However, there is one exception to this rule: our planet. These boundaries and limitations are fixed.

Okay, so we did actually discuss competencies in the end.

THE END

Index